The Fever

A ROMANCE OF THE RED ROCKS

A Novel, by James A. Myers

and his Village

"Kachina Woman" a 16 x 12 oil on canvas by Steve Simon. Kachina Woman is a hoodoo vortex at the mouth of the Boyton Canyon, sacred to the Native American tribes of Northern Arizona. The painting appears in a collection of Sedona beauty: "The Spirit of Sedona, art and verse by Steve Simon." www.SteveSimon.com

ISBN: 0-615-72730-1
ISBN 13: 978-0-615-72730-1
Printed by CreateSpace, an Amazon.com company

Parable of the One and the Many

The wise fool Nasreddin is
working as a ferryman.

His passenger, a scholar, wants to
discuss grammar and linguistics.

Nasreddin says he has no use for such tools.
The scholar informs him he
has wasted his life.

"Have you ever learned to
swim?" asks Nasreddin.

"No!" the scholar scoffs. "I have
immersed myself in thinking."

"In that case," Nasreddin replies,
you've wasted your life.

The boat is sinking."

In reality, you and I, like Nasreddin the ferryman, have many of the same personal questions, and **many** of the same potential ways of wasting our time on stage. Nevertheless, there just may be **one** outstanding answer, as some wise seers have seen. The lives of Anna Pagani and John Malachy arrive at different thresholds that open a fresh perspective on this possibility of survival for Mankind. That is what is currently at stake in this romance.

A foretaste: Looking out the window, looking ahead to death...

She does not want to do this. Deep in her gut she has the fearful intuition that yesterday's telephone call could wind up ruining her life. Minutes before the Jet Blue A320s Airbus thunders into the blackness above New York's John F. Kennedy tarmac, the dark haired, unattached woman in seat 6B feels relieved that the seat next to her is empty. She is used to being alone; she hates uncertainty. She actually prefers isolation. Her life is waiting to take off. She has a rendezvous with death. Inside she trembles.

She wears a white silk scarf around her neck. Both her fists are mildly clenched in her lap. She doesn't want to do what she is doing. She has no choice. She hasn't worn a scarf around her neck in years, but this menacing night she feels vulnerable. She thought that she had accepted her crimson fate long ago, but this night she has to protect herself against a possible ugly reaction.

A dark-skinned, Indian looking, man comes down the aisle. Her heart skips a beat. He looks like Amit.

The courier who delivered the plane ticket that evening had said, "Enjoy the Red Rock Country. It's wild." She knows almost nothing about where she is going, except that she is going to a sad ending. She has no interest in red rocks. Her mind slips back to one of the darkest days of her childhood. She can still hear her mother's sick cough.

But first, dear readers, let us glance back to where romance stories all began.

Imagine the eternal before. There are only the related vibrations. Bang! Bits fly into relationships, *"Let there be space and time."* Boom! *"Matter and energy"* For billions of time-years the Cosmos rushes, expands, gases condense, key elements coalesce. Then presto, life emerges when two bacteria hook-up. Hardly a romance, you say. But a dramatic start to the Great Story one must admit.

Eventually, once upon time, on a planet, in a small solar system, in a milky galaxy, the ballad of *Homo sapiens* begins to sing in dreamtime. A riff of intuition proclaims: *Something big is at stake.* A defining juncture is dawning. A small band of hominine females <u>helps</u> a sister in her late teens bring forth a girl child. The newborn of this <u>collaboration</u> is given the name Eve. As often happened in that primeval savannah, the demon of death steals away with the mother's *anima.* Not to worry, the alloband of young females share their breasts with baby Eve. The milk of maternal kindness flows into the gathering process. In the garden savannah, Eve becomes the mother of an emergent species, *Homo sapiens.*

Only after millennia does the offspring of her consort Adam come to pride himself as *sapiens* (wise). However, with the slippage of time many have cause to wonder if Adam's offspring, made of clay and breath, have enough wisdom to escape a final, atomic, Earth conflagration. This fall of man snuck upon the stage amid many missed connections and disconnections.

Eventually, out of chaos, a small mutation comes to pass: Europa loses the heel of her boot. It becomes Sicilia. More millennia slip by, and the wail of a marked Sicilian girl baby pierces the sterile operating room of the General Hospital in the Bronx, USA.

Listen in as the Song of *Sapiens* struggles to hang on to some sort of melody.

"No, mother, no," the sobbing girl pleads, her face wild with fear. The coughing mother pulls on.

"We all want the same things. We're all human," the frustrated woman coughs again into the chilly, gray Bronx morning. Her gloved hand yanks forward her sobbing daughter's bare hand. The middle aged woman grouses on in a Reality that she has little idea about, if it hears or cares. She is an immigrant who never had the blessed burden of religion. A Sicilian of peasant stock, she wears her every day, gray, ankle-length wool dress with a two-inch black belt, black street shoes, and black cotton gloves. The noisy New York morning is already heavy with the fumes of city buses and the smoke of apartment chimneys. She spits at a fire hydrant. "We all want people to respect us. Why can't people in this country be kind?" she mumbles to the brownstone front steps. The warning wail of a police siren pierces the unclean air. The evil empire is shouting back its warning. She coughs on, "I have no choice. It's gone on too long. Yesterday was the last straw."

In Gina Pagani's heart, the memory of her daughter rushing into the apartment from public school, her little eyes crying uncontrollably because they called her "a witch," plays like a Greek tragedy. Gina's kind heart had constricted in her breast. It was a clarion moment, and the courage to act had welled up in her flooded heart, like waters breaking a rift over a dam. She was not by nature a fighter, but she had to stand up for her daughter. At that challenging juncture in her life, Gina had heard the insistent call of what she had to do.

Years earlier, her own life had been ravished of choice. Today she is fighting back with a daring decision. She had known for a long time that the kids at PS 13 had been bullying and poking fun at her only daughter. She had come across the smutty posts on Anna's Facebook. She knows what is at stake if you leave it to the wheel of fortune to make the choices. In a sense, this is Gina's moment of spitting in the eye of those who would hurt the wounded.

She had kept her tongue, knowing that her husband, Luigi, is an intolerant man. He scoffs and belittles people who dump their woes at the feet of others. To be sure, the face that Gina Fava Pagani parades this day runs cross-current to the natural disposition of this once good-hearted, Sicilian hill girl, who had been given in marriage to a headstrong city-man. She was a poor, hillside maiden in need of someone to provide for her financially. But today she is yanking on with love for her daughter and spite for men who hurt women.

The Favas were olive farmers in the steep Sicilian hills. The stingy soil was hard to work, having been covered by volcanic lava several times. At that time Gina, the youngest of a family of seven, is a comely, dark-haired girl with a fair complexion. Her bloodline courses back to both the Romans and the Normans. She is sometimes sweet, sometimes hellion, and sings like a nightingale. She is known for her upbeat personality with close family ties.

She lives like a wildflower in full bloom. Through their child-hood years, Gina and her blond-haired, fair-skinned, blue-eyed playmate, Carlo Verdi, roam the hills and swim naked in the mountain streams. The Verdis are poor Northern Italians from the alpine country north of Milan. Carlo and his family come to Sicily when Gina is six-years-old. Gina and Carlo grow up elfin friends. At fourteen she opens her unbroken treasure to her friend, under a green willow tree along a singing mountain stream. She sings the happiest song of her life. It is the song of young love. Her dream that day is to never forget that spot where the branches of a tree smile down at you, the ground tickles your bare bottom, and the wind plays softly on your white legs. But, as most of us know, the worm of youth turns, and the light inside can be dimmed, by the older people who want to control you.

When Gina is fifteen, a drought withers away the Fava fam-ily orchard – a sinister omen in the fecund mind of a girl at the peak of puberty. Her family is no longer able to support their six remaining dependents. She is marriageable. She has the body and milk of a woman. A marriage is arranged with the well-to-do Pagani family in the port city of Siracusa. Her heart, like a weeping willow along a sad river, droops to the ground. Destiny demands that she leave her family, her beloved olive hills, and the mountain air that opens her mouth to sing. Worst of all, she has to say good-bye, probably forever, to her friend, the only boy who had entered her treasure trove.

She has not yet met her city husband-to-be, but her heart has a premonition that when she does meet him they will not have the sort of soul-body relationship Carlo and she had shared. Carlo was a Gaia child who also is at home near the trees and the streams. The exile to the city is a loss Gina may never recover from. Her wildflower of love withers that winter and the nightingale will not sing the new spring, as we shall see.

These sad memories are raging though Gina's mind that gray morning as she braves on through the congestion and noise of the city people, selfishly jostling one another. She is no longer a singing flower girl. Her oldest sister, Cecilia, had moved to Augusta, an industrial city, north of Siracusa, when Gina was a guileless girl. Cecilia died five years later of influenza.

The Pagani family of Siracusa was an old line of mechanics. The local jest was that they had fixed and sabotaged the broken chariots of the Roman legions. The Pagani Garage took care of the city buses and vehicles. Luigi Pagani was small man with an aquiline nose, and, whoa, a hot-temper.

Shortly, after he and Gina were married, he had a shouting argument with his father Guiseppi. The angry youngster immediately took passage away to America, dragging his hapless wife with him. They had no relatives, no friends in the crowded American metropolis. And Gina hated the repulsive smell of the air from the moment she got out of the taxi cab in front of their sixth floor walk-up. She knew she would not sing here. She had barely hummed in Siracusa.

Mechanics were in demand in the City, and Luigi was, after all, a city-boy-mechanic. He could turn a wrench. He found employment at the O'Sullivan garage in the Bronx. He felt at home in the noisy fumes and smoke of the city. Gina grudgingly breathed in the grimy air with depressing resentment. But in the end, it was not her lungs, but her broken heart that took her. Luigi always claimed that her cough was in her head. She didn't sing because heart remained back in the hills where Carlo remained. Besides, Gina had it in her mind that she had a contagious disease, like the lung disease that took her sister. Unschooled, she believed that disease can be transmitted, as it were, mentally. For fear of spreading the disease, she did not caress or kiss her daughter.

Ever since being stripped of the idyllic relationship of her hillside days, Gina had submitted to the yoke, as women have done for long years. But this particular dismal Bronx dawning day, she is anything but submissive; neither is her befuddled, kicking, eight-year-old daughter. For Anna, what is going down is an unfair wrong that her young heart can't imagine ever accepting, or forgiving. That bleak morning she senses that there is a lot at stake. Tender of age, she is being dragged across an unwanted threshold, and pulled toward an un-chosen road. Her ability to trust is being trampled under life's feet. Why is this happening? The red blotch is not her fault.

It was on that day that the soul of a turtle named Anna took almost final refuge in her shell.

Mother Gina knows her man better than the streambed knows the stream. He will be furious. *He might even take a swing at me,* she ruminates, as she strides on resolutely. *He's done that before. But the time has come to do something. Pshaw, I should worry? Ha! You can count on it. It will be the same as always: He'll come home from work. I'll confess what I've done. He'll throw his arms in the air and shout, "No, it can't be." He'll drink some wine and fall asleep in his chair, and come to bed fumbling for me to comfort him. The morrow, he'll up and go to the maintenance barn to work on those oily trucks.*

She yanks her dragging daughter's hand onward into the dirty din of the city.

Luigi Pagani had grown up where the mafia appeared to have the covert blessing of the clergy. Many of the people feared, even hated, both power-groups. Gina's poverty-stricken hill family also would have little to do with them, although Gina herself had a more tolerant disposition. She was by nature a people-female, but once in the city, she had to be cautious. Luigi's father, Guiseppi, had been a good mechanic, a respected laborer and jovial with his family, but he detested priests – especially the Papists. He spat when a priest walked by. The back-fence talk was that a soft-fleshed, middle-aged priest had messed with Guiseppi's youngest brother Benito, when Benito was seven and preparing for first Holy Communion. People said that Benito was never right in the head after that time. Gina was convinced that most abuse is insidious, and nearly indelible.

The majority of the people who live around the Paganis in the North Bronx are Irish or Jewish – God-fearing, church-syna-gogue-goers. There are not many "Eye-talians" in the neighbor-hood, so quickly little eight-year old Anna felt like an outsider. Perhaps if they had belonged to some faith community, young Anna would have experienced some sense of connection. But she had her unfair birth blemish. Life is capricious. She didn't understand. And, to boot, she wasn't slim. Mama's manicotti with ricotta, eggplant, sardines, spinach, and cheery-tomatoes was needed comfort food to Anna, who sat the school day stiff, scared to move. She always felt on edge, emotionally threatened by the bullies.

As her mother yanks her through the neighborhood to St. Cecilia School, young Anna harbors a clutch of doom in her unripe body. Her life is crossing a dark chalk-line on the sidewalk. She will no longer be walking to PS 13 with her friend Billy. She had been happy to have a boy as a friend. Some girls didn't. Now she won't. Maybe never, ever.

It has to go without saying that little Anna had often cowered at the way she was treated at Public School 13. Agreed evolution has her quirky ways. Lady Luck had laid the red blemish on baby Anna without a note of explanation.

Naturally, the girl doesn't want to leave Billy and the handful of girls she knows – they're her only friends. They're the only people who make her laugh. At that time of her life, friends are hugely important to a little outsider. Of course, if she stops to think about it, PS 13 isn't exactly a nice place. But it's the only place she knows, and is known. Home is a hell, full of shouting too much of the time. Her headstrong mother and stubborn father shout and gesture at each other. Why her mother thinks the Catholic boys will be kinder, she can't understand. She's heard that Catholics burn girls at the stake, for silly reasons.

Anna certainly has no doubts that her father detests priests and distrusts anything Roman or religious. He will be loudly angry at her for going to the nuns. Deep down, she loves her funny father and wants his love. Yes, he has a stupid temper, but he is sometimes sweet to her – at least accepting. He is the one person who ever calls her "the apple of my eye," even if only when the words smell of wine.

As her mother registers her as a "non-Catholic" in Sister Mary Immaculata's office, Anna's first training bra squeezes her chest. She teeters on the verge of fainting. When she sees the narrowing of the nun's squint and feels the burn of her stare on her neck, Anna experiences, yet again, the stigma of being different, not right enough. She is no stranger to that feeling. At that instant, she sides with her father about people who talk about gods and cloudy mysteries. She agrees, "Baloney!"

Nevertheless, life's female story flows on. Her years at St. Cecilia's leave only faint, mixed watermarks on the submerged pools of Anna's soul. No way had she wanted to be there – true, the Catholics weren't quite as nasty to her, but they still pointed, and their lips still mouthed: *Gross. Sick. Ugly.* Sicilians, some say, have a propensity to distrust what is not work, women, and wine. Anna is not by temperament distrusting. Still, it is an heirloom for a girl to need to protect herself. Below the smothered hurt, she is like her mother used to be when she was young – kindhearted. But in the school of hard words, teenage Anna grows even more leery of males, young and old. After all, we have to be open to the possibility that Anna's inner pain might have simply been a little girl's need for a father's affection–or perhaps any male presence in her life.

As you hopefully know, the statistics for sexual assault, domestic violence, child abuse and stalking – to name just a few deviations from the path to beyond – are hard to swallow. Yet we are asked to digest them, like bitter herbs. The footprints of the violent are plastered across the daily rags. You probably know someone who has suffered more than her/his share of inner hurt. You may know an isolated person who couldn't take it anymore and took her own life. Ours may not be the worst of times, but it doesn't feel like the best of times. Yet, some say we may be on the edge of a new break forward.

Much to Luigi Pagani's relief, young Anna was allowed to go to the neighborhood public high school. But that didn't turn out much better. Teenagers can be cruel. After all, they grow up surrounded by a lot of selfish role models. Besides, once a young person like Anna feels like an outsider, it's not easy to feel whole, accepted, one of the normal band of kids. You suspect that you must give off an unseen stink: *Stay away. I'm not like you.* Boys who had teased and made fun of her neck in PS 13 were now even more brazen in their bullying in her freshman year, even though by then her figure had become like a young Italian movie-star's. When Anna put her mind to something, she achieved. It's survival.

Fortunately, having a strong bloodline back to the Romans, Anna fought back in her own way. She found a safe grotto in books and learning. She found a stopgap self in reading, starting with the Greek epics. She grew into the romantic Arthurian legends, and on to Edward Grimbel's *Young Adventurers into Science.* Even during those bewildering years in high school, she found escape in silly mental conversations with Galileo (wronged by the clergy), Isaac Newton (whom she thought cute), Einstein (whom she couldn't figure out), and Marie Curie, (the poster female for her future). Madame Curie did not have a rose garden life, but she was resilient, eventually winning two

Nobel prizes, one in physics, one in chemistry. They, the scientists, seemed like safe people; not emotional types who would bully a girl. **The call** to be a scientist fell on fertile ground, took root, and a protective persona came to life. Life does seem to nudge us, doesn't it?

Many psychologists would have diagnosed that Anna was repressing an iceberg of alienation. Nonetheless, like Cinderella, Anna found in science her stand-in for a Prince Charming. In the world's eyes, she skated through high school at the top of her class, thrilled with all she felt she was learning about the physical world and the expanding cosmos. *Knowing is as much fun as sex*, she periodically tried to convince herself. She felt different from most of the giddy girls who babbled about what they did, or valiantly refused to do, with their boyfriends. The watchdog at the doorstep of Anna's mind protected her. He barked if she began to slip into woolgathering about the girls' gaggling and their salacious adventures.

She was curious; after all, the world below the bellybutton is a wild cosmos that comes with the original equipment (minus instructions). Nonetheless, she taught herself to pick up a book and begin to focus, determined that she would someday show her father that she deserved more credit than he had given her – and more attention. Some aunt told her that Sicilians were born scholars. Still, in the unplumbed cavity of her female regions, she twitched with a pestering desire for a real boy-girl relationship – a pestering that reminded her of those unseen Greek Sirens of the night. Bravely, she fought off those Furies with a resolve to show everyone that she was not a freak. In actuality, the tender turtle within was moving more deeply into her shell.

Anna's father had a fatal "industrial accident" in her senior year of high school, and his body was shipped back to be buried in the Pagani family plot. He hadn't always been what neighbors might call a good family man; he was consistently opinionated, even harsh. They called him in Sicilian: *a shit-kicker*, which wasn't all that bad in the culture of godfathers. With his work, his wine-buddies, and his occasional Zorbaesque trysts with lonely, needy women (almost expected in that passionate, patriarchal culture), he had given little quality time to his only daughter, who often sat alone in her small room fantasizing and hoping that her father would say one of those funny sayings that would make her feel special. It had happened only rarely. Still, she had relished him in his sporadic Mediterranean moments. An empty sensation spread within her as she watched the plane with his body lift off the runway at La Guardia airport. You probably are not surprised that the *going on* of her father's physical remains was an enigma to a young woman, with little spiritual education.

Besides, there was the suspicious specter of injustice about this "industrial accident." God and the world weren't as provident as the good nuns at St. Cecilia's had liked to paint. For the next many years, these bitters of disillusionment will linger, as hidden burrs under the saddle of her psyche. The life of an outsider is no picnic. To make her cup even bitterer that senior year, she was passed over for the class valedictorian honor, even though her grades and records were far above the boy chosen. She presumed the teachers were afraid of the public's reaction to the crimson Gorbachev-like mark on her neck. Of course there was the possibility of the "boys are always better" bias. Nevertheless, she was showing them that achieving isn't just a boy thing. For Anna at that time, achieving was the only wing she had to fly with. The bullies had crippled her relationship wing.

The world turned; Anna won a scholarship to New York University and chose to major in physics, the science in which she felt most at home. Ever since the days of Newton and Descartes in the sixteen century, the science of physics has been materialistic, mechanistic, and deterministic. In her young, profane mind, if someone used fuzzy words like *God, soul, spirit* in earshot of a scientist, her mouth could be washed out with Fels Naptha soap. Materialism was in. Only the visible existed. Anna's upbringing had taught her to distrust the myths of the clerics and soothsayers. Actually, her education had taught her to suspect anything fuzzy, undocumented, or romantic. *Love* was not an element of the periodic table.

Let me tell you, as if you were from another time warp, the ostrich head-in-the-sand routine is not an easy strategy for a hormonal bosom of eighteen years, especially after the 60's revolution; more especially if you have regularly suffered as one of the passed-over girls, standing unasked on the dance floor sidelines. She knew her biology; the youthful mammalian urge to "do it" is female as well as male. So are sexual curiosity and the desire to be one of the group. Yes, she is interested in what everybody else claims to be doing. Naturally these drives swash across the synapses of her brain. But the underbelly of this story is that Anna, the marked one, the ugly duckling, never felt appreciated by any male.

As you might have been able to foresee, Anna's maiden taste of the forbidden was a letdown. *Is that all **it's** about?* She asked the morning after losing her virginity, sitting up in bed, knees clutched to her chest and cheeks wet with night tears. She didn't feel at all special; she hurt, a feeling she should have been used to. *Perhaps*, she wondered, *because I am flawed, I drew the short straw – Bradford Finch. He probably couldn't make it with any of the pretty, cool girls. Maybe he didn't even know the right way to do it. Or maybe I just wasn't ready. Maybe I'll never be. Lots of famous scientists survived without sex. It's only animal, you know.*

Through the years, she has observed the carryings-on of other girls and boys as basically a bystander. There had been no sexual revolution in the Pagani household. Female desire remains a burning question in most post-Victorian environments. Many claim that the popular culture's causal approach to the riddle of intimacy remains a daunting challenge. Certainly as a student of science and a visceral female, her deep mind knows there is something alluring about sex. She just isn't sure if she is emotionally equipped for it. Still, like good research, she feels that intimacy calls for careful attention. Even as a scientifically-minded coed, Anna believed that, actions elicit reactions. Allow a guy to touch a private body zone, and you'd damn well better be prepared for a response. Men are animals, and animals catch signals.

At that time of her development, unscientific notions like *non-harming, commitment, fidelity* have no place in her thinking, and show no signs of soon being part of her thinking. Still and all, she is by nature modest and sensitive. And despite her upbringing, she is not given to judging others. If people could see into the protected core of this young, bullied woman, they would see a lovable person. But who has the time to look inside a pretty woman?

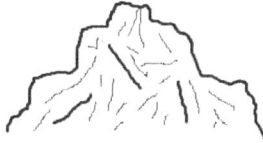

Anna graduated Magnum cum laude, and was hired by The New York Institute of Theoretical Physics. Right from the beginning, whenever Anna sees her new boss come in wearing his white linen Gatsby touring cap, a shiver races up her spine, and a sick page in her memories flies open. A page she desperately wants to forget, but can't ever tear out of her book of evil. For several reasons, in her mind, Wyatt Jones and Nick Mellon are kindred demons.

Nick Mellon was wearing an identical white cap that fearful night when he dumped off her roommate at their rented flat in Brooklyn. Cassie was disgracefully disheveled and wreaked of alcohol and sex. As a little girl, Anna had heard her mother, scream at her father, "You're the devil's own." Anna didn't believe in demons, but when she saw again and again the visual image of a man dropping a hurt woman on a couch, she recognized the hellish presence of evil. In her shocked psyche, the man in the white cap became an indelible incarnation of the satanic.

Cassie had talked about Nick before she agreed to go to a 1920's party at the Beta Gamma fraternity. Anna hadn't liked the vibes she picked up: He was handsome with wavy golden hair, popular with the gang of girls who put a lot of stock in money. He boasted that he was determined to make a mountain of money as an inside trader in San Francisco. She recognized the type: outwardly cool, inwardly egotistical. It had surprised her that Cassie agreed to go. Granted, both of them had basically no social life, except their own close relationship. As college seniors, they were at the top of their hormones.

He had also smelled of alcohol when she opened the door. He said nothing. He just dumped Cassie on the couch and scampered off, like a naughty dog that had just peed on a fire hydrant Anna hoped she'd never see or smell him again, or his likes.

Cassie Middleton was a California girl, though not your classic Baywatch babe. She couldn't even swim; say nothing about ride a surfboard. She grew up in Compton, California, the daughter of a Jamaica born taxi driver and a Swedish immigrant waitress. Her skin was a beautiful light brown, her hair a saucy dark brown. She walked with calypso and had the body of a model and the mind of a Nobel laureate. Like Anna, she was on a scholarship; she studying International Relations. They met in the NYU library when they were sophomores, and often grabbed a quick lunch in the library cafeteria.

When they were seniors, they decided to rent a flat in Brooklyn, close to the subway into the city. They were both secretly attracted to each other, possibly even physically. Nevertheless both were driven to succeed in the man's world. Both came from immigrant conscious environments and knew that a lot was at stake for them as outsiders. Only once did Anna see Cassie completely naked. And the beautiful image never left the sanctuary of her memory. They had been out for a run, and accidently came upon one another in their small bathroom shower. As Cassie stepped out of the shower, Anna experienced a surge in her body that most of us would recognize as desire. She immediately retreated. Fear won the moment. In truth they had the kind of connection with one another that many of us would call **love**. Cassie was the best, and only, real girlfriend Anna ever had. In a more privileged world, they could have easily become lovers. But they, the underprivileged, chose to stay simply soul sisters.

Two months after money boy dumps her on the couch, Cassie tells Anna she is pregnant. Someone had spiked the punch. She only remembered being led into a bedroom. She refused to consider an abortion. Anna admired her, but wasn't sure where she stood. Having a child by a man who worshipped money as well as himself was a big hurdle for Anna. She sealed her lips, but couldn't seal her mind. His memory was locked in.

About two months later, Anna hears a scream from the bathroom. She rushes in to find Cassie wailing in tears, and looking down into a toilet filled with blood. "I lost the baby. I lost my baby," Cassie repeats over and over and over. She is in shock. It is a scene and a wail, no woman could ever stifle.

Several weeks later, Cassie drops out of school. When Anna gets back to their flat, she finds a note saying *I love you.* Cassie has packed up her things and walked away into the gray winter mist. As Anna stands in the silent apartment, her senses bringing back the smell and dark color of blood, she feels a piercing pang of lost love. They had lived emotionally close, especially before the devil dumped Cassie on the couch. Anna trembles as she remembers. A part of her heart melts into tears running down her cheeks. Her heart begins to freeze tighter.

Anna never heard from Cassie and often wondered if she might even have jumped off a bridge somewhere in California or just walked off into the desert. Chiseled into her consciousness were new tablets about men who love money and the dangers of casual relationships. It was as if what happened to Cassie had happened to her, Anna. She would never tell anyone about Cassie.

That is one of the reasons she fears Wyatt Jones. He is a Nick Mellon who loves money and thinks nothing of using women. It is her guess that there are a lot of those animals prowling the city. Sometimes she sees it in their eyes as she walks to work. If the reader is a woman, she may well see what Anna was seeing. Most men don't see with those same perceiving eyes.

Fortuitously, at that time, Amit Gusain walks into Anna's life. It is another threshold time; she is crossing over the life marker of 'no-longer-student, now-adult-and-employed.' That's a big one, isn't it? Amit will become her colleague and friend, at least for a while.

Amit drew his first breath in one of the most malodorous armpits of the world, surrounded by rank poverty, rampant prostitution, and killer diseases. His father's Hindu family originally belonged to the revered Brahmin caste, but had fallen upon hard times. By the time of Amit let out his first cry, the family had been reduced to subsistence survival. Amit's father pulled a rickshaw through the streets of what was then Bombay, and died an early death of malaria. Amit's mother, a devout, unschooled Hindi girl from the countryside, had the maternal sagacity to urge her children to pursue learning and knowledge. Her oldest son, a handsome, caring boy, made the wise choice to listen to his mother's advice. He worked assiduously at his school lessons, yet always had time to laugh with his friends. His dark eyes danced like a happy Shiva, but did not miss seeing the squalor and suffering of his neighbors in Dharavi.

On his morning walk to the municipal primary school, Amit passed through one of the sprawling city's numerous brothel districts. One day he smiled kindly at a Muslim waif peering out of a narrow alleyway. He would never forget the hope that sparkled at that moment in her dark eyes at his simple kind smile. From then on, seven-year-old Adveena was there at the alleyway, waiting for her brown skinned hero in his shiny white school clothes. After a while, she started walking by his side, reaching up for her ten-year-old friend's hand, and they walked hand in hand.

Precocious and serious minded about his studies, Amit applied himself, first in the University of Bengal; then he applied to Stanford University in Northern California, and got his PhD in record time. He was hired by the New York Institute of Theoretical Physics the same June as young Dr. Anna Pagani. The tenured scientists called them the "Whiz Kids."

Anna felt attracted to Amit from the first day she met him: He was tall, dark, and handsome, with wavy chestnut hair, and full of fun. She loved the masculine timbre of his deep baritone laugh. She hadn't been around many people who laughed as readily and heartedly as Amit. In addition, there was a magnetic *je ne sais quoi* quality to him. He never spoke badly of others. It was a time when she was walking the tightrope of smoldering hormones. Rightly she wanted connection. She didn't understand it, but looking back, it might have been Amit's non-material values that crowned his cloudy mystery. She hadn't known people with strong positive beliefs, either. Or maybe it was his dark brown complexion that endeared him – it made him also an outsider. She cringed whenever Wyatt, her dumb boss, referred to him as "the dark one." Wyatt was one of those self-conceited guys who pride themselves on their sense of humor.

She also had a sneaking suspicion that Amit found her attractive. Sometimes she caught him smiling at her when she loosened her hair at lunch or walked in the park near the Institute. He seemed to feel a warm respect for her and was at ease talking with her. He enjoyed joking and laughing, but also had a pensive bent. She liked him a lot; more than any man she had ever met. He was more soul-searching and open-minded with her than with the other men. Yet he was different from both her and the other classical physicists. He had his quirky ideas.

By the time they met, Anna's body had matured winsomely, and she had outgrown the edge of her anti-religion conditioning. She didn't deem herself either an atheist or an agnostic. She was a nose-to-the grindstone scientist, that's all. Still, for her, words like *love* even *relationship,* were in the column of those don't ask, I don't know, questions. Her childhood had made her timorous. She really didn't understand her philosophical male-companion from mysterious Mumbai. She privately admired him for his interest in what the others called "the spooky physics" (quantum physics). For her, their gender entanglement was indeed unsettling, but secretly tingly, even if quite confusing and a little threatening.

Nevertheless, in our world of norms, Amit was married. And we live in a world of shifting, evolving norms, don't we? Through the graces of one of the University of Bengal professors, a marriage had been arranged between the Amit and a fair-skinned, round-faced girl from a well-to-do manufacturing family. The young girl was basically uneducated, but pleasantly pampered. She was a commodity widely sought in India as a docile wife. Thinking himself a kind of Renaissance patron, the professor only wanted to further the future of his promising student. At that time, arranged marriages were the only game in town, so young Amit had no choice. He went along with marrying a girl he hadn't even met until a few weeks before the festive wedding ceremony, despite the secret that in his heart, his memory still clutched the warm hand of the little Adveena, who was blossoming into a beautiful young woman. To his boyish heart, she had felt like **true love**. One's first love is surely one of life's eventful stepping stones, is it not?

Things did not fare well for the newly married, ex-pat couple in the Big Apple. Despite her materialistic upbringing, Shakti chaffed at "America's atheistic culture." In clear-minded moments, Amit suspected that, under her veil of anti-Americanism, she missed her sisters, and the sensual smells, exotic sounds, and spicy tastes of Mumbai.

Anna could see that the relationship was not fulfilling either of them. She felt a sincere empathy for Amit – one of her untypical emotions. Silently, she puzzled over the riddle of relationship. As the seasons changed those first years, her concerns deepened. Eventually, Shakti asked to be 'released,' and return to India. Anna never quite fathomed the technicalities of such an arrangement, nor did she feel any closer to understanding male/female relationships. But Shakti did return to India, and Amit continued to laugh with Anna and the others. Nevertheless, he behaved as if he were still married. Anna felt stranded, verging on anger. It was an anger she wasn't able to express even to herself. Most of us have been there, and probably still do repress some of our most hurtful emotions.

Anna knew that Layla, the other female physicist at the Institute, had moon eyes for Amit, but Layla flirted with lots of the guys, including their boss, Wyatt. She comes off as an immigrant, with an attractive body that she plays like a chess piece. Not surprisingly, she invests a lot of time with her personal trainer. Her body is her queen-piece. Anna doubts that Amit is the fooling around type. He is serious-minded like her.

Layla usually felt uncomfortable around Anna. In her needy Lebanese mind, the Whiz-girl was just too "goodie-shoes." Shit, she actually seemed to like work, as if she might even do it without pay. Besides, she dressed like a dork: black stockings, almost flat shoes, and minimal make-up that was about as unexciting as her white lab coat. Girl Layla loved shoes, especially high heels and tight skirts. She wasn't tall – only 5'4. She thought her hips a little too wide. But on high-heels, her hindquarters had attitude, and she knew it. She fearlessly flaunted her asset. At heart she was just a shopkeeper's daughter.

In Layla's mind, Anna had to be lonely. Everybody needs somebody. Hell, the Greeks knew that, didn't they? And as far as Layla knew, no one was tending to the dork's physical needs. Certainly she had to have them, but, some say that some people can drown their needs in work or play. Nobody seemed to know what is boiling in the hot caldron below her dork's navel. We all get *the hots*, Layla believed. The dork has got to be unhappy.

Still and all, Layla had to admit that Anna was never catty, never downing, not even underselling her contributions to the Institute, which she knew were few. It was almost as if Anna accepted her for just who she is – not much to rave about. She presumed that workaholic Anna didn't see her as a woman recklessly hungry to be loved and taken care of. Layla knew she was a woman whose deep-self feared she was silently running close to empty. *If she knew me, she probably wouldn't be so accepting.*

After graduation from Stanford, Amit had become increasingly intrigued by quantum physics. Most of the older scientists smirked off his non-mainstream (non-Newtonian) interests as hippie-like, presuming that India is still a culture catching-up. Mainstream physicists have no interest in the observer and consciousness as real parts of reality. After all, that's what physics is about – explaining reality. For them, the real big questions are about splitting the atom, or the commercial possibilities of gravitation experiments. But Amit had come to define the new physics, as he understood it, as "Seeking the smallest answers to the biggest, burning questions." That expression, the burning questions, inevitably brought a frown to Anna's brow. It sounded like religion masquerading as science.

Soon after she was hired, Anna decided that she should get an apartment within walking distance of the Institute. On inclement days, she could take a taxi. Born a city girl, she was privy to the folly and frustration of a car in the city. It was as stupid as bringing the notorious bull into a china shop. Truth was: she was afraid of driving. If she had a mechanical gene, it hadn't surfaced. She considered herself too mechanically inept to drive a car.

She found a one-bedroom place on the Upper East Side. The expense scared her to distraction. It would take half of her salary each month. But she bit the bullet and leased-to-own the apartment. The kitchen was tiny. She had no plans to entertain. The little living room was her refuge at night. She listened to some classical music, read some professional journals, and indulged in some science fiction. The plausible prospect of extra-terrestrial life in the cosmos gave her a rush. Occasionally she would order some manicotti or lasagna from the Italian deli down the street. She knew it was bad for her figure, and a contradiction. She'd just promise herself to run extra the next day. After years as an outsider she was used to her own company.

Toward the end of her first year, she read H. G. Wells' *The Time Machine* and Arnie Spheeris's *Andromeda's Future Trek*. Spheeris stirred up some unacknowledged female coals.

Usually, once read, Anna's books were recycled to the library. She has read *Andromeda* several times over the years. Andromeda, also a woman of flagrant contradictions, was possibly a kind of closet alter ego. The author's science wasn't that advanced, and the prose not very poetic, but to Anna, the relationship sounded heroic – an Arthurian idyll of intimacy. Ann never thinks of herself as romantic. She is a scientist. Still, some of us who can read through the lines of her story have a suspicion that another fair princess sleeps in the scientist's depths. Perhaps, she dreams, Amit will awaken her.

In the book, Ava Gold's father, Captain Herman Guldenstern, is a fighter pilot in the East German Air Force. The only pictures of him in Ava's mind are in uniform: black airman's cap with a silver insignia, black shirt, black jodhpurs, and black leather boots. The only colors she remembers are the campaign ribbons on his chest. Even the short riding-crop that he carries is black, as is the gloved hand he routinely slabs it into. He is a stern, disciplined authoritarian. He never held her, nor ever kissed her. Neither did her Prussian nanny. In Spheeris's book, her birth mother is missing. It is *Herr Capitan* alone who determines that his only daughter will enroll in the East Berlin Institute of Military Strategy. She likes to please her father and is used to army life. The captain is delighted when she elects to go into the Europol Space Mission (ESM). Ava has accepted the Spartan life that destiny appears to have lain out as her path. To all the world, she seems like *the natural*. The tight-lipped life is in her genes and her memes.

Upon being accepted into the elite and highly secretive ESM, she assumes the name Andromeda. Each cosmonaut commander bears the code name of a constellation or a galaxy. A near twin of the earth's Milky Way, Andromeda is one of the hundreds of billions of galaxies in our universe. It is a spiral galaxy of a trillion stars. As a figure in mythology, Andromeda is the princess of bravery who is chained to a rock in the ocean as a sacrifice to the male sea monster, Kraken. Moreover, Ava chose the name for what it means: *Andros* (man) and *mendomai* (to think) – She who thinks strong like a man. The name became her persona. The soft female became the hard male mask.

Jason Kenny, the Iowa farm boy who enters the book, is the son of a nurse. (Little further character explanation needed.) His father Joseph Kenny is both a veterinarian and a corn farmer, well known in the area for his gentleness. Jason gets his B.A. in interpersonal psychology and his M.A. in naturopathic medicine. After years of academia and cultural mayhem, the big-and-strong corn-fed Iowan feels lost. He just wants to get away from the jarring news of political scandals, the disgrace of the poor getting poorer, and the violence diet of the media soothsayers. He had grown up watching *Star Trek*. When it got to the point where he just had to get away, he applies to the ESM. His qualifications are a dead-on match for the needs of a small, highly-trained crew, in cramped quarters, for long periods of time. He gets the job, and shows up for his first intergalactic mission, bumbling and lumbering, in a spacesuit he can hardly steer. A different somebody, he's a welcome addition to the crew.

He first encounters Commander Andromeda as he boards the spaceship *Kaiser Wilhelm* for his mission away from it all. He has been briefed that she is one tough bird. What is more, she doesn't even look female in her official space suit, even with her helmet is off. She has what he judges to be a professional smile. The timbre of her voice announces that she will call the shots. Americans in general don't like authority. They are the people who rebelled against monarchy, tyranny, and whoever thinks himself, or herself, top dog. Jason is American, but he is also an Iowan – as broadminded as the plains. He is not small minded about others. Not even Germans, even though his five uncles had fought to unhorse the Aryan *Ubermensch* who had rained hate upon Europe.

Their mission is to out race a Russian rogue spaceship to the Sea of Craters on Mars. (Coed Pagani, had once seen the Sea of Craters through a telescope.) Soon after the initial hurtling through galactic space, the buzzer in Jason's cubicle office sounds. He asks for acknowledgment and realizes that it is his commander herself. He presses a button and the infirmary door slides open enough to let in the space-suited, East German commander. She explains that she is in great discomfort. She has some kind of annoying itching that makes it almost impossible to sit still. Can he give her something to stop it?

"I'm sorry to hear that, Commander Andromeda. But I'll have to have a look at it before I can determine what can be done. You'll have to remove your suit and uniform."

She winces. He turns his eyes away while she who thinks like a man removes everything except her dainty red panty. When he turns to inspect her rash, his eyes widen in wonder. The transformation is unbelievable! The strong looking commander isn't there. Before his eyes is a delicate young damsel – slim, small-boned, with soft white skin, and blotches of red (reminding Anna, as she reads, of her own blotch). The commander's pixie-like, short-cut blonde hair reminds him of the golden silk tassels that crown the slender cornstalks of his native plains. It's love at first, naked sight.

She lets out an impatient puff of breath. *Herr* Commander is embarrassed and feels vulnerable. He puts together a naturopathic unguent of four medicinal herbs in a base of avocado oil. There are red blotches of the edema almost everywhere: on her breasts, down into her pubic triangle, and especially on her back. With an edge of irritation and authority, she tells him to apply the salve to her back. "I can handle the rest, Lieutenant" she says with teenage-like testiness. "But my back is driving me crazy."

The first touches of his hand twist her neurons tight, stiff-necked, and angry as hell. She is shocked, alarmed, and frightened at being touched by a man. Men **don't** touch **me**! But Jason had been brought into the world by a gentle Sioux midwife, who eased him into a pool of warm water, and passed him to a circle of loving hands. As he touches, a presence leaks out of his fingertips. At first, inside the commander's mind, she is flailing. *Damn you.* Then, deeper inside, the girl within the woman's body says *Yes* as she senses his gentle respect that softens her body and warms its way to her heart. She has never before experienced the intimacy of a tender touch.

The black box of her mind retrieves from her academic days something about the necessity of touch for human well-being. She had laughed at the English idea back then, but now she just wants his fingers to go on, and on. She heals quickly, crediting the touch more than the sweet-smelling balm.

Eager for his gentle touch, she invites him to a *rendezvous* in her compartment. The first time things are awkward. The next time, once the metal, airlock door slides tight and the lavender-scented oxygen resumes it softening effect, they move into their own new ritual – a spontaneous exploration. His mind eventually christens it their *rite de passage*, their crossing of the limen of desire. He delights in peeking at her soft nipples. The girls he had encountered as a farm boy were strong boned farmer's daughters. She now just yearns to be touched. It makes her feel special. She feels valued as feminine.

The ritual begins with her coy smile. Her signal that she is comfortable with him and is giving him permission to do what no other man has ever been allowed. He slowly and deliberately begins to open her space suit, the protective camouflage bearing her commander's insignia – the first of seven veils before the final fig leaf. She follows suit, opening the Velcro straps of his official identity until they both stand as revealed as Adam and Eve. (The first time, Ava didn't take off her red panty. Then she did, with a shy smile.) She transforms into a delicate Medici Venus, the apotheosis of modest beauty.

Each time she slowly guides him to her bed, holding back the opening to the white lace tent that creates their secret cave. For an unhurried spell, they lie, looking into each other's eyes, quietly exchanging secrets – their innermost feelings and never-told fears. It's like they are moving around in each other's soul space, oblivious to the suns, moons, stars, and cosmic solitude that the *Kaiser Wilhelm* is speeding through. As he traces his finger over her flesh, he whispers *Ava.* She purrs. In his mind, he hums *Getting to know you*, admiring the delicate slope of her soft shoulders. In knowing her, he is getting to know himself. He can't find the words for the core of the female mystery: Gentle?

Delicate? Fragile? Moreover, he remembers the saying *the soft will conquer the hard.*

When the golden girl of space reaches a plateau of desire, her wetness spreading, she glances at his tumescence and, rolls onto her back, whispering *I want you inside of me.* After they come together, her body glistening with an inner after-glow and a Cheshire cat smile, she moves her back fluidly into his front, and he wraps his farm boy arms around her in the hug of two spoons. She drifts off into the star system of the satisfied.

The first time she read it, in her early twenties, Anna had made a pencil notation after the last sentence, as she always did to let whoever bought the used book at the library know what she thought about the book: A romance. This author thinks that mutual attentiveness with a man brings out a woman's true nature. Hogwash. Women must learn to swim with the piranhas. Still, she keeps the book. To this day it sits on her little library shelf.

Life, as we of the Malachy clan know, can be a greased pig, hard to pin down and full of surprise wiggles. My ancestral family has a long history as Dubliners. Mael O'Morgair (Anglicized to Malachy) (1094 - 1148), was the Archbishop of Armagh and the first Irishman canonized by an Italian pope. Like Boniface in Germany, Malachy was a reformer of the lax life and a promoter of monastic contemplation. He preached that life was a struggle between the forces of the light and the Great Deceiver from the dark fires. At the time of the deadly potato famine, the Malachy clan made the mighty decision and immigrated to New York City, a city brimming with greenhorns, kith, kin, and blue-collar jobs. It was one of those: *You gotta do, what you gotta do* decisions.

Early on in my own life, I had to face such a decision. As a young Catholic boy I had lived sheltered in a haven that had all the answers. My mother said I was born with a serious spoon in my mouth. One of my high school teachers said I would have a wrinkled brow when I grew up because I frowned a lot. Like a docile boy, I had wrapped myself up in the life of Holy Mother the Church, my schooling, and my sports.

In college, I got hooked on surfing the Internet news, even though I sensed that I was being seduced by the chronicles of the dark side...a kind of social porn. I told myself that someday I'd do some writing about the American culture. I had loved Robert Bellah's *Habits of the Heart.* I've come to think there's a twisted addiction to the news. It certainly panders to the violent and prurient. Maybe the public pulp distracts one from his private lonesomeness. The news seems to loom like the culture's beaked hawk of the nether world. Personally, during those waning moon nights in the Big Apple, I was without a north star. I began slipping into a kind of sloth, giving up sports and exercising. "I am just too busy, man." My health, both physical and mental, sunk toward a low-ebb. I spent my days medicated by the fluorescent lights of classrooms and libraries. I soothed my psyche afterwards with a couple of pints at some Irish pub.

By the time I finished my bachelor's degree, I was sick of Sin City. The Euclidian mind can become a monkey on your back. I had, per force of the culture, bought into Descartes's fallacy: I am because I cogitate. I cogitated a lot, but I wasn't happy.

When it came my time to hang up the life of undergraduate academia, my tender self, with its own inner famine, decided on the West Coast city with a lot of Irishers, and regular Gaelic activities – San Francisco. Moving west wasn't easy. Moving on never is. But I burned the boats of my youth and set out in search of a new harbor – away from those East Coast money-crazy Molocks, puffed-up Narcissi, and trolls of Priapus.

Immigrating to the city of the golden bridge and friendly fog, I was not expecting Utopia or Camelot or Shangri-La … just a perch where I could see the light of connecting and contributing. However, shortly after arriving to that city where little cable cars climb, on one of those famous foggy nights down on the waterfront in North Beach, I found my twenty-three-year-old butt perched nervously at the end of the long, curved bar. Yes, I was trolling. I was still woefully wet-behind the ears, and still lacking in the social skills that educators say you can only learn by failing.

To this day, the *Buena Vista Café* is one of San Francisco's most crowded Irish watering holes, internationally famous for its Shannon Airport Irish coffees. You can catch the nip of the Irish whisky in the air, and glimpse the frothed cream floating like a swan across the dark coffee, ponded in the small glass goblet. To be sure, it is an elixir. I look into the crowd and see a lass advancing toward me with swaying hips that rival the loins of Cleopatra. Her body motions announce that she is a risk-taker. In truth, imperceptible to the insecure me, she is just a female parading a girl's insecurity. Her fiery red hair and lively green eyes make her a magnet for men's attention. I am thrilled when Allie O'Grady joins me at the bar. She exudes a scent of musk – that musk that jams the male regulatory signal console, even of men with all their synapses matured. I wasn't yet one of those mature guys. Life can be a struggle, but there are moments that call for surrender.

A native Sunset girl and educated in a local Catholic school, she is gainfully employed as a stewardess for Aer Lingus and is interested in sports. Sports had always been one of those distractions that kept my mind buoyant. She had given away her prized cherry in high school, as was expected. When in Rome, the young stewardess accommodates those guys with the expensive looking Captain's uniforms. She considers bedding down to be job security. Truth be confessed, young Allie turns out to be almost as naïve as I was.

It didn't take long before we wound up in the sac, like babes in toy-land. It took even less time for Allie to become pregnant. We were married in St. Mary's downtown. In a sense it was a shot-gun wedding, but we didn't think of it as that. It was one of those crossroad times that you are forced to make a decision. Life is full of those crossroads that force you to make a hard choice. It's choices that alter the course of your life. We both came from a culture that expected marriage, and was death on abortion.

In a sense, we had no choice. Besides we were both raging with young hormones; and raging hormones can feel like wisdom. The fact that neither of us really knew who we were would only come to light years down the river of our lives. We were typical young Catholics who knew the rules, and did what the fates destined us to do.

Allie retired from her job and settled into being a full-time mother to Matt, and almost two years later to Noreen. In some senses, she was a natural, at least as a mother. I guess most women are. But we were different, Allie and I. Men and women are, aren't they? Women can be in the moment – bathing the infant, playing with the rubber ducky, absorbed in Oprah's guru. Life had no pestering questions for Allie. She wasn't interested in philosophy. She didn't need a *theory of it all* to explain what she would do that day. Meaning was not one of her important words.

I, on the other hand, compulsively continued wanting, like Icarus, to fly with my wings of wax, into the burning sun. I taught classes in Comparative Religions and Journal Writing, (considered a spiritual skill in the city that made Haight Ashbury a hippie haven). At that time, I still wrote in my journal, not as much as in college, just a short few lines when something struck me. My pen wrote very little about my inner life which had sort of slipped offline. Those journal entries, with traces of my life journey, are somewhere in a steamer trunk. I still don't feel inclined to go back to the story of the past. Better perhaps to envision the future.

Nights and weekends, I went to State to get a master's degree. I was neurotically busy – being busy is what psychologists call "a personal trait." (A male trait?) In hindsight, I suspect it is a male defense mechanism. Hell, I didn't know who I was. A man can hide in the bulrushes of being busy. Naturally, I rationalized that I was doing all of this for Allie and the kids: If I get another degree, I'll bring home more bacon. I presumed it's the bacon that keeps a family happy.

Time flew by, as it does when you are young and running around trying to find an identity you can hang your hat on. Wow, where did it go? Matt grew tall, graduated, and got a job with the San Francisco's *finest.* Two years later, Noreen, who had studied literature, graduated and ran away to a job in Minneapolis with an advertising company. As I said, Allie had never needed an explanation of what it's all about, nor was she inclined to concern herself about the big picture or some ultimate reality. Yes, mentally, we were miles apart. The carnal romp had been a nightly adventure in the beginning. According to some canons of biology, it was successful: Allie's and my genes will pass on. The afterlife never seemed to be one of her unvoiced questions. Getting through today and blotting out tomorrow, until tomorrow, that was Allie. She could skate through a day of pop tarts, school buses, cleaning ladies, girls' lunches, afternoon gym, and prepare a respectable evening meal. It's the bane of lower and middle class women. Wool gathering is a luxury they can't afford.

Her one *bete noire* in life was her hips, her weight. She freaked out every time she stepped on a scale and saw that she had gained a pound. (And then we went on another Dr. So-and-so diet.) I didn't seem to be an answer to her acceptance/security concerns, and maybe she had to be culturally desirable, in case of future need. That may well be a modern female survival meme. After all, a girl never knows if her mate will return home true: an eagle could swoop down onto her sparrow husband in flight, a hunter could shoot him down in the woods; a woman of pleasure could coax him into her wanting bed.

After Noreen's birth, Allie's pleasure thermometer cooled its youthful heat. To be frank, I don't think Allie found me all that exciting or proficient after Noreen. Then, I guess I gave up trying. Eventually, the midlife female change came upon her just after the nest emptied.

One gray day she went out for a drive on Skyline Drive, which she often did "to clear her head." I was away for a week-long conference on eschatology. She had taken some of those damn prescription drugs her therapist had prescribed for anxiety. Her car went off the road and down the embankment. Her body, once beautiful and sculpted, was a crushed mess. When I got the news, I rushed home. With tears in my eyes, I had to identify her. I realized that even though our marriage was not the greatest story ever told, we did have a genuine physical chemistry, at least for a few years. In retrospect, I realize that those tears in the morgue were also tears for my own failure. I had never learned to give her the gift of presence. In a sense, I had not really been present to myself, say nothing about being present to the ambient world.

The police recorded it as an accident. It had rained that morning. The road was undoubtedly slippery. Nevertheless in my mind it will always be a suicide, possibly prompted by an unconscious death wish. A silent killer wish spawned by a life without a defined direction. Again, I have to feel that I failed her. I hadn't been attuned enough to her lack of vision, her emptiness. I was only a shadowy presence to her – too wrapped up in myself, and my books. But can one really be responsible for another's soul? No, but one can contribute more than I did.

Nostalgia is the coming home of loss. For months I mourned my failure. It was as if a part of my soul both died with her and broke open. I suppose you could say that her death plowed me open. I would lie fallow for a winter or two; and another woman would sow some seeds of maturity into the soil that Allie had left open in my spirit.

The Sunset redhead still looms as one of my non-wins.

It is mid-afternoon on late February day in the red rocks of the Sedona high country, still chilly. I'm looking out the bar window at the enamel-blue sky that is spread across the valley which I temporarily consider home. Oh yes, reader, I'm Gwen Dykstra. For me, a fugitive from that world of boys high on gynecology, life here is palatable, though far from satisfying. I suffer from your garden-variety loneliness. This afternoon I'm high with the energy of a morning hike out the Soldiers Pass Trail.

The *Cave,* originally *The Lonesome Cowboy Saloon,* where I work, is pretty empty and quiet. The crowd will come into in about two hours when the feature film lets out. My attention snags on a guy coming in the front door. There is no spring in his step. He isn't a local. I've been tending bar here long enough to read bar people like an animal reads potential meals. My bet: New York or maybe West Coast. He is dressed in a brown bomber-style, leather jacket and an open-collared white shirt. Good looking, but a cowboy down on himself if I ever saw one. Of course, as they used to say in the schoolyard, "It takes one to know one." His brown modish-looking hair is longish the way I like it, and I catch the greenish hue in his hazel eyes as he takes a seat at the bar. Easy guess: Irish. No wedding ring. I'm experienced at fleshing out people – well, men at least. I still don't understand women. Not even my kid sister, who has come out of her own mess, and is now standing on her own good legs. I wished I had them. Nevertheless, I like women too, although I'm not ready to go there. I don't think.

I've been working here at the *Cave* almost four years. It's a good location right in the middle of West Sedona on State Highway 89A that comes down from the old silver mining town of Jerome, goes through town, and up Oak Creek Canyon to Flagstaff and Historic Route 66. I really get a kick out of that old mining town, Jerome. The very thought of Jennie Banter's early 1900's bordello up in the Crib District brings a kind of wetness to my mouth, and regions below. The cribs being the shacks where the soiled doves plied their trade with the female-starved mine workers on "Husbands Alley." I sometimes fancy that I would have enjoyed living back then in the "wickedest town in the west." It's rumored that the murdered Jennie's ghost still haunts the *Lace Room* in *The Mile High Inn.* But a modern-day gal can't make a living there.

Jerome has changed from a frontier town with a 100 prostitutes to small town of tourist shops and art vendors. And society is tumbling into a new sexuality that few of us, if any, understand. I think it's somehow shallower. And I guess I have to confess that I'm not at all sure I could tolerate being used by well-oiled men, night after night. Once in a while, sure, maybe. But I do fancy the way those gals dressed-up and flirted. I'd been a nurse, got burned out, and came to Sedona to find a new life. I get a kick out of listening to the troubles of strangers like the guy who has just climbed on a stool at the far end bar. They make me forget my own foibles.

I check my hair in the mirror, and head toward him. I wink at him as I approach, "Howdy, partner. What can I do for you?"

I can still see Gwen's first kittenish smile like it was yesterday. She's an unforgettable, complex gal. And to this day, several years later, big John Malachy still goes to her from time to time, like a little boy who needs to reassure himself that mommy is still there. At that time in late 2008, my life was running on fumes only ... too much academia and news too discouraging from the cultural warfronts. That morning, for example, there was news of another 14 year-old girl gang raped in Philadelphia. Five teenage boys held her down and proved their manhood to one another. It frightened me. I didn't know what I wanted, or who I was. I had always been living a script written by someone else or some institution. I never had to work at who I am. By that time I was ready to trash that catechism of childhood answers. But I couldn't quite. Now several years after Gwen's first smile, a new version of who I am seems to be struggling to break ground.

Like Sisyphus with his stone, I've had the seeker-sickness. I've been banging my head against that stone since I reached the age of reason and first Holy Communion at seven-years-old. When I met Gwen Dykstra, the sickness was buzzing in my head like a swarm of killer bees. I suffered from the guilt that I am a loser who might never beat those bees.

I still hear her sweet voice, "Let's face it, Mr. John Malachy; we're all made of the same stuff. We all have the same needs, the same desires." She winks, serving me my second vodka tonic with a lime twist. An obviously, sensual barmaid's wink, but not a blatant come-on, just enough to stir the homunculus to attention. And my carnal prowess has been at parade rest longer than Oprah's relationship guru would recommend.

Gwen is a kind of exciting sea nymph. You know the ones that lure mariners to their destruction – the ones who both excite, and frighten. Yet even in my self-absorbed state, I could catch glimpses of the vulnerable *puella fragila,* at the edges of her voice, and her cautious eyes. By dint of my failed relationships with both Annie and my daughter Noreen, I'd come to believe that women are easier to hurt that we men realize. It's common knowledge that the bite of the male's snake leaves fang marks in a woman's psyche. "We're all human, with the same hungers," she continues.

Gwen isn't that old, but the bloom of youth is starting to fade on her face. Still, there is a soft aura of resignation on that ordinary, Midwestern face, undoubtedly gathered in the school of life's knocks. That afternoon, her ginger-ash blonde hair hangs down past her shoulder blades in a loose ponytail, fastened with a turquoise clasp. Her trim body is graced with small, still peaked, breasts. It's her deep sky-blue eyes that draw me in, calling to me, with a soft, shy, yet genuine, acceptance. They are eyes one seldom encounters in the maddening crowds of a city.

I hope she likes me, a shy voice from the hold below is saying. Out of the blue, I wonder if the magical light of the surrounding mountains might have something to do with that sparkle. I know that from the moment I arrived in Sedona, I felt something strange – a summons I wanted to resist. Ever since my college days, I no longer think of myself as a Catholic, but I do still have subtle "spiritual" roots from those innocent times.

"The problem, if you don't mind my saying so," she adds, "is that nowadays, it's frightfully difficult to find that yellow brick road to the Emerald City. God knows, I've tried enough brick roads, and I don't feel anywhere closer to finding that mythical Grail, that brims with answers. Believe me, it's easy to lose sight of what we really want – what our spirit really forages for." (*You got that right, girl. I don't know what I want. Of course, I know what my body wants,* my mind chips in.)

"The din outside," Gwen says with a quick nod of her head, "drowns out the wise woman within. **That** I know from experience. But we can't give up, John, can we? We <u>must</u> keep on seeking. Or we're wasting our time on stage. And the whole human team could wander into the bogs. Lots of other people need people like us who have hit deep potholes, but keep on trucking." I sense then and there, that both of us seek the same mythical lost ark.

Ah, the yellow brick road, my mind muses, fascinated by the moving-feast of her upper body, *I used to believe it existed, but my faith is getting thin, and thinner. The gal's right about the noise. You can't hear yourself in this media-bombarded culture. God, it was so easy to believe when I was young. An Eternal Boy in me still craves that certainty.*

It might not have been the worst of times, but it wasn't the best of times for the American culture. The economy was tanking. A lot of people were losing their jobs and homes. On top of that, a whole lot of people's sons and daughters had died or got maimed in Iraq. Add another questionable war in Afghanistan that is bleeding the country even further. Meanwhile people have almost confidence in the elected leaders of the country, especially after the recent spate of "love-guvs."

But here in the *Cave* with the mellow soft lights and fireplace burning behind her, one easily gets the sense that there is a sensitive vein (and more) below her tight purple skirt and modest white blouse. One senses a something that some would call soulful. Adorned with her corral-colored macramé bracelet with its small silver *Pisces* charm, she evokes the image of the saucy barmaid in *He Who Saw the Deep* (The Epic of Gilgamesh). My father loved to quote passages from world literature. My head still rings with his strong, tenor voice: *Beside the sea, she lives, the woman of wine. Sidhuri sits with the golden bowl and the golden vats that gods gave her. She sees Gilgamesh coming toward her, wearing skins, the flesh of gods in his belly, but despair in his heart, and the face of one who has made a long journey.* (I have little doubt that I remember those lines so well because I seem predestined to a similar long haul.)

On other future nights, saucy Gwen will conjure up the image of the Greek goddess Iris, serving nectar to Zeus from her ornate pitcher. She has those museum book Greek curves, like Milo's Venus. Clearly the tomes of mythology and history teem with such women, endowed with presence and understanding – those hallmarks of humanity, undoubtedly born long ago in a circle of sisterly caring. After all, it was a female who gave birth to this primate who knows that he knows, (even if nowadays he doesn't seem to know where the hell he is going). No one can deny the fact: *First man* emerged from a woman's womb, and drank in the longing for relationship at a woman's breast.

The iconic barmaid motions to my woolgathering glass, "You ready?" It's mid-afternoon of my second day in Sedona, and I am the wounded hero wandering, somewhat dazed, on the outskirts of anhedonia – that loss of the capacity to experience joy. The spark of life's meaning had gradually slipped out of my life.

In reality, m*eaning* is now a mere pilot-light. The sad woe is that this lost wanderer doesn't realize how much in need of a maternal ear and heart he is. I nod an affirmation, not so much for the drink, but for her soft company. Carelessly, I had been unwittingly shying away from the gentle sex, having fallen into licking my wounds of failure.

"What brings you to town? The film festival?" she asks.

"More or less. To tell the stark truth, I don't know what brings me **here**, rather than someplace else. A few minutes ago, I walked out of a boring documentary. Maybe the film was okay. Maybe I'm what's not okay. A travel agent talked me into coming here."

"Sounds like you're carrying some hurts. I know hurting. I'd guess we all do. Hard to escape these days, isn't it?"

"Oh, yeah, a long story."

"I like stories," she says as she sets another drink down in front of me. "On me."

At that moment, an epiphany opens a crack in some door: This place, this woman, are sending signals, like angels do. Not the ones who announce, but the ones who stand and hear. In my heart of hearts, I feel that the place is trying to light a silent spark inside me. I had felt something strange when I first laid eyes on these spectacular red bluffs.

The barmaid and I exchange stories, and talk to and at one another with our eyes, with our bodies, with our hearts open. She's a real good story sharer herself, and boy, does that gal have stories. Don't get her started. Though with me that afternoon, she didn't talk that much; she let me talk. But I caught the sense that this gal has seen and suffered. I also hazily recognized that I wanted a woman in my life.

Some of her last words to me as I moved toward the door of the *Cave* were: "Get out and hike while you're here, John Malachy. I find it a great tonic for a sore soul."

On the ride back out to the resort, I stare at the world of the red rocks standing strong in the changing light and shadows of afternoon. I have a sensation that the landscape wants to tell me something. I never had a feeling like this in the maddening city. By the time the shuttle gets to the entrance to the resort, I feel almost human again, and I haven't felt human in quite some time. A few years ago, Gwen had also been down and bummed, and came to Sedona at the insistence of her younger sister, Sally Stevens, another outdoors gal who has traveled the less traveled road, but cares about her unorthodox older sister.

It's October 2008, the seedtime of my passage through the rabbit hole to the dramatic wonderland of the red hills. Again I'm poised on the cusp of a life change, though I don't clearly see it coming. But Gwen has handed me the red rose of attentiveness. No sweeter rose. (I will return to talk with this empathic barmaid many times in the handful of years that follow.) Gwen also has her wounds and that familiar dull wanting within, as do many women moving upwards in the years, in a self-occupied culture. Possibly it hurts more in those women whose bodies have never felt the fullness of life growing within. For sure, many have only tasted the thin barrenness of shallow relationships. Sadly, Gwen still falls into dumb choices, but soldiers on.

Mitzi Stein, one of the gals getting off the shuttle back at the resort hotel, invites me for a soak in her hot tub. My imagination perks up, but I'm not up to the temptation, even though my body knows it is dragging an unwanted, rusty anchor. Perhaps at that juncture I am worrying that I might be a little rusty in the sheets. I fear failure. It'd been a while. Secondly, I've downed a couple of vodka tonics at *The Cave*. But the bottom line is that I sense that Mitzi just isn't going to turn out to be *"the one"* for me. Sadly, my silent intuitive self is heavy-hearted, admitting to myself that Gwen probably isn't *the one* either. I don't quite know why. She listened to my words, but I don't think she heard *me*.

Perhaps there is no *one* for me. Perhaps that *chemistry* stuff is a myth. Perhaps life is destined to pass me by. Besides, I believe, in the crevasses of my mind, that walk-away sex leaves rueful dents in the person left in the cold sheets. It's as if the heart of the person used wakes up to the realization she's been had. She's been a thing. Yet the culture, or perhaps the media, claims that many women are forced by circumstances to surrender to being just things of flesh. According to the paleontologists: *Sex for food; food for sex*, is as old as these hills.

So I crash the couch for an hour. When I awake, I turn on the TV. I know I watch too much news, but then I tell myself that I need to know what is going on in the "real" world. All the same, the majesty of this expressive high country doesn't fit with watching the major media news, which depresses me anyways. Most of it is about violent reactions in a somewhat bizarre culture – a culture perhaps sliding down the slope toward annihilation. Some doomsters say *probable* extermination. On the other hand, others believe there is a growing remnant of people who know that the stakes are high and worth working for. I have to admit that, for me, evolution seems to be losing the direction that got us to where we are. The bonds of relationship that held us together seem to be fraying.

The local Phoenix channel isn't much better: rapes, murders, break-ins, and political scandals. Sedona doesn't seem to have a news channel. Having no news channel feels like la-la-land. So I watch an info piece on the area. The section on hiking the hills catches my attention. My inner Merlin and creaky joints, from a life too slowed-down, whisper: *Better for your health. Man putting on years.*

Later, sitting under the stars on the deck of my casita at the entrance to an awesome canyon, I watch a romantic silver moon rise behind a tall, rock spire that seems like the fabled Zen finger pointing at the moon. I make a short entry into my journal on the big questions and answers that had once guided me through the narrows of youth. The Sophic barmaid's words about losing track of what we really want had stirred up that pesky swarm of buzzing bees. The moon is romantic, but I no longer feel the romance with life that I felt as a boy.

Just before I was getting ready to go back to the resort hotel, and after Gwen tells me to get out and hike, I asked her about the prices of real estate in Sedona. "Oh, they're all over the lot," she says. "They say there are some great buys. The banks are hurting." She talks about Bob Dorian and his partner Catherine Reilly who come in regularly for the happy hour. "He's one of the most knowledgeable realtors in town. He seems to have a knack."

The next morning, I awake discombobulated and angry at myself for having some brandy from the honors-bar. I guess I was fighting off the fantasy of Mitzi Stein in her hot tub. To my chagrin, there is a red light blinking on my bedside phone. I push the button, wondering who even knows where I am. "Hello, this is Bob Dorian with Red Rock Realty," the tape begins. "Last night Gwen at the Cave said you were inquiring about real estate in Sedona. I'd be glad to show you a few places, if you're interested. It's a good time to buy, and Sedona bewitches. I came here nine years ago without any plans of staying, but I caught the fever. Give me a call if I can be of assistance, 928 204 7397."

I lie there anxious, something moving in me. I'd only had three vodkas and a couple of brandies. But I sense that it is more than the drink that stirs restive. Something untapped in me wants to see more to this land of weathered red mountains. The place seems so unconcerned about change, so stable, so different from the way I feel. Besides, I hardly feel jazzed about sitting in a dark movie theater again, when the light outside is so entrancing. I'm only going to be here for a few days. Heck, those nature movies on TV aren't the real thing. This place feels like the real thing; there is something different in the atmosphere. As if from dreamtime, the scent of Mitzi Stein's cloud of Channel-#-something comes back. Maybe I should have just done it. It seems pretty normal these days, or so they make you think. But no, maybe I don't know who I am, but I don't want to go in that aimless direction. I want something more.

I shower, shave, and order breakfast. After some coffee and a Southwestern omelet with Navajo blue corn tortillas, I return the realtor's call. When I meet him in the hotel lobby, Bob Dorian looks successful – short graying hair, well-barbered, average height and lines, obviously in tight shape. He's dressed very professionally, yet comfortably in an open collared dark blue shirt, and beige, pressed chinos. His blue eyes and smile are made for sales. He's got personality plus, which isn't common in the teaching profession. He takes me, in his upscale jeep, with custom get-in steps, to several tempting homes that do indeed seem good buys, compared to the Bay Area.

When he takes me to Lomas Serenas, at the base of Elephant Rock, he says something about this little enclave having a reputation of being a close-knit community. Zing! An arrow lodges in my heart: people, community, connection. However, that region of my brain that is supposed to recognize the big picture doesn't exactly stand up to dance a stack of barley. But, unbeknownst to me, it has heard the comment. I may not know who I am, but from time to time, some deep regions of my consciousness suspect who I'd like to be – if I ever stopped to listen to myself.

After we see about six places, Bob invites me to go hiking the next morning. I accept, remembering Gwen's advice. He and his partner meet me at the front door of the resort as the sun is peeking over the red hills. Catherine is fashionably slender, lean-and-limber looking. She dressed in form-fitting light khaki jeans and a cream-colored crewneck blouse. Her designer sunglasses are pushed up on her light-ginger blonde hair, which is pulled back and twisted into a braided ponytail that gives her age a touch of mystery. Her whole ambiance exudes the feminine, yet something unsettled. She looks younger than he. As we go out the back gate of the resort into Boynton Canyon, I am very conscious of her graceful gait and nice lines.

Bob is a talker and obviously in love with this canyon: "According to legend, this canyon is the birthplace of the Yavapi-Apache nation. A great flood had been prophesized. A wise old man carved a boat out of a cottonwood tree, and sealed his virgin daughter in it with some provisions, and a woodpecker riding on top. The rains came and water covered the whole world. When the waters recede, the log comes to rest on a high cliff back in this canyon. The bird pecks it open, and beautiful First Woman emerges. She becomes lonely and does some ceremonial dances to the gods. Shortly thereafter, she becomes pregnant by the Sun and brings forth a son, the father of the 'old people."

To myself, I say, *Bob, I'm not interested in buying this canyon. Ease off.*

Catherine points her long, tapered finger up to some cliff-overhangs in the red mountain walls. "Back in history, the beauty of this Garden of crimson rocks, tall green pines, and happy animals summoned and hosted the archaic people of the high plateau." She spoke with a kind of soft reverence that made her seem desirable and cultured. She didn't sound like a salesperson, just a woman with eyes for beauty. "They came to celebrate and seek guidance. To them these red mountains and shady canyons were, and still are, holy – promoting wholeness – which they call *hohzo* – balance or harmony. This canyon was a meeting ground for many nations – the Hopi, the Zuni, the Anasazi, the Navajo, the Yavapi, the Apache, and the Sinaquans. It was a crossroads of peaceful trading and some misty loafing – a patch of earth un-bloodied by war." Catherine pauses as if to honor the holiness of the place.

"Those early sojourners," salesman Bob rushes in "left behind their symbols, etched and painted on rock message boards. The symbols say that in this wild, yet habitable place, there is an answer to constantly wandering. When I first came here, those petroglyphs said to me: Stay with me. Put down your roots. You do not have to keep moving on." He was smiling. I knew he talked partially from his heart. He did have a knack for the place. We walked deeper into the changing light, the friendly trees, the majestic walls, and the daunting quiet. When we reached a clearing with ten or twelve sitting stones arranged in a circle, Catherine said, "This is a medicine wheel. Let's sit and meditate for a few minutes."

Catherine Reilly's mother, Mary was a blue-blooded Quinn of Boston, and a graduate of the Harvard Law School. When she married Brendan Reilly, a popular young Democrat, it was a Boston social event. Brendan was a handsome, ambitious bonvivant with the gift of gab and a gregarious sense of humor. Little Catherine had adored her red haired father who swung her up in the sky when she was three, and danced a reel with her when she was six. When he ran off to the West Coast with a rich, young blonde starlet, eight-year-old Catherine couldn't understand. After only a few months she began asking her mother what happened. *Why did he leave us?* She kept on asking, but never got an answer that explained her heart's question. Some questions echo for a life time, as you may know.

Mary, her mother, was first and foremost a professional woman. Catherine was raised by Clare, her nineteen-year-old, Irish *au-pair* from County Cork. With Clare's simple common sense and strict discipline, Catherine, to all admiring eyes, grew up normal. She attended the best Catholic convent schools, and went all the way to Boston University, where she majored in American History. In a class on the American West, she met Sean Brady, whose eyes had the same wildness as her father's. With Clare's common sense, ringing in her mind, Catherine resisted Sean's physical advances. Sean was an Ulster Protestant, but not really into religion. He agreed to convert, to get what he wanted. He was twenty-two and she was twenty when the Cardinal of Boston pronounced them man and wife. He was twenty-four and she twenty-two when the County Clerk pointed to the dotted line on the divorce papers. Again a disenchanted Catherine jabbed the sky: *Why?* She hadn't trusted Sean. She had seen his eyes scanning many a pretty behind, a couple of times too often. She knew what he wanted.

Perhaps her call to *Go West* had to do with the Sean-wildness-thing, (they had met in the *American West* class). More perhaps it was her immigrant roots that made the West her destiny. Her great grandfather, John Quinn had gone west from Ireland to North America at a time when the smell of famine was in the air. After the divorce, Catherine went first to Santa Fe-Taos, and loved the art and spiritual feel at the Buddhist ashram. She drove her white Mustang convertible through the unique lands of Utah, Idaho, and Montana. It was in Colorado where she read a story about the Schnebly family, whose life there was devastated by an anthrax epidemic that wiped out their cattle, and led them back to the red rock country of Arizona. By this time, she was getting tired of being always on the move. The Schnebly story of their inter-faith struggle, pioneer days, and the lure of the red rock landscape, called. She responded, another fever victim.

After the canyon adventure, at Catherine's suggestion, we break the morning fast at the *Mii Amo Café* in the spa on the resort grounds. The food is fabulous, but Catherine is equal parts – enigma and entrancing. I can hardly keep my eyes off of her. I feel jealous, wishing I had someone like her in my life. She talks a lot about her mother and their first visit to Enchantment. I feel that she wants me to know her. Wishful thinking, I'm sure.

That night I write. My imagination remembers her every word. The images of a naked Catherine under jets of water cleansing her oiled body won't quit. I'm not sure whether it is the magic of the setting or the sheer sensuality of Catherine, but something rumbles like a pre-quake in my psyche. I'm on the edge of telling Bob that I'd like to buy the town house he showed me in Lomas Serenas. He did have a knack for matching buyer and product. But I don't. I don't know why. I do know my daughter Noreen will have a fit if I sell the house where she grew up. Maybe I just don't like Bob's hustling me.

Catherine's mother, Mary, had developed breast cancer. She retired from her stressful routine, and made the decision to devote herself to her spiritual health. Shortly after she learned that Catherine was pitching a tent in Sedona, she arranged to spend a week at the Enchantment Resort. Cancer survival magazines tout *Mii Amo* as a transformative retreat that enhances serenity – if you can afford it. She could. Her maternal heart also knew that connection with her daughter would be the real chemo-therapy she needed. She was educated enough to know that it's relationships in the end that heal.

As Catherine recounted the visit, her mother didn't do a lot. She did go to the ceremonial Crystal Grotto, a rounded mediation room, open to the sky. She did write an intention for the "worry box" at the entrance. Catherine was sure it was about her daughter's footloose life, not about her own dying problem. Catherine's note that morning was an intention for her mother's health. She admired and loved her mother, but was drifting away from her Boston moorings. That evening, in an Enchantment group experience, she smiles as the smoke rises into the canyon sky. The therapist is burning the intentions from the worry box. She remembers the pampering her mother insisted she do at the spa. The sensual seduces, and she decided to stay in Sedona for good.

Sally and Gwen Dykstra grew up on a dairy farm in snowy Wisconsin. In Gwen's own words their mom was strict as hell. Their father was out with the cows at five in the morning, came in for breakfast at eight, and went back to work. According to her, it was what people called the 'work ethic,' and they went to church on Sunday. "That was more social mores than a religious experience, if you know what I mean," Gwen explained.

On the television at the *Cave,* where Gwen works, there's constantly news about guys wronging women. She'd like to ignore it, but can't escape it. Most recently, there was a story about the struggling, mature single mom who had a long affair with a married politician because "it got me away from my humdrum life." The guy used her for over a decade. In the dairy culture, infidelity is seldom talked about in the presence of the men. In the heartland you know when to keep shut your mouth. Women, of course, talk about it amongst themselves. That's what women do, isn't it? They talk to one another. And like it or not, they accept that their men, like their bulls, have animal drives. Little Gwen was never sure whether the bovines in the barn dared to moo about being used. In the flurries of winter snows, infidelity is swallowed as a male privilege. Fidelity hardly sounded like a sanctimonious word to a dairyman's daughter.

Gwen's Aunt Bea, her father's sister, was the flip of her
mother. She was happy and bubbly with Gwen and Sally. Bea
was a nurse. One of Gwen's fond childhood memories is snuggling up in the abundant bosom of Bea's white uniform. When
she came for a visit, Bea always asked about the girls' school
progress, about their friends, and their fun things. She made
them feel listened to. So, at about age seven, Gwen heard the
call to be a nurse.

In high school, Bea had fooled around with Buddy Hazard,
the best dancer in the whole area. Buddy told her she had the
softest white skin he had ever touched. After high school, she
went to nursing school. She was a born caregiver, like Florence
Nightingale. Buddy came up to visit her from time to time, and
they messed around. In her senior year, she discovered she was
with child, and married Buddy. She lost the baby in the sixth
month.

Buddy was a long-distance trucker, on the road most of the
time. The loss of the baby shook them both to their unfledged
cores. Bea knew that Buddy had a weakness for young runaway
hitchhikers. She knew he took pleasure in touching the soft skin
of a teenage girl. For several years, Bea worked twelve-hour
shifts as her way of protecting her mind from her situation. She
didn't feel that she had any choice. And other people needed her.

One raining night on a mountainous Montana road, Buddy's
rig went into a long skid, crashed through the guard rail, and
down the embankment. As fickle fate would have it, he survived; wouldn't you know it, the teenage girl in the sleeper died
of a concussion? The Montana coroner's report showed that she
had recent semen in her system. She was fifteen. Bea and Buddy

separated, and eventually divorced. Discouraged, Bea moved back to snowy Wisconsin, close to the Dykstra's.

Gwen is one of those people who need to stay close to kin and friends. Whenever she goes home, Gwen visits Bea, her once cheerful aunt, now a sad, broken spinster. Gwen would love to see her aunt find some kind of special relationship. Gwen herself is a tangle of complexities, but she believes everyone needs someone they matter to. For sure, the phantom of Bea's life is a weird skeleton in the closet of Gwen's mind.

After her graduation from nursing school, young Gwen wound up working in the trauma center in Omaha Central. It was an all-consuming, exhausting, paradoxical life. The nurses felt they were doing some good, but some days the losses seemed to outnumber the successes. As a natural giver, Gwen worked hard, unwittingly sacrificing herself for the sick and dying. She has never regretted doing that. She only regrets doing it stupidly. She had failed to take care of herself. She burned out young. She often tells the guys she meets at the bar, "You have to take care of yourself, my friend– one of Nature's laws."

As she saw it, the medical world is like a little land of Oz – doctors, surgeons, anesthetists, radiologists, technicians, and on down the corridor – a kind of secret society. Nurses are trained to stay in their prescribed boundaries. They bitch about the pecking order, but fear to cross the line, during the day. They need the job, financially and emotionally.

You have to understand that there are two basic types of medical males: First, the faithful ones – the **tier-one** majority, truly married, truly dedicated to healing. Then there are the **tier-two** guys, who fill in the gaps. They are the cheaters: those who love the money, love the title *Doctor*, and think nurses should consider it an honor to go to bed with them. So, Gwen, who was weak about the donuts and coffee in the nurses' room, wound up working off her stress with some those tier-two types, and a few techies, who claimed they were unattached. Several of the other nurses advised her to use a vibrator, but Gwen loves the touch of flesh. She had studied a lot of biology. She well knows that we share 98% of our DNA with the chimpanzees, who are notoriously unruly when it comes to copulating, and love being groomed. As far as she is concerned promiscuity might well be a hanger-on from our pre-hominid days – even for gals.

Nights home alone, she gets angry and discouraged when she listens to the news. It's like *Shit, the politicians, big athletes, movie stars do it. Nobody seems to care*. It's unfair. For over a decade, Gwen lived alone with a three-legged dog, a cussing parrot, and another scaredy cat that spent most of her life hiding under or behind the couch. Gwen's relationship life was a rollercoaster, with more downs than ups. As she tells the talkative guys at *The Cave:* "Nothing brings on a down-mood-swing as a wounding relationship. People know how to hurt you, don't they?"

When she was diagnosed by the hospital psychologist as bipolar, her younger sister Sally convinced her to move to fervid Sedona. Sally believes that the vibes of the great outdoors are the best medicine in the world. She loves this bioregion because it makes her feel good about herself and the planet. That was five years ago. Now Gwen is the happiest barmaid in Coconino County. She is still looking for Mr. Right, or possibly, Miss Right. But she is gun-shy of those uncharted waters. The whole world around her seems confused, clueless. Relationship seems more of a risk, than a benefit. She is well aware of the perils of romantic adventures; several of her friends had waltzed into the devil's den and never recovered.

Across town, out at the Yavapi College campus, a tall, gray-haired man walks across the parking lot. He is an elderly teacher and executive. There's a twinkle in his eye, and his dying body has a happier than usual stride. He has just seen a mule deer and her two milk-chocolate-brown fawns with their white spots of youth. They had stood motionless just inside the edge of the stand of pines near where he parked. He loved animals. As he opened the OLLI (Osher Lifelong Learning Institute) door and stepped across the college threshold, where the days of senior seekers would come, Aubrey prayed his morning mantra: *Grant me the courage to go on this day with a smile. May I do some good today for at least one person.*

On the plane back to San Francisco after my escape to the red canyon country, I'm on a restless edge. I have two vodka tonics. That night I toss and turn for hours before succumbing into a deep dream. It isn't quite a nightmare; nor is it your sweet dream either. I wake up sweating, frightened, remembering the canyon, the enigmatic, sensuous, spiritual Catherine, and the house in Lomas Serenas on the edge of the forest wilderness. That house in the community where people talk to one another.

That first day back to the everyday ways of moving through the days, I go to the Pacific Coast Highway and walk along the ocean for a couple of hours, lost in my challenging conundrums. The ocean is another of those earth mothers that sing lullabies to the wandering tribes. At some time in life, we all have these *crossroad* decisions, when we stand stroking our chins. I'm sure you have stood there – afraid to make a mistake. You probably will agree that it would be nice to have someone to talk to and even hold your hand, and look lovingly into your eyes, as you look into the possibles of the future with it many arms reaching.

My heart thinks it knows what I want to do – what my life energy needs to do. But I'm afraid. I remind myself that change is always a bugaboo. Yet my heart feels that part of my scourge is the fever of the fear of failing. I'm afraid of letting my kids down, again.

That night I have a couple of brandies. I call my Matt: "Son, I'm thinking of selling the house and moving to a beautiful place in Arizona called Sedona." There's a moment of silence.

"I've seen pictures of the place, Dad. Looks awesome. Great place for a getaway. And I think you can use a change. You've been almost a zombie since the accident. Why don't you consider renting out the home. If Sedona doesn't work out, you'll still have a home."

My daughter Noreen is not home. I'm relieved and leave her a message on her answering machine. To be frank with you, my daughter and I have never really been close. I'm sure it's mostly my fault. I'm not really good with women. Maybe they are too complex for me. Noreen is like her mother – a wild Irish rose that can't understand a man with his mind in the library thistles. I soften my worries with another brandy and white crème de menthe.

The next morning there is a frantic red message on my machine: "I think you're crazy as a loon. If you want my vote, which I doubt you do, No! Damn it, no! But you'll do what you want. You guys always do. I'll just have to marry Pierre and stay here. I won't have a home anymore." The phone goes dead. My head starts to ache as if being squeezed in a vice.

I have an acute sense that I've got to change or I won't be good for anyone, including myself. I shower, shave, and make a pot of coffee. My soul is in overdrive. Movement, that's what I crave. Slowly I start to wander around the house, sipping my caffeine. In every room, I find the ghosts of failure. *I'll never heal here. In the pure mountain air of Sedona I'll have a chance.*

Finally, I take out Bob Dorian's card and make the call that I fear doing, but fear even more not doing. I need not tell you that the memory of Catherine's story about her visit to the spa is enticing. I see showering in the wall of Vichy jets after her skin had been mollified by a juniper-berry and rose-milk rubdown. She is not easy to forget. Actually, it is the ladies with the unclear edges who are not easy to forget.

According to *the Dineh people,* only the Creator knows where the beginning is. The Dineh (Navajo) sing chants telling that from the Mind of the Creator came the Holy People who were to put the world in balance *(hozho).* First man and first woman emerge from the previous worlds (plants, insects, animals). They build first house *(hooghan)* and chant the Blessing. Spider woman teaches them to weave, and Changing Woman is born at the start of the fourth world. She is impregnated by the sun and gives birth to two hero sons who battle and slay the evil monsters. Changing Woman gives man corn and domestic animals. It is **her** blessings that *the Blessing Way* asks. (The Navajo and the Vavapi are neighboring tribes and share similar creation *mythos.*)

The Begays are Navajo. They could teach us much about the way of Man. For almost two centuries, the Begay clan has lived in the Crystal area just north of Window Rock, Arizona. They are weavers, noted for their un-bordered rugs, with wavy horizontal bands of rust, black, red, blue, and decorated with geometric designs, especially the squash blossom. Grandmother Sanhkyo Begay had been elected to the tribal council of the local chapter of the Navajo Nation. She was an elder. After her daughter Nascha gives birth to Kai, grandmother Begay sings <u>The Blessing Way</u> and <u>The Night Song</u>: *"Happily may I walk. May it be*

*beautiful before me…behind me…below me…above me. May it
be beautiful all around me. In beauty it is finished."*

Kai Begay grows up an invisible reservation girl who learns
to weave as a child and rides the school bus two hours a day to
the high school in Window Rock. The reservation circle of the
women is her safe house – her mother, her sisters, her aunts, her
cousins. They often circle their looms and gossip in groups. In
her senior year of high school, Kai begins to go with Billy Deer-
foote, and is ecstatic when she first misses her time of month at
nineteen. Billy is a good soul, but without direction. There aren't
many opportunities for advancement on the reservation if you
don't like farming. Many of Billy's friends have hung up their
moccasins and left the reservation. Few return. Billy chooses to
stay. He is a family soul. Grandmother Sanhkyo presides at Kai
and Billy's wedding.

Kai names her daughter Nascha after her mother, the real
warm spark in her heart. Kai and Billy live in the Begay hooghan
for a year, which doesn't help Billy's self-image. He stoically
resents the control the old women have. To him, it's not modern.
He also hates farming, so he is essentially unemployed on the
reservation, where he feels disenfranchised. He takes to drinking, winds up killing a boy in a knife fight, and runs away –
never to be heard from again.

The heart of the deserted single mother cracks open like an
egg hit on the frying pan's hard edge – a fissure that feels as big
as a canyon. Her nights bring trembling tears. She feels deserted
beyond repair, and decides to take her daughter away from the
muddle that has cut the legs out from under her. Yes, Dineh
women, like grandmother Sanhkyo, have some control. Still, in

the back rooms of life, men still hold the cards that trump the queens.

With Nascha strapped to her back, she thumbs rides to Flagstaff. One truck driver tells her that he will buy them both supper if she will sleep with him. When she gets out of that truck in Flagstaff, she makes a mad dash for freedom, her baby rack bouncing on her back. The next day she finds an ad for a live-in housekeeper in a place she has never heard of. She gets a Dineh cousin to drive her for an interview.

The man who opens the door in Sedona looks old, even though he had once been a wild Italian youth, who had entered the moist cave of many an adoring Sicilian beauty, eager to leave her childhood behind. Back then he was handsome, sensitive, and already acclaimed as a talented artist. Painting was his burning passion, and he had a lust for travel. He traveled and painted, and was smart enough to put the money from his paintings into a bank account. When his health began to worsen, he moved to clean air of the high country, for his lungs, seeking Nature's cure.

A few years later, and in failing health, when he answers the door to the timid Navajo girl applying for the job of housekeeper, he looks at her and the ebony haired child strapped to her back. The perceiving heart of the sick man sees a girl who needs help; his artist eye perceives a poignant painting: classic Native American mother and child. The painter calls himself an atheist, but, old and slipping toward the final door, he has a lot of the spirit of the mountains in his heart. He hears the winds in his mind. Besides he has the eye for color, texture, and youth. To him, youth is the mirror opposite of death. Though he tries, he fails to see into the heart of the matter of death. For him, painting the world beyond the passage would be sacrilege of art. His old soul welcomes the sight of youth.

And so, the seed of a fragile bond, between a man who knows he is dying and a young woman who knows she has a daughter to live for, falls into the soil, and germinates. He buys her a loom. Inspired, she weaves him the best Crystal rug she has ever woven. Her child, Nascha, grows to love "Papa," who teaches her to paint. Sometimes he takes her for a walk into the reality of the landscape, and points out scenes that would lend themselves to a good canvas. She, in turn, loves to tell him the stories her mother constantly passes on to her, especially the story of Changing Woman.

I'm sitting on my back deck, watching the purple dusk arrive and chuckling at the irony of life. Now, after having lived all my life in bustling metropolises, I, John Malachy, live alone in a small town miles from any crowded city? This sudden switch still tickles mi fancy. And wouldn't you know it, when I opened the Sedona area telephone book, there wasn't another person with the surname Malachy in the whole of the northern high hills. For the first time in my life, I was as bare and exposed as a leafless tree in winter. I found myself without family, friends, to say nothing of a community of studious minds. Without any close relationship, a guy, hard and soft wired for connection as I am (we are), I was skating on thin ice. Sometimes I ask myself: What happened to you? Did you just decide to drop out of society? Are you afraid of getting involved again? Or just perhaps, like the prophets who had to first go into the desert, has my fervid destiny called me to these rugged mountains?

You see, after my wife's suspicious death, I drifted in the down doldrums, like a loose sailboat, for many confused months, with no North Star in my firmament. I wandered around with little direction, easy to do when your moorings are mostly in your rational prefrontal cortex. Bewildered, and bewitched by doubts, I wasn't sleeping well and didn't feel like eating. I began to lose

weight, and mumbled with the slightest annoyance, *What da f...!*
I'd lost my courage to face my smoldering Irish anger, which
was mostly aimed back at myself. You don't need to be Irish to
know that feeling. My physical body limped fatigued.

Luckily, the kids Matt and Noreen, were getting settled in
their own lives, and naturally they wanted to be let go. Basically
I had only myself to worry about. To boot, the country was in
sick shape. It worried me sick. After many depressed nights of
getting cozy with a bottle of the Bacchus, I made what might
seem to any of your normal minds a snap decision: I quit my
teaching job, and decided to travel. My life just shouted: Saddle
your ass and move out.

The atmosphere at the college was another part of the goad
that drove me out. An older teacher was waging a campaign of
skepticism against the idea of global warming. A young teacher
took up the cudgels and organized the students to carry plac-
ards around the campus: Save the Arctic Fox. Save the Beluga
Whale. Save the Emperor Penguin.

Then nineteen-year-old Margie Pepper hung herself in the
girls' locker room. She had been a placard carrier. Most people
blamed the tragedy on the fact that she was being needled for
being gay. I liked Margie. She was in my seminar on *The Dawn
of Religion.* She was cute, with a winning smile. Deep down, I
feel she worried about the future. Some days, I do too.

Those tensions, along with my deflated emotions, had me feeling like St. Sebastian at the stake, bleeding from many arrows.
My subterranean mind seemed to know that it was time to get
away. I had a buddy at the college who used to repeat: "All life
is perspective. Perspective is a way of seeing the broad picture, a

way of perceiving interrelationships, a way of discovering what matters." My quiver of perceiving arrows felt empty.

. Certainly the economy and the banking crisis were also on my mind. Moreover, I just had the itch to get out of my mental Dodge. Or like Odysseus I was being forced to take the journey to a home that might have meaning. After Allie's death, I had no special connection, no significant other. And I had no confidence in myself. My soul was at stake, my journey uncharted. I decided I needed to escape.

My friend, Patsy Sullivan, at the Downtown Travel Agency said, "Go to Sedona over in Arizona. I loovvve it over there. Next week is the beginning of the film festival. It's a good show. And, believe me, the place is drop-dead gorgeous. Be sure to take some hiking boots. The mountains and canyon call people off their couches and out of the woodwork and into the wilderness. It'll be great for what ails you."

So I went. I saw. Sedona conquered. I was hit by what the locals call: "the Red Rock Fever." You go to Sedona for a week, even a weekend, and you wind up buying a house, or you leave and come back in six months– to stay. The accidental malady is well documented and common. That visit with Bob Dorian to that gated subdivision near the red hills was no accidental summons. The finger of reality was pointing to what felt like a manifest destiny.

I'll grant you that for all my boyhood involvement with religion, I don't think I ever had anything close to a *spiritual experience.* Hey, don't jump to any conclusions. Those first months in the high desert, I didn't have anything one might call "an experience." Mother Nature does things coyly, almost shyly. Her come-on can be hard to hear if your ears are full of emotional and cultural wax. Her push is feather light, but she **does** like to nudge, believe you me. She can be effective, just as she can be blocked. Unsuspected by me, another, exciting young woman with the dancing green eyes was on her way. She will turn out to be the Hermes sent to guide me. Indeed she will crack open a new escape hatch in my psychic dungeon. (More on that shortly.)

I'm still not ready to wrap words around the term *spiritual experience,* despite the fact that I'm becoming convinced that we all would smile from a deeper place if we were tasting some of that seldom sampled dimension. The human need for "the numinous" may well be as ingrained as the need to propagate. (Of course you are free to argue that.)

Of course, the sex urge was under Victorian wraps for centuries. Maybe the time for a Sixties style shift to a different taste of experience stands in the wings of evolution. The humdrum of materialism isn't cutting the mustard for many. I begin to sense that spiritual (or "meaningful" if you prefer) experiences are both too diverse, too personal to pin to the mat – especially in our clamorous culture with its individualism. I am beginning to suspect that *spiritual* is a communal gig, as well as an individual, hard-earned trait.

I know there is a cohort of thinkers who think that sex also was communal in the beginning. Could be, but I don't think we are the same selves we were back in the walk-out of Africa. Paradoxically, the ability to see the invisible is an ability we could have inherited from those original people, but we lost it along the way. The magical presences of the earth have taken the back seat since "science" took over the reins.

It brings a smile to my heart when I recall that Moses met his numinous mystery, his Yahweh, in what the Sinai poet called "a burning bush." The biblical chronicler talked about a voice from out of Nature that addressed the escaping leader, (no, probably not a flesh woman). However, the Emily on her way to me is indeed flesh. She will become my burning bush, my female Yoda teaching me to fight the mindless evil.

Regardless, something deep, perhaps even arising from an inherited prior sensitivity, had slapped me awake when that Phoenix-Sedona Shuttle van first pulled into sight of these soaring red hills. Bathed in the intense, afternoon high desert light, Sedona was doing her dance of the Seven Veils, shimmering on the blue horizon, her ageless clefts enchanting!

That dancing apparition awakened a layer of me I didn't know was slumbering. It took a few worried nights for me to gather the courage to stick a toe into the prospect of seeing something new. If I ever do get foolish enough to try to *define* "spiritual experience," the phrase *the ambient world* will belong in the mix. As you may have noticed, the temptation to reduce the mysterious into words is one of my addictions.

There seems to be a gathering of minds that suspects that one catches glimpses of the numinous (aka the Spirit, God, Yahweh, Allah, the Father) in the rocks, the trees, the birdsong – and the kind-hearted people. The rocks are not God. Nevertheless, it may be that the luminosity of the rocks, the whispering wind in the trees, the warm sun on the back of your neck, and the piney smell of the land after a soft rain that prepare the heart to hear, like the farmer prepares his field for the seed. "The old people" called Nature's fore-play, *earth wisdom.*

I can't find a word for the opposite counterpart of being present. I've heard labels like: robotic-routines, running on autopilot, default-awareness, conditioned behavior, or preprogramed scripts. They are all antonyms of *attunement*. Does the Gotham of concrete and glass dumb-down our ability to see the invisible around us? Does it cloud our portals of perception? I don't think it is right to say that the city closes us down to the signals coming toward us. Golly, the City swarms with interesting people. Maybe you think that way too. You wouldn't be reading a romance of perception, if you weren't somewhat curious about the messages coming at you. You'd be watching a "reality" show or mud wrestling.

Back in academia, I sat through a course on *The Contemplative Life*. I didn't have any interest in being contemplative. In fact it seemed like something medieval. But it was a three-credit course at a convenient time slot, and the teacher had a reputation of being easy. She was a gray haired woman, a veteran of the Golden Gate be-ins of the 60's. She still lived in the Haight. She spent a lot of chalk on the literal left brain and the big-picture right brain. According the gospel of that time, the two physical halves of the brain had two distinct ways of seeing the world.

Now with all the mind widening research, those hypotheses are considered too rigid. We don't have two brain-minds. We have a lot of complex parts working together, although there are areas that contribute more to language and linear time ("left") and areas that are more involved in pre-word imagery and direct experience ("right")

The sun has set and an almost sacred stillness hangs in the forest behind my safe-house. I feel that here in Lomas Serenas,

I stand at the edge of the mystique that this more-than-human bioregion is trying to nurture in me a new way of looking at life. A new seer, whom I had no clue of when I made the decision to leave the sweet clams and salty seafood of the San Francisco, is emerging. Sometimes I don't even recognize myself. I've even begun to need less escape into the fog of alcohol and blotto mind.

B.E. (Before Emily), I lived the left-brain-way (to continue the metaphor). That's what our education stresses. The right-eye with its pre-verbal ability to relax into direct experience with childlike freshness is under-educated. The right-hemisphere can see the vast forest, not just the tree in front of itself. It has a kind of diffuse focus. In the wilderness, on the switching bends and rises of the trails, I am beginning to have a hunch that one can catch glimpses of that immanence which points a finger to the transcendent something more. With some practice, one can smell something divine in the trees, in the canyons, in the winds. (*Practice* is an old revered word, quite monastic.) To do so, one must turn down the volume of mind chatter, which is often judgmental of both self and others. (*Meditation* is another of those oldie words.) As Emily's books will say the one-eyed way is an unhappy way. Her clear-blue-mind is a much better guide.

The owl, that paragon of perception, hoots out in the darkness. It's time to pack it in. Tomorrow is another opening of another present moment. Perception as a continuum between the two poles, once simplified as *literal* and *holistic,* beckons as a better way. Balance between the two has got to be the secret. I have lived imbalanced to the bookish left. The red rock country is summoning me to *experience* in the balancing right way.

As I fall into the valley of forgetting, it is raining. The dance of the drops on the acrylic skylight is soothing. I know the trees and the animals are happy. I imagine a young doe sticking her tongue out to catch a drop of wetness.

Sometime in my first months in high country, I met Paul Jones at a talk in the library. The talk was on Sedona Schnebly. Her bronze statue in front of the library had captivated my imagination the first time I saw her. Paul lives near Lomas Serenas and is also an early riser. He hikes with his dog most every morning. We now often meet and walk into the wilderness together. He is well educated, an avid reader, and a man who takes the mind seriously. One of our first early morning hikes is a vivid memory: There's fresh light behind and between the trees, but the round, yellow sun hasn't even peeked over the Rim. It's a moment when the mystery of the earth meets the numen of the changing sky and the universes beyond – truly a time of transition. It's the time when the mountain lions are slowly putting paw in front of paw, heading to their lairs in the high caves after a night of hunting survival. It's the time when the dawn twins, light and warmth, will make their tip-toe entrance into a waiting world.

We are walking up Chapel Road, heading out to that unique promontory called Chicken Point, which looks over the expanse of the landscape that makes one feel like a king surveying his realm. The low, namesake, rock configuration does resemble a brooding mother hen. But it is a little close to the edge for this chicken. I'm not what people call "Brave-heart." I walk with fears, some of which I'm in touch with. Fear of heights is up-there with fear of falling and fear of failing.

Paul has just seen *Avatar* in 3D and is stoked and verbal. "It's a new way of seeing, which opens up the world around us. In 3-D, we step into a dimension of depth that makes you feel you are right there, surrounded by the scene. "Jeepers," he says, "2-D, the flatlander's screen version, doesn't hold a candle. We lose so much of the richness of life when we don't see depth."

His words, *surrounded by the scene,* went like a laser beam to my chest. I felt a shortness of breath, and my heart nodded: *So that's it! The place is surrounding me and working on me.* Gwen had said something that first night about the power of the place. It hadn't registered. I still find it hard to believe. No previous place in my life had felt like a palpable presence that works you toward some new way of perceiving. The cities I'd lived in were just there to be survived. If anything, they wear you down, not build you up.

That night I compulsively seek shelter in my study, hoping to puzzle together Paul's words about "ways of seeing." I felt uneasy, almost guilty about growing up and remaining a "flat-lander.' Some vague memories from my class at State on the great Hebrew scholar of relationship stirred. They were trying to get my attention. Being alone in my ivory tower, the silent space brings back memories, even ones long gone cold.

When I first came to Sedona, I'd got lucky. I told Bob Dorian, my realtor, that I would need to add a study/workspace, and he said, "Go Southwest. Billy Hawkson is the best." Tall, dark eyed Billy had left the Hopi reservation as a teenager, got a job in construction, and then branched out on his own. People say the Hopis have an inborn sense of the power and personality of nature and the surroundings. They sense the importance of inner peace. When I met Billy, I was impressed with his calmness. It was his idea to have my study a separate building, accessed by a short covered walkway lined with native plants– wildflowers, flowering cacti, and a few culinary herbs. Now I enjoy the scarlet spikes of the Indian paint brush flower and the pine-like fragrance of rosemary. I like trekking into my private Garden of Eden.

The building itself is a mud adobe with wide windows that capture the majesty of the red rocks. To the northwest, I can see almost forever, through distant mountain gaps and beyond. Sometimes I catch a thunderstorm dancing and rumbling on the mountain tops, followed by a rainbow across us all. To the southeast, I see close up, and virtually personal, most of the expressive rock formations. A couple of them are touted to house the acclaimed energy spots. In one corner of the room, I have a Hopi kiva (a beehive fireplace), and in the front center, a large desk made from polished ponderosa burls. Along the back wall I have my dear friends – books, books, books – loaded with words, word, words. Oh, I love my courtesans, who lounge in the white, peeled *latilla* bookcases. These pine pole shelves match the ceiling between the horizontal ponderosa *vigas*, the backbones of the rear portion of the room. In the front portion, I have a cool retractable glass ceiling which opens electronically when I want to hear and smell the hills outside. There I'm like a child of Nature close to the breast of nourishment.

For all intents and purposes, I had flown to Arizona a head-case. My once mental self, lived trapped in a cage of problem-solving self- talk: a cultural condition that may be on the way to epidemic proportions. Despite all that, my first few months in Sedona, continuing into that first year, there came to me a silent trickle of subtle sensibilities, especially on my dawn walks. Right from the beginning, I was drawn to the silent light of dawn. At that time I had no clue about the power of the ambient world. To think in terms of the trees, the birds, and the arroyos perceiving and expressing was another "you-gotta-be-out-of-your-mind" idea, akin to pagan animism or to witchery or even voodoo.

To level with you, by that early walk with Paul, I hadn't caught on to what was happening to me. We might not focus on it, but while we are knotted up chasing our squirrelly tails around in multitasking and grabbing the goodies, we are being addressed. Our consciousness is blind to that presence that early men called "Spirit Nature," who wants to nudge us with her fairy-godmother's wand, especially if we are in one of her magical places. Lucky for me, I had begun to put my boots to the earth daily. There was a restless wind in me. Of course, in the beginning, I rarely paused to sniff the cool scent of the pines, or listen to the birdsong singing to the rising sun. I was just doing what everyone seemed to be doing – hiking. When Paul said something about the "right brain way of seeing," it rang a bell that I knew was sounding for me. A fresh way of seeing the world was playing in the edges of my consciousness.

I had done some more reading on the different modes of the mind: brain lateralization, after my course on contemplation. I was aware that I had lived classically addicted to what they then called linear language. After all, that's what our education systems teach, isn't it? I've already said that, but education seems so important. Now cyber technology has further empowered logical thinking at the expense of holistic experience. Here, after a few years of wandering in the red rock wilderness, I can see that soon after my feet were in touch with the earthy soil of the upcountry and the singular light of sunrise, the animate and articulate surroundings were leading my feet in a more balanced direction. The right hemisphere was emerging from its dust bin.

That night after walking with Paul, I returned to my study, poured myself a small brandy, and pulled out my Buber notebook. Paul had used the expression: "ways of seeing the world around us." His words had strangely looped me back to Buber. As I plied my course notebook, I realized that, starved for relationship, I had focused on Buber's *I-Thou* – the human to human bonding. My logical mind was confident that I had captured the essence of one of the most profound seers of relationship. I was surprised to see that I had two-pages of notes on Nature. But, holy cripes, I had missed the pre-liminal or pre-threshold stepping stone.

According to Buber, a certain dawning awareness allows one to cross a *limen* (doorstep, sill, or threshold) into a new way of perceiving. To perceive is to interface with information. To be in touch with information is to be alive. Nature, physical beings, can **open the door,** and prepare us to say *Thou* to another particular human being. For Buber, it is an attitude of responding – wordlessly – to the rocks, plants, animals that meet us and send signals to us. The signals come not from Nature, big and blurry, but as unique **particular** beings, for example, that tall, oxygenating pinyon pine that leans to the left, or that little, white, mountain daisy with a missing pedal … so cute in her hurt, so singularly tiny.

On the trail to being a little more sensitive, I was struck by a day in Buber's biography when he failed. Failure is my hairshirt. He had been to a Hasidic event and returned home with a religious buzz on. A young man awaited the learned young scholar's counsel. Martin talked to Meje, but he was too wrapped up in his own buzz to really be present to the young man. He was into himself. (That sounded distressfully familiar.)

Months later, Buber found out on the street that Meje had foolhardily died on the warfront, having no reason to live. Buber knew he had failed the boy. He had not been "present" to him. That missed connection became a turning-point, like his misconnection with his mother. Buber decided to turn away from 'religious' experience, and turn toward his own backyard, the world around. He turned toward a new way of seeing. He talked of life as "a narrow ridge." Certainly one needs balance on a narrow ridge.

The Meje story spoke to my heart. As I've mentioned, Yahweh spoke to Moses from some burning item in nature. That the Power of the Universe speaks through the surrounding world is a mind altering theory. I now believe that it is far from being some pious shot in the dark. Some scientists confirm that everything emits waves of information. Fritz Albert Popp, a German research physicist called these emissions: *biophotons.* These scientists have done experiments showing that there is an ongoing conversation between the light in me and the light in the world. According to these frontier sciences, the world around even influences our genes and DNA.

At first, I wasn't at all comfortable with these hypotheses; they went against the grain. But something in me kept on mumbling: *Give it a try. It will never be easier than here in beautiful Sedona.* According to one of the books that my coming Hermes would soon put in my hands, I had to start learning to be present to the trees, the mountain daisies, and the scurrying cottontails. The claim is that learning to be wordlessly absorbed in "individuals" in Nature is a primer in the ABC's of human relationship. I sure needed some help in that area. I was tired of being lonely. There is nothing like loneliness to bring a person to his knees.

At this point in my journey, I conjecture that Mother Nature is not the only preparatory (liminal) experience. Undoubtedly there are other *limens* that allow us to cross into the garden of heightened consciousness. Perhaps, for example, doing the wave with a busload of Patriot football friends at the Super Bowl could be an ecstatic (out of your small self) happening. Woefully, there are some celebrities and some ordinary Joe's probing thresholds like drugs, alcohol, erotic pleasures to escape the cramped mind. But for me, the silence of the canyons is like a monastery for the mind. As I remember from that college course, contemplatives sought the sweetness of silence and stillness.

So, to my surprise, Buber had seen the stepping stone of confirming the non-human world: the world of Doric columns and cats, rocks and plants, stones and stars – each with the own **bestowing** being. I wasn't clear on this concept of bestowing. Then I awoke one morning, as the sun was smiling over the Mogollan Rim, and the pines were standing in their morning meditation, awaiting the warm rays of the sun. A gentle eureka warmed my brain, "Quiet, stupid. Don't say a word. Don't even think. Just be here, now, as that tree over there is." Out of the corner of my morning eye, trying to practice my new wide-angle perception, I could see a pinyon pine across the street from my driveway. It was as unique and curvy as any Hollywood model. I quietly felt the dignity in the branching tree with its arms pulled in every which direction by the times and the weather.

Not long down the road, a woman named Emily would cross my bow and further shake up my normal, blinkered way of looking on the world. I would begin to wake up to the enlivening sensation that my life was possibly opening to a new direction – I was starting to appreciate the encompassing earth. The Catholicism of my youth had been laced with rationality: decreed dogmas, ethical strictures, and political stances. Basically, as a boy, I bought that whole package, being at heart a youngster who liked to be comfortable within the group-think (color that insecure). I might have been occasionally tempted to raise my hand to question the church's treasure troves, while children around the world were dying for lack of food. Or I wondered why caring women couldn't lead the liturgy. But in general, I was docile. I knelt to kiss the bishop's ring. I seldom wasted time in the seemingly shallow waters of just being. Catholics have a vocation **to do**. Jesus was a doer. I'm grateful to my parents for raising me in the church of the 1940's and 50's. It made me who I am – a wannabe Samaritan who wants to care about others, like the Galilean did. But society and learning and I are ever evolving on. The Church is still back in the old boys club of cassocks and male-only *pontiffs.* The Latin savvy among you readers will recall that *pons* mean bridge, *facere* means to build. So, a pontiff (bishop) is a person who brings two sides of the river together. Modern society needs "pontiffs" on every corner, if we are going to turn the corner. Sedona the place is in a real sense a pontiff.

Plainly, like a spiritual purgative, even from the first days here, the color and the stillness of the red rock energy has been trying to straighten me out, despite the gnarly way the twig of my youthful mind was bent. Still, even here in this silver-tongued air of the highlands, my bookish bent hangs on by it fingernails, hoping that perhaps in this amazing context, I might find some Euclidian answers to the burning questions. Ever since I arrived, like a split personality, I've spent hours in my glass-roofed study with my head bent over a new book. I persist in my small-minded, self-seeking pursuit. It's another kind of fervor. Still, nowadays when I raise my head and see a shy mule deer doe looking at me from the edge of the pine trees, or a curious blue jay looking at me from the branch of a juniper tree, the arising mind in me occasionally wonders what's going through their heads. Do they really perceive me as I perceive them? It probably isn't apparent to my neighbors but I am having a frightful time crossing that bridge to seeing the world as alive. That's a process of baby steps, or should we say quantum steps.

If some of these ideas seem too far out to you, I can understand. Sometimes I feel like giving up and just lapsing back into the old way of looking at reality. It's so much easier to be normal. But then I see what's going on in our society, I get a little burst of courage, or maybe it's fear. I cheer myself on: We need change, and let it begin with me.

Paul's words about the ways of knowing were like John the Baptist preparing the way for her who is coming. But he had not really prepared this sundered man, wandering, under a cloud of probabilities, for the **wild woman** who came.

Shortly after I settle into my study and take up walking with Paul, a cannon ball shoots across my bow. (If your life hasn't had a cannon ball crossing your bow recently, a reminder: Keep your head down. They come out of nowhere, like tornados, and they can knock you off your pins.) Mine came as a petite, honey-blonde, Tennessee firebrand.

Back in the hills where she comes from, it is commonly claimed that Emily York is a kin-descendant of the World War I hero, Sergeant York. Alvin York, a God-fearing hillbilly, didn't believe the Almighty condoned killing. When he was drafted, he tried to avoid the war fields, and registered as a conscientious objector. He was turned down because he didn't belong to a church of registered pacifists. Watching his buddies being decimated and dying in the Meuse-Argonne battle, he, like the great Greek Achilles, found the courage to decide and act. He slipped around behind the German lines and began shooting with such marksmanship that all 132 enemy combatants immediately surrendered. At his Medal of Honor ceremony, he explained that he did it to help end the war and minimize the killing. He was a man with backwoods convictions, perchance an endangered species.

Emily was born into a poverty-stricken, single-mom home on a dusty piece of dirt outside Nashville. Her father had already deployed before she was born, and never returned from the first

Gulf War. Her mother, Addie, was uneducated, and worked as a cashier at Mac Given's gas station. She also had come through the up-and-downs of hillbilly life. As a teenager, she could be a hellion, but often flipped into a morose mood. Back then the term bipolar was almost unknown.

Some say that in grammar school, girl Emily was shyer than a country mouse. Others say that as a high school cheerleader, her hormones exploded, and she was the life of the party. She was by nature sensitive, caring, and outgoing. Her mother died of a broken heart when Emily was away in junior college. Addie had long struggled with bouts of depression. Emily often says that her mother died of ignorance. Nevertheless, the world rightly wonders how this honey-haired gal got to be the spiritual Amazon she is now, considering where she started. She has to be one of those amazing-grace stories.

To this Yankee boy, her story sounds like that classic Southern story of female grit. You know, the Scarlett O'Hara fiction that buoyed a nation bleeding with civil wounds. But believe me, when this petite pistol, who emits sexuality in her gait and clutches values in her breast, shoots across the bow of my life, the groin animal groaned. The beast of hibernating carnality let out a weak growl, and began to stretch. The beast is hungry for values, hungry for any meaning, hungry for the touch of a woman. Seeing her delicate, soft shoulders, I fancy I have courage. Then again, I am aware that I have a lot of coward neuron cells. Yet at that initial encounter, the beast within feels like Rip Van Winkle stretching awake from a long sleep. Moreover, aware that this beast's ability to reach across the between to a woman has been in the sleep mode, I freeze. Relationship is such a minefield.

Here's how Emily comes into my life: One bright, balmy morning, shortly after I arrive in Sedona, and purchase my town-house, I hear the front doorbell chime. I am in my black boxers down in the think tank Billy Hawkson has recently finished. I pull on a pair of gray Russell sweats, and go to the door. Through the peek-hole, my eye sees an impressive-looking woman. She's not petite, but she projects an aura of intelligence and competence. Scandinavian, I surmise. Curious, I open the door.

"Good morning, Mr. Malachy. I'm Sally Stevens, I live over on Quail Run with my husband Brad. Welcome to the neighborhood." (Ah, I recognize the name: she's Gwen's sister. I've picked up some of her sad story.) She looks winsome with her long, yellowish-blonde hair, and wide-set Nordic blue eyes. She's nicely dressed in a white tunic top, white tapering pants, and belt of silver loops resting on some strong, shapely hips. In most male-female encounters there is, I am convinced, a silent sexual undertow – occasionally confessed, usually unacknowledged, but inescapably part of the dance. It may be part of the animal dance of the genes to propagate.

"I hope you'll come and join us some Friday evening for the wine and cheese get together." She goes on to explain that she is on the board of the Women of the Red Rocks, who once a month, invite a popular speaker. This month they have invited a gal from down South, and want to have a good turnout for "this bold young woman." One of Sally's sorority sisters heard her in Chicago. The sister said the gal really helped her simplify her life. Simplifying life appears to be one of Sally's agendas. My mind wonders why, and what does it means to simplify one's life, if that's even a realistic option, in this day and age.

Consciously, I tell myself I will go just to be neighborly; I've read enough about the deleterious effects of isolation – both for the soma (body) and that other human part, the psyche. But damn, I like my quiet time to pursue my studies. A wine and cheese get-together sounds a little frivolous, a waste of valuable reading time. After all there are big questions in the folds of the *Sapiens* wager. I watch the news. I know we are in trouble. I need to work on those questions. That very morning, I'd been knee deep into Heidegger's *Time and Being*. He wrestled, like a Sumo philosopher, with the question of our sense of being. My own identity, of course, is still tied up in Houdini knots. None-theless I tell Sally, disguising a grin, "Yes, I'll come to both. What time did you say the wine and cheese starts?" It would be orchestrating on the obvious to say that my body-mind-spirit was searching for something, or someone to plug the black hole of my spirit. I was *hors de combat*.

The clip in my fantasy regularly replays that meeting with the Tennessee Joan of Arc. De rigueur we had to wear name tags. And believe you me, Emily York is no Tennessee walker. Her short-cut blonde hair bounces with vixen cuteness as she bounds up and down the aisles. Dressed in a tight blue skirt and a white linen top, with a red silk scarf loosely flapping around her deli-cate, alabaster neck, she moves with the fast, feline strides of a lissome cougar. I don't know where the thought emerges from, but I think: This gal is a fighter. I bet she's suffered, perhaps even been ravished. She's kicking and scratching back at the mindless system that hurt her. She's shouting: Wake up! Wake up!

My animal appetites spring alive and send a message up to my heart-center: Hear Yee, Hear Yee. Big stakes possible! Mister Failure, don't blow this one. This hottie prances cute, as shiny as a queen's button. Your life needs shiny, needs stoking, a voice within prompts. That afternoon, Emily doesn't talk a lot about herself. Her passion seems to be about how ignorant we are about our equipment – mostly meaning our minds and emotions. To my own surprise, her words cut like surgical knives, poking around in my slumping psyche. My caveman sex tooth for someone young and sweet certainly has something to do with my interest.

Some crazy how, she, like a sponge diver, grabs my mind, and yanks it to the surface. Vaguely, I hear her say that most men are like bulls in heat. She also believes that women are cowed by the big-money men who sit behind polished corporate desks. This gal is a dragon of female fire. In the sixteenth century, the church burned witches at the stake.

I presume Emily went at least to some community college, but I get the impression she is a down-home, self-made, bootstraps tigress. She makes it clear that she has come to the searing conclusion that our toxic "American-muddled-mindset" is crippling us. "There's an apocalyptic battle between the Good Mind and the Evil Mind storming across this land," she intones. And she seems convinced that she has been drafted to do battle with the fire-breathing dragon of ignorance. America has to be liberated from its self-shackled empty-headedness. So, the Joan of Arc of mindfulness takes the stage like a Lady Gaga. For many of the souls of the presumably gathering remnant, she taps into an empty hole in the human heart – the modern void.

She is handing out her one page summary, responding vigorously to the high-fives, and freely touching people on the shoulder. She's electric and as explosive as a cherry bomb. I'd never seen every day looking women so whipped up. The scene is like a teenage rock festival or a paid-for political rally. My mind decides that these gals must have some wordless needs or some unspoken hopes. If you listen to the dark side media, you have to worry that the dark is already sniffing its day of triumph in the prevailing winds. But these women here are in essence shouting back, *No way, Great Deceiver.*

Young southern blondes have never been my go-to fantasy, yet at that moment, with the afternoon light soft outside, inside my undernourished urge is on the whet. Undoubtedly the silly grin on my face betrays my gathering randiness. Admittedly, I am weak in the knees from my failures. My lonesome life is on the shore of an island called no-hands-touching. Whatever this crowd-pleasing chic has to say will be cool with me. I'll buy a set of encyclopedias if that is what it takes. Wow, with her heart shaped face and cute little pointed chin, she promises to be exciting. She discharges a sassiness that would challenge any man's dander. My lonely man's dander is like yeast in the pizza dough … about five minutes, and rising.

She begins to shout over the buzzing crowd: "The handout I'm giving you summarizes a game plan to lead your life into simpler, more peaceful pastures. These are personal life-strategies that really hunt. I know these practices can chase away the dark birds of prey from the branches of your minds. They clarified my skies. But as we say down home, the proof of the catfish is in the eating."

(I watch her shifting her weight from one foot to the other, alternately exposing her tilted neck from one side to the other, at first blush so demure, yet ever so teasing and tempting. Her body language gives off that naughty thirty-something scent.)

"We'll start with #1. the breath, and move on to #2. attending to the surrounding sense world, very important, #3. body and emotion awareness, #4. personal and social attunement, and finish with #5. visualization. It's all plain talk, as simple as Daniel Boone's coon-skin cap. It's about de-cluttering your mind. And, believe you me, folks, if you live in Uncle Sam's land, you got clutter-galore in that noisy-mind."

In Yankee-land, where the Malachy immigrants put down their roots, Southern girls loom as part of the plantation legends, somewhat similar to the Salem stories. Emily York is not a sweet, submissive, Southern, antebellum, long dress lady. She is like the determined Georgia woman of *Gone with the Wind*. Not my cup of tea, even though, I have to admit, the little lady is sweetly put together. Moreover, she's a threat to my theory of it all, which has me and my fellow patriarchs at the center of it all. My memory of that classic movie is that those Southern gals eventually neuter a man's spirit. Emily is sexually provocative with a titillating riff of danger. She's the lion. I'm the Daniel, who is not where he feels safe to be, in his time of change.

Like a dutiful ex-teacher, I have foolishly taken a seat in the first row. Before I know it, her wide, Shenandoah green eyes are glancing off my name tag and swaggering into the windows of my insecure soul. The winking dimple on her pointed chin heightens my excitement. Desire begins to rise up in my loins, like an awakening kundalini serpent. Signals between a man's loins and a pair of cat green eyes travel at nano-speed. Women sniff desire, like German Shepherds sniff illegal immigrants.

Subconsciously, lightning flashes across my limbic synapses. My wanton voyeur moon sails over a bed where a young, white body lies. Who knows, my fantasy mind rages on: She just might need a roll in the sack. It might be a break from talking, talking to a tangled crowd of minds in search of new ways out of their empty lives. I know I get tired of talking, talking to my tireless self. And I might discover that isolation in my cool study is not the ticket to happiness.

As you can see, my animal wanting is tugging at the leash. I'm conjuring up that this little woman wants to be wanted, like most everybody else does – at least in my moon-sailing. Gwen says we all want the same activity. I feel the storm winds of encounter, rattling the shutters of my soul. My body freezes up, unsure.

"Mr. Malachy, would you be kind enough to read aloud for us the first page."

A boyish smile melts my face, as I call a huddle of my inner guys: Some shouting, *Go for it. Win the lottery.* Others saying, *You're losing it, Mr. Mal.* Slowly my gathering testosterone releases my face, while she waits out the long, boy-girl moment. I recover my balance, wink at her, and stand up to the challenge. After all, I supposedly have the teacher DNA. I quickly scan a few lines to get the lay of the land; then I begin to read aloud: "The human mind is the pinnacle of fourteen billion years of evolution. It is now capable of the most creative, most loving, most forward-planning deeds. At the same time, the rowdy, untamed mind is the shadowy seat of our worst crimes, evil actions, and self-inflicted stress. Because we are not attuned to our minds and the world around us, we are not at peace with our selves or our planet.

Mind is what the neurons of the body-brain do; our conscious self emerges from this physical activity. Untrained, unschooled minds easily morph into the storm troopers of the evil empire. The evil empire may sound like poetry, but it's as real as John Glenn's step onto the moon. Monkey minds swing from old wild thoughts to new distracting vagabond thoughts. The way of **mindfulness** is a venerable wisdom, and now a cutting-edge scientific tool of personal and social well-being." (End of first page.)

I decide I've played enough of her game. I am tempted to stick out my tongue at the she devil who inflames my imagination. I settle for winking at Scarlett O'Hara again. Her fair, rosy face deepens. I know I've touched one of her moist spots … we all have them.

As I start to sit down, I spy a woman sitting in the second row off to the right. Her face is half hiding under a helmet of dirty blonde hair, cut short, straight at the neck, and front bangs totally hiding her forehead. Not my first choice in hair styles. I like the wild Farrah Fawcett types. She is slender, under-endowed, and conservatively dressed. She sits motionless, looking down into her lap, where she slowly fumbles her fingertips.

This place of strange energy is obviously awakening more than my contextual mind. Like a confused King Kong, my male mind approaches a roar: *What is that woman doing here? She doesn't even seem to be paying attention. She must be hurting on the inside if she is here.* (She's motionless.) *Hurt has a thousand faces, and a million responses – some people act out with aggression, others withdraw into submission.*

There is an empty seat next to her. I hear the conscience-nudge to go sit next to her, and say hello. After a fashion, my male unconscious is guardedly awakening to the prowl, even if my conscious self is not aware of it. The male moth is naturally drawn to the fragile female flame. Still, the butterfly of compassion has not yet eased out of his chrysalis. Like a timid sheep, hardly a ram, I rationalize that it might be gauche. After all, I tell myself, this is a gathering for women. There are only a few token men. I recognize Brad Stevens golden crew-cut head. The men probably are husbands and guests of the women on the board.

I recall walking out later into the brisk, stimulating late afternoon light, thinking about the lonesome woman playing with her fingers, a nervous form of self-touching. A year or two down the road, I might try to concentrate on my breath and watch my parade of emotions without judging. Emily would lay great store by both strategies, but I am still, at that time, an untried mind. But Emily's noble Gandhi words are as clear in my head as the sun setting over the Rim that night as I walk home: *Start the process of being the change you wish to see in the world.* We had scored, she and I.

When I get home, I'm in need of some psychic space. I don't remember seeing much of the splendor of the western sky nor rising Alpha Centauri on the way home. I had walked AWOL in a mental semi-fog, her words jamming my mind waves. Falling lost into thought-loops is such an easy mode to slide into. Call it the zombie mode. The Tennessee volunteer with her green eyes had unleashed my reptile-mammal neurons.

Yet my rational cortex knows that young Emily is unfortunately a don't-go-there for me. But a body in heat feeds on fantasy, like a bear feeds on honey. It blows my mind that I could even dream naughtily of her. I am a changing man. This damn high country is already loosening some tight screws. Despite all my inner turbulence, in some fold of my mind, that cute seed-thrower's message has landed safely onto my rocky, leave-me-be soil. Somehow I accept this modern-day Joan of Arc's message, as if it was sent especially to me. For some portentous reason, I'll never forget you, Emily, and your challenge to change. You have awakened my juices and spun me in a new direction.

Right from the start, I decide to dutifully embrace Emily's premise: We live in a culture jammed with a storm of static, in a mindscape of constant pop-ups and spam. The sneaky presence of a sinister energy the desert people called *Beelzebub* is alive and streaming. The empire's mission statement maintains: If I say it often enough and loud enough, the masses will swallow my idols, my icons and my delusions. On the other side, Emily of Arc waves the banner that this tangled mix of ignorance must be pruned and weeded. Her words make sense. Females, as we men better know, can upset apple carts.

As the genii of the under-mind are wont, her words continually come back. In my head she is saying, "Evolution doesn't do quickies. We can't quickly change this skewed system that wants, like a Pied Piper, to lead our dumbed-down species over the cliff's brink. Our minds must awaken! The way of mindfulness is the open portal. We enter, or we perish." (In one of my dreams, a shadowy-me-figure stands up, and walks toward the preacher's podium. It feels like a kind of conversion experience.)

The next morning, the light of day enlivening my spirit, I awake peaceful. I have no defense against the cutie's assumption that we need to do something about the fog in our minds, or we run the risk of forfeiting our humanity. She's right – there **is** a lot at stake. Sedona seems to be sending the same message – at least to those of us who get the call to settle here. Carl and Sedona Schnebly got that call, and a recall. Yes, I've lived with my fair share of head fog. Suddenly I feel like life is pushing me out of the comfort zone. I protest, Why me? I like comfort. I'm used to it. I know that I have a hunger for clarity.

I simmer in the sheets without stirring; my mind lollygagging: Yes, our collective hive mind is threatened and timorous. Maybe we have to choose: *To be or not to be.* Either to courageously place a few, small pebbles on the mosaic of kindness; or slip down the dark way. We can go mind berserk and shoot at a group of students at a bus stop, as someone did in last night's 7:00 pm news. Even the shared mind of a place like Lomas Serenas has to struggle for connection. A common pitfall for gated communities is to give up and slip-slide into insular dwellings. I don't think people like the Stevens want that.

That little Tennessee gal has lit a fire under me. There are layers to this process we call mind. We don't fully understand these evolving layers, say nothing about teaching the upcoming generations about the reptile brain, the mammalian brain, and the current, battling theories of the human frontal cortex/mind. If you must know, I am not ignoring that it is something akin to the reptile layer that finds Emily so desirable. Even a reptile yearns to reproduce. I grin, imagining Emily's retort: *A reptile has no conscience. Conscience, Mr. Malachy, is the mountaintop of the species who thinks he is the summit of evolution, but acts like he's the pits.*

Last night, I had gone to my think tank and slid back my retractable roof to look up at the evening star. I had to concede that the little Southern she-devil is dead on: *Homo sapiens* better wise up, or as the media says: Get smart. She is repelling and provocative, at the same time. Her talk continues to burrow into my consciousness. Maybe she has been sent to bring more than my mind alive. After all, the body and mind are not two, but one.

The image of her childlike body off in some hotel bed reminds me of her visualization technique. It seems promising. It may be a balm for the toxic reactions lying-in-wait in my burnt-out psyche. Allie's death still hangs like an albatross around my mind. I've been carrying the cross that I hurt her by my impassioned searching. I feel myself waking up to the need to start with healing my own wounds. If I heal, I will have the strength to not harm others.

The bouncy blonde from the hardscrabble South is perhaps what my Catholic parents might have called "an angel"– a presence who comes into your life with a message. My resolution is to give Joan of Arc's ideas an honest-to-goodness try. Perhaps she is the reason the universe has called me to Sedona. I needed some sense kicked into me. I know my mind is a waste land, even a war-zone. As I climb out of bed, her #2 point – *attending to the surrounding sense world* – slips into my awakening body.

A couple of nights later, as I am walking over to the clubhouse for the wine and cheese, the sunlight is long, deep into its descent into western horizon – an orphic time of day. The trees are deepening the satiny cast of the late afternoon, inviting me to stand and reflect. I stop, and lift my eyes up toward the Mogollon Rim, that escarpment that towers over the north side of town. The rugged cliffs rise up to the Colorado plateau, a 600 million-years-solid hunk of the North American continent – a kind of rock of the ages.

My eyes follow the flight of a raven high in the sky. What is he after, I wonder? My mind recalls the biblical raven that brought nourishing help to Elias in the desert. Is this messenger a sign? Will I bump into someone nice? Encounter a mature woman who can put up with a screwed up loser like me? I feel a new energy stirring in my spirit.

A week or so after being shocked awake, I come out of dreamtime angry with myself. Opening one eye briefly, I see the red
light of the little alarm clock, 3:14 am. The day before had been
an arduous day, hiking Sycamore Canyon in the morning, meeting the cable repair man around noon, and reading Alan Wallace's *Embracing Mind,* one of the five recommended books on
Emily York's handout. Wallace is both a scientist and a teacher
of Buddhist meditation. He writes about the contemplative sciences, where neuroscience and Eastern wisdom converge.

In stark contrast, the Internet news of the yesterday hangs
heavy in my gray matter, like storm clouds: teen pregnancies
are up, job openings down, suicides of soldiers returning from
far-away wars are skyrocketing, and the nation's debt is over the
top. Dusk had come darkly the night before, and I dozed off in
my chair on my observation deck. I could not recall coming in
to bed. When I have too much wine, my memory goes south. I
have to face up to the fact that I need to shape up. In that department, I'm still heading in the down direction. I know it's about
drowning my fears and insecurity.

I don't open my eyes wide, nor turn on a light. I just lie there
chafing to berate myself for my lack of self-control. Wine is on
its way to becoming an Achilles heel – Achilles the guy who
would be invincible. In the backroom of my mind, a deal to

have a dry day is being struck – again. I lie there alone, soul-searching my feelings, trying not to be judging. That's what the guru books say: *without grasping on to judgments.* I question whether the feeling in the pit of my stomach is because I am a failure or because I am lonely. My drinking feels like another failure. Oops, I am slipping out of the "clear kind blue mind," as Emily's book describes the mental state I am supposed to be striving for.

Lying here, my eyes closed to the world, aware of the silent emptiness of the room – of the house – the little homunculus heart inside my chest is wandering on the edge of fear. It is the fear of facing one's aloneness, or maybe it's a fear of relationship. I wonder how many lonely people are lying in dark rooms around the world, feeling like this deserted island of a man. Maybe there is a John Malachy somewhere in the suburbs of Dublin, tossing and turning, unable to sleep, berating the drink. The woman with the helmet of dirty blonde hair, sitting alone in the lecture hall, shuffles through my mind. I bet that's why she was there. She too is an island.

I've waded through a good deal of reading about the origins of the human race. Clearly we spent a lot of time in close need of one another, for well over 100,000 years. We've only been "bowling alone" for some recent few decades. Evolution continues to weave the need for social contact into the warp and woof of being human. I tell myself I should be getting more involved in the community, but somehow my self-confidence has gone limp. My alcohol failings seem related to my isolation. No contest, judge. Guilty as charged. I'll try.

The dark thoughts and sad feelings begin melding into one another. In the background I hear the sound of a spattering rain on the acrylic skylight in the bathroom. It sounds like a Morse code message. Outside the pre-dawn wind rubs the branches of a pine tree softly on the side wall of my bedroom. For a couple of hours I drift in and out of sadness, in and out of shallow snatches of sleep. Standing silently in the darkness next to my bed, I imagine the demon of discouragement with his thief-like smile.

I awake again. The clock says 5:56 am. Soft rays of the rising sun are slipping through the open slats of the plantation shutters that protect my bedroom. The rain has stopped. My body doesn't feel rested. I feel the tug to wallow in my *poor me* downheartedness. I've been here many times of recent. But, trying to be courageous, I whisper the prayer of the prophet Samuel: *Here I am. Speak,* and roll my bare feet onto the cool tile floor telling myself that I don't have to live yesterday. I only have this one day to live. This is the present moment. I know it isn't just a question of not drinking too much wine. I have to do the positive. I resolve to try to be kind to at least one person this given day. Perhaps I'll pass someone on the trail and get a chance to smile and say, "Have a great day." I'll take one small step out of the bog of isolation. That's the tonic my lassitude needs. I regret that I didn't say hello to that lonely, finger-fumbling woman. We all need smiles. Smiles are like multivitamins. In a way, dear Gwen who sent me out hiking is right. The wilderness embraces, and brings solace. Out there, one feels a sense of vitality. I got to get going, and hit the wilderness trail.

I drive over to the Thunder Mountain Trail, planning to stop at the library afterwards. The leaves are changing colors. Even as a boy, fall has always been my soft favorite – a season of briskness after the sluggish heat of summer, with turning leaves and football. Now in Sedona the magic seems magnified. It's October 2009, and I'm beginning to feel somewhat at home in the high country. My spirit has recently been stirred up by the Tennessee epiphany who shook me out of my drifting. I've reserved another of her recommended books at the library. *My Stroke of Insight* is by Jill Bolte Taylor, the Harvard-trained neuroscientist who suffered a stroke, losing the left half of her brain.

I arrive at the library a good half hour early. I love the statue of Sedona in her laced-up boots, ankles-to-neck cowgirl outfit, her feminine breast emboldened in bronze, and a candid, Missouri smile. In one hand, she has an apple outstretched to the needy, in the other a basket with more fresh fruit from the Schnebly orchard. A lady pioneer in 1901, she knew people living on the frontier had to take care of one another.

When I approach the library's shaded, front portico, I see a lone, young woman seated on one of the two stone benches. She is engrossed in a large book on her lap. Her face is tented in medium-long, ginger-blonde hair. She is conservatively well-dressed. She doesn't have that hang-loose, New Age, lean with long hair look that I've come to accept as "Western." I peg her as Chicago, or Minnesota, possibly Boston. She looks quite demure. So despite being a moth who is easily drawn to the eternal fecund flame, (you may have sensed that) I decide to honor her absorption in her tome. Perhaps it is the softness and stillness of the autumn portico. I somehow do catch the title of her book, *Alchemy and Mysticism.* That ups her aura in my book. Yet I sit down on the other stone bench and try to get back into another of Emily's next recommendation, Andrew Newberg's *How God Changes Your Brain.*

I find my bookmark and open to the section I had been reading, his paragraphs on yawning. Yawning in a brain/spiritual book is an idea that tickles my funny bone. You have to be kidding, Andrew. And believe it or not, the girl yawns. (Perhaps she only sighs. But a small sign is good enough for most male moths.) I audibly chuckle. (Of course, it's partly staged.)

"What's so funny?" she says, lifting her open, young face from her book.

"I was just reading about yawning, and you yawned."

"Did I?"

"Yes, the book I'm reading says it's good for your brain."

"What's *your* book?"

I give her a quick synopsis of the quest for mindfulness, mentioning *Kirtan Kriya*, a kind of meditation that incorporates breathing, movement, mantras, mudras, and chanting.

"Your book sounds more interesting than mine," she says, getting up and coming over to sit next to me. Sometimes the flame also wants to be connected to a candle.

We quickly fall into a seamless exchange of personal thoughts – rare for strangers on stone benches. We are like long-separated twins, who have bumped into one another unexpectedly. She is attractive, something I hadn't focused on consciously. I scan the nice lines of her face, trying to convince myself that it is her mind that attracts me.

She introduces herself as Iliana. "That's not my real name. I got that at my rebirth from my new-birth mother." All of this doesn't really register with me. I'm still absorbed in liking her, and trying to put a finger on why. I mean besides the obvious. "I'm here for a vision quest retreat out at the Secret Mountain Wilderness Retreat Center."

Then the library opens. We both rise to go in. "Can I give you a hug?" she asks. I smile, and she gives me a genuine hug, saying, "I need hugs at this time in my life." I feel a surge of closeness with her. In her eyes, I see something special: *She's a seeker.*

Several nights later, in the softening light of falling after-noon, I walk down to the Lomas Serenas clubhouse for a Friday night wine and cheese get-together. I feel a need for compan-ions. Not by bread and wine alone does man find whatever he is questing for. When I come in, I recognize Brad Stevens. My mind slumps to a comparison: He's a tall, strong guy with a kind of quiet smile, a youthful head of close-cropped, golden hair, and happily married. I'm an early-fifties guy, with dull chestnut hair lazily hugging my neck, and an ordinary body and face, both with signs of *ennui.* I'm flying solo. The difference, as my inner critic concludes is my insecurity. Brad has a look of self-confidence, with a slight, sad moon over his shoulder. I'm told he is a serious student. I'm interested in what I hear he's into: the social structures that support happiness and long life.

When I was just a pup, my father used to say, "John was born with that serious frown on his face. I think he inherited it from me." (Irishmen, as the world knows, are not a pint shy of retell-ing any tale.) Nevertheless, becoming aware of my conflicted emotion is, in reality, progress, believe it or not Mr. Ripley. I tell myself it is progress because being attuned to one's emotions is step #3 of Emily's strategies, which I'm trying to get into, although it is still her #2 that intrigues me. Sedona must have a hand in that. I count my lucky stars and my heavenly hills.

My father, Leo John Malachy, was a hard working world literature teacher and moderator of the high school newspaper. He loved to recite passages from his lectures. I think he missed his calling; he was a born thespian. My mother was the real heart of our home. (What else is new?) Helen Jane had thought about going into the convent, but somehow her destiny called her into nursing. Things seem to happen for a reason, don't they? She met my father in the hospital, where she, a twenty-year-old nurse, fresh out of nursing school, was caring for his mother. Leo Malachy, the concerned son, had gone to Albany, New York to get good care for his sick mother. He wasn't an especially talented or handsome man, but he had a vein of caring that made him sort of special to those who looked into his eyes. I am one of those lucky ones, born into a "secure-attachment" home. No troubling questions in the Malachy household: God the Father is up there, long white beard and all, looking over us – anthropomorphic as hell. If we obeyed the laws of the church (no meat on Friday, no artificial birth control, and no attending Protestant weddings) and, of course, His commandments, we'd get a nice piece of real estate in the hereafter. How much rosier could life be for a young boy?

I do remember a silly boyhood scruple. I wasn't supposed to *play with myself.* Handling the plumbing fixtures was somehow dirty and sinful. Even then, I found it ironic that my tiny genitals were "myself." I could touch my arm, my belly, my nose, my back-ass – none of those were *myself.* So yes, I had a slightly tweaked introduction to the world of sexuality. Never mind, crazy as it may sound, I am more glad than sad that this twig was bent in the direction of restraint. I can imagine how many more mistakes I would have made without that childhood notion of purity and self-control. But not even the fear of hell disarmed my God-given concupiscence. It seems to be there for a reason.

At that stage of my life, my father was one of my heroes of a thousand faces. He was a man who loved the outdoors, although he seldom took me along. He was a loner, who worried a lot. He was super conscientious about his lesson preparations, and he loved to tell stories. His all-time favorite Aesop fable was the one about the slave Androcles who befriended the lion with the thorn in his paw in the forest. The kind slave was later thrown into the arena of Rome to be mauled and eaten. When I was about three, Dad would get down on his hands and knees, and play the lion: "What was the amazement of the spectators," he'd recite, "when the lion after one glance, bounds up to the slave and lies down at his feet. The lion had recognized his kind friend."

Dad wasn't exactly what you would call religious, although he did go to church on Sunday, taking a three-pointer (rump on the pew bench behind him, instead of kneeling straight up). It wasn't what you were supposed to do. I was a little embarrassed. (My literal mind tends to be tough on people. Even, I confess, sarcastic.) He did get down onto his knees when he got out of bed in the morning and before he got back in at night. No one knew what sort of exchange went on during those silent kneel downs. He never talked the church talk. He did nothing exciting except go to work every day, "chopping wood and carrying water," as the Zen people say. He gave us a chicken-in-the-pot, good lower-middle-class life. *Thanks, Dad.* He died young, I wasn't twenty.

I was emotionally closer to my mom, who worked hard keeping the house clean, washing and ironing the family's clothes, cooking our meals, and washing our dirty dishes. She even ran the sheets through "the mangle." That was before we could afford permanent-press sheets. She had what I now consider the good fortune to come from a working-class family, or as she called it, "the other side of the tracks." There she developed a resilient backbone, one of those traits not passed on by genes. You have to build your own. She had put herself through nursing school by working as a servant girl for a family on the wealthy side of the tracks. Still, she had a sense of humor, which I also didn't inherit. She once told me a "dirty joke" about a priest who slipped in the mud, shouting, "Jesus Christ. God Almighty," to the shock of Mrs. Gilhooley, who was passing by. Mom said that poor Mrs. Gilhooley had misheard: What Father O'Brien actually said was, "Cheese and crackers, got all muddy." Of course, little Johnny was not to repeat that story. I suspect I got my interest in religious studies from her.

She was a stickler for education and saw to it that homework was done every night. If I got good grades, she smiled and hugged me with her strong arms. Almost by osmosis, I took to heart that there were three big questions: **me, my God, my destiny.**

Of course, I didn't talk to Brad Stevens that night about my upbringing or my existential confusion. Life had taught me not to talk about the things that really matter. Insularity is a closet rubric of individualism. Be not an open book. Hide what people might use against you. One can't forget the dogs that eat dogs. Nevertheless, here in Lomas Serenas, just like Bob the realtor advertised, I'm beginning to feel an acceptance, a kind of community. That seems to fit well into the *geist* of the red rocks country.

When I got home, I went out to my back deck to clear my head. It was on a dark night like this that I first saw the big, red gleaming eyes of an owl in the forest. Perched in forest tree, he was solitary and solemn, his body motionless, except for the slow rotation of his head and neck. His *Hoo H'hoo* brought back one of my father's rhymes: There was an owl who lived in an oak. The more he heard, the less he spoke. The less he spoke, the more he heard. Why can't we be like that wise old bird? For my father, the owl was a symbol of the virtue of being quiet. He knew the owl was the favorite feathered creature of Athena, the goddess of the Greek acropolis where wisdom was venerated.

May and June had sweltered, hot and dry with westerly winds. Now, the second week of July, the season of the monsoon thunderstorms with southeasterly up-flows is bringing more rain up from the Sea of Cortez. My friend Paul likes this annual meteorological wind shift. He tells me I'll be a true Arizonan when I take rain dances seriously.

The day launched with brilliant blue, sunny skies. As morning melts into afternoon, galleons of storm clouds begin to move toward a collision with the Rim cliffs, I'm standing on my back deck, I feel the excitement the indigenous people must have felt as the power of Nature gathered around them. It puts me in a good mood to feel a part of something much, much larger than myself. I'm sick of unimportant.

Soon the sound and light show gets serious: a throaty boom of thunder rumbles against the Mogollan Rim, echoing in the canyons, and grumbling through the trees. The sky splits with crisp, blue peals of electricity dancing on the red cliffs, and the healing rain falls fast and furious into the storm drains and the forest arroyos. Then, as suddenly as it exploded, it stops. The world returns to a friendly stillness, and a rainbow arches across the land. This place is definitely atmospheric. I feel I have somehow arrived.

That evening I go in and watch some news, trying to avoid having a drink. It is one of my "dry days." I'm trying to get myself into what I call *Right body*, rewriting a bit the Buddha's eightfold path. The news doesn't help. It brings on cultural angst. Read society's lips, my mind niggles: we are a troubled tribe. I don't know what to believe about our future. I take a walk in the night air, but it doesn't help much. I take a shower hoping that will relax me before climbing into bed. I resist the impulse to have a brandy and white crème de menthe.

For a couple of hours, I fight myself to find a comfortable position and come to terms with *Nyx*, the shadowy goddess of the night. I'm unable to keep thoughts about bank greed, wealth inequality, and those five great extinctions out of my rowdy mind. Of course, biologists say there are throngs of species ending their days, every day. Some wags talk of a Mayan Armageddon. Something much larger than my little self seems to be hanging in the balance. Exhausted, I fall into the hole of dreaming, and I find myself up in a tree.

My dreaming self has a solid impression that I am in an acacia tree in a grassy savannah environment. I feel rather nervous because the tree canopy is thin and the trees are spread out from one another. I feel exposed. I have a strong sentiment that I am in Africa. I can hear talking and soon a party of about thirty men, women, and children comes through the tall elephant grass to the east. They seem to be telling one another stories. Some seem to be almost reciting oral-traditions, handed down in a sing-song way. Others seem engaged in everyday gossip.

A couple of men carry wooden poles on their shoulders. A large bleeding animal hangs between the poles. Young women hug infants to their chests. Older-looking women, conceivably grandmothers, walk holding the hands of toddlers. Some young men carry clubs and tools that look like spear launchers or dart throwers. Another group of young, barefooted women in deerskin dresses, falling just below their knees, are bringing animal skin totes. Based on what I have read my mind guesses that the skins are filled with tubers, berries, and other edible forages.

A tall, wiry man, dark-skinned, graying at his temples, raises his hand. The group stops. The sun has begun to set over the acacias. He looks around, taking in everything around them. Then he slowly nods, nods twice, and the group breaks into action. Damn, they are going to camp down not far from my perch. Everyone seems to know his or her job. Some senior looking men clear a swatch of ground, and begin cutting and preparing the kill.

The tawny women find a spot under the tree next to me, and resume trading their tales. I can't understand a word. They begin to sort and organize what they have gathered. Obviously they've done this before. Even I can catch the timbre of sisterly solidarity that comes up from the group. Perhaps intimacy is a better description. The professor, who gave the talk last week at the college, had used the term "gregarious" when he talked about the primitive peoples he had lived among. He had also alluded to something like the power of femaleness. Some teens scurry laughingly off and return with twigs and lightwood for the fires. Some mature men come back with larger pieces of wood and begin setting up three fires. I sense a psalm of togetherness rising from this "residential unit" (that's the term the professor used). The psalm is full of a kind of unabashed happiness one doesn't hear much these days. So simple and so united.

To me, the scene I am privy to seems to be shouting: *Eat your heart out, modern man. Life might never get much simpler than this.* My dreamtime fantasy imagines a Merlin-like heavenly voice saying: *This is the way I wanted this little planet to be. Of all the trillions of my creations, I tried to make this one a special place. But it seems like the train is jumping the tracks. My free will wrinkle may have been a mistake. But hey, you don't know the ending. That's my secret.*

Through the tall grass to the west another "residential unit" of about the same size emerges. From the way they are greeted, I get the impression that they have somehow been invited to share. Some of the original unit hug members of the incomers, maybe brothers and sisters. They don't all look like kin, though some do. Right away the newcomers join in the tasks at hand, and soon gather in gender groups. The men cook and distribute pieces of meat to everyone. The women give each person a handful of assorted vittles. I see one comely young woman with depleted breasts give her child to a younger girl with well-rounded breasts, who immediately gives her milk to the child. It's a touching scene. If I listen carefully I even hear the child chomping amid the revved up chatter. I guess he is a boy.

The shared meal goes on for a long, leisurely time. The sun is already setting in the western sky, coloring the savannah pink and gold by the time everyone is pitching in to clean up the area. They seem to care for and steward the place. Night moves silently in, with only a thin crescent moon. They divide into two groups. I can't tell, but I suppose that they are moving back to their original bands. Each group has three fires, and they arrange themselves head to toe in a triangle. I think I hear some animals moving about in the darkness, but it's hard to see. I am disappointed because the whole bedding down ritual is something I am keenly interested in, not having done that in a couple of blue moons.

I can sense that everyone seems to have someone to snuggle with. There are several clusters resembling modern families, and some pair-bonds like one reads about these days. But I don't get the impression that the young people are what we like to call monogamous. I'm getting angry at this dream. For me, the physical clutch was becoming hot again, and I'm not seeing any. Surely it's happening. Somehow it doesn't seem superficial, or shallow. It is not what we'd call "cheap."

The next morning I sleep in. The sun is up, and the sky is that fabled Arizona ringing blue. I feel rested, but isolated. I have the Lomas group of acquaintances, but it is thin, not deep. I have no tap root person in my life. Of course, maybe those hunter-gathers in my dream had the whole "residential band" as their anchor relationship. That's another possible: group sex like a loving commune. Sounds like fun, but somehow it doesn't sound like me. The question of the one or the many is probably a never-ending song.

Time hikes by slowly in the ageless high hills, but it definitely keeps climbing. I have fallen for the clean blue air, the warm golden sun, the cheerful green wilderness, and the silence of the stars. As the pages of the calendar blow by, I am spending almost as much time out in nature as I am in my book room. But, almost three years after my great escape to the country of red mountains, I'm sitting with several old buddies in hops-smelling Haggerty's Bar in upper Manhattan, where we have gathered to attend Eddie McMahon's funeral. By then, I luckily, or maybe thanks to the Tennessee pistol, am feeling better about life and myself. The high country also appears to be the tonic my deflated spirit needed.

We had been together in the undergraduate dorm of Manhattan College. Most of us had been raised Catholic. We dated girls from the nearby Mount St. Vincent College, and had sing-along Kum-ba-ya liturgies on the floor of the student union building. We stayed up at night, sneaking beers, and discussing the eternal paradoxes, and of course the inscrutable other gender. The college years can be a wide-eyed philosophical time of life.

By the time I get word about Eddie's premature death, I am hungry for some kind of familiar connection. I'm also genuinely aware that I am frightened by death – one of those hidden bugaboos about which the little inner voice says: *You know you've got to look it in the eye.* Early on out of academia, my youthful attachment to organized religion had steadily been sliding downhill. That part of my Sisyphus psyche was losing. Then, after Allie's suicide, if that was what it was as I believe, I didn't have the courage to believe in much of anything, let alone face mortality. But now my courage is making a soft comeback. Sedona is not really a fever. It's a slow arousal. It's like a subtle foreplay.

"Death is a fickle mystery, isn't it, John? Why Eddie? Why him?" Tim Larkin is asking.

"You got that right, my friend. It's a furky, murky mystery. One of the many. We have problems with mysteries, don't we? Hell, I spent my youth memorizing the answers to **the essential questions**, as if *the Temple Gang* knew the right answers. Now I've turned my face away from those childhood answers. But damn it, those old questions keep coming back, like the proverbial bad pennies. Now, as I am stepping into midlife and start looking down the hallway of life, they persist in bugging me even more. They're like those unseen sand fleas Arizonans call 'no-see-um.' They're pains in the neck." (I was drinking a Guinness for old time's sake.) "I try to hide from those pesky concerns, but they are like death, we can't escape them. Since my life fell apart, I've wrestled, time and again, with figuring out if God exists, who I am, what am I supposed to do, and where's it all going. I occasionally catch myself singing in the shower, *What's it all about, Alfie?*"

"What was it Brother Luke used to say in his theology class? 'Aaah, the big challenges of life: my God, my blue heaven, and how I buy stock in it,'" Bill Sullivan, sitting on my left, asks and answers from his memory.

"Something like that. Hearing you voice them, makes me realize me how self-centered those concerns are. They're all about the individual, the almighty me, aren't they?"

"Kathy's going to have a rough time," Jack Reynolds chimes in, with the genuine care of a friend in his voice. "How old are the girls now?" he asks, wiping the beer foam off his salt-and-pepper mustache.

"I think Maureen is thirteen or so, and Bridie is almost eleven," Bill answers.

"It was such a shock. Hell, guys, I was skiing with him last winter up on Windham Mountain. No way did he seem sick." Reynolds looks genuinely grieved; somehow our college togetherness had taught us to care about one another. It's a ripe time of life. We were like the guys and gals now coming home from the wars in the foreign mountains. They are trained to an honor code: Take care of one another. Never leave a fallen comrade in the field.

"The type of pancreatic cancer he had is rare, but aggressive – slow to show and quick to kill. It's one where you never hear the hoof-beats of the four horsemen coming."

"I have to admit it was a nice mass," Tim confesses. "First one I've been to in years. Father Dunstan sure believes Eddie is already happy in heaven. I didn't know that Eddie and Kathy still practiced the faith and had the girls in the Holy Rosary Convent School."

"Funny isn't it? Eddie seemed like one of the least church-minded guys in our group. He was happy enough with his sports and his chemistry. Yet he was one of the guys who seemed never to have wavered in that faith of our fathers. I guess actually, there are quite a few who still hang on to a lot of the old ways. Sometimes I suspect that they are just on automatic pilot, unable to get off the dime. We were conditioned, weren't we? It sure was easier to just take life on faith."

"I guess we have to call it that, John. Hell, we were teenagers. We believed; no questions asked. We didn't have to work out our own answers. We were spoon-fed. Yet one has to admit the original message is among the most inspiring, positive messages ever spoken. The Galilean tapped into a deep human vein – love for the others. The rub is you don't hear the original flavor much anymore. They killed the messenger, and what is happening to his message is an even sadder story."

"Damn straight, the message is a huge loss. However, now that I have the luxury of hiking in the contemplative silence of some majestic red spires, I'm catching restful riffs of new, yet old, possibilities echoing in the ancient canyons and speaking from the cliff-faces. Funny what fresh wind blowing through your ears can do – gets rid of the old cobwebs and jamming static."

"Sounds like you still believe in some message, John."

(I can feel an emotion tiptoeing across my face – not sure whether it is embarrassment, pride, confusion, or uncertainty. I still don't really know who I am. I still haven't found whatever I have been looking for. I guess I've bragged too much today about my progress.) "Yes, I guess you could say that," I respond with a hesitation. "Not the old way, although sometimes I miss some of those old ways. I tell myself that **some** human community of belief would be better than nothing. But at times I feel kind of naked, out in the cold. My neighbors are friendly, but we don't talk seriously, like us guys used to in the dorms. Nevertheless, as I said, since I moved to high hills, I begin to see the journey in a different light. There may be no "**final answers**," as that *Who-Wants-to-be-a-Millionaire* lady used to jab – worded answers, that is. Still and all, I don't think we need to walk in atheistic darkness. There are crumbs to follow. The Galilean left crumbs. The Buddha left crumbs. Nature leaves crumbs. I'm picking up crumbs as I walk with a still mind and try to merge into the world around me, even if for only brief spurts of non-trying."

I had the sense that my old gang was with me. The human needs sharing. We had once shared so openly. That trust was coming back. And I knew they were interested in where I was, as I was interested in them. So the tower of me, babbled on. "A little Southern bombshell opened my senses to the community of trees, rocks, birds, and winds that encircle me. I'm now on the outskirts of feeling a kind of community of beings all around me. Hard to explain, and hard to snuggle into, but I beginning to suspect that we need to be attuned to the land, to our place in the universe, as a prelude to the big challenge – getting in tune with an-other. And yes Buford, I'm talking about women – those gorgeous, enigmatic, scary, ball-busting beings."

"Amen, amen, my friend. You have to love'em," Buford booms, with a baritone slur.

"As I probably said a Guinness ago, guys, I sure miss a community of dialogue. I mean thinking-and-feeling people who are working out their own answers. I'm personally coming to some working hypotheses for my own life. They're still tentative. But where can one find such a community of dialogue, as we young bucks had? The church of our childhood is becoming like Humpty Dumpty, whose fall seems on the edge."

"I guess in Europe he's already egg-shells," Tim says, half joshing, half serious.

"Yes, and if one listens to the news, you have to think that spiritually this country is like that legendary herd of white elephants heading for the cliffs of death. I mean f'ing around and violence to others are as American as apple pie used to be."

"In any event, I still hear the apostles saying, 'Lord, to whom shall we go? You have the words of eternal life. And we have believed.'" Reynolds adds.

"Aaah, I just don't know," I reply. "But as I said, I do feel that moving out into the hill country has started the worm turning in my spirit. I often remember Moses climbing the mountain to encounter that infamous bush. Now and again, as I hike the red mountains, I sense the chaparral along the trails whispering to me, as if she were a voice for me."

"Come off it, Malachy. You've always been a wooly-headed loner. You need what we all need. You need to get laid." big Buford Edwards interjects, with a hoist of his beer.

"Amazing isn't it, what we had, but didn't know we had it?" Sully helpfully jumps in.

"Yes, a special relationship, wasn't it? A group thing! Before we got sucked in, and blown out into the system that homogenizes."

"Yeah, we had something like the Marines *esprit de corps*. We didn't bowl alone. As they now say. *It takes a village* to do anything of value," Sully always seemed to hit the nail.

The group seemed to sense that we had reached the suburbs of past joys that had doubtful futures. Back home, most of us lived in worlds where people were shy of trust, and soul terrified of being just another *it*. Tim Larkin seems to sense the thin ice and rushes in save the situation, "Are you still doing that journal writing, John?"

"Off and on, I try. Just short squibs of what I find in my reading, or ideas my mind cobbles together. Sometimes I like to capture memorable moments, or people who stick in my mind. But I'm going through the long dry haul, the writers' desert. I haven't really been able to pick a pen and seriously write in a long time. Any life has roadblocks, right? To me, words like lethargy, lassitude, and *tedium vitae* come quickly to mind. Allie's death really broke my moorings. Yet, out in the canyons, my mind muses about what might bind those loose thoughts into a book – *The Book of Malachy* – down the long, lonely winding road. Yes, damn it, Buford, I'm lonely. I admit that to myself, seeing no Saving Grace on the horizon. Grace being a woman."

"That's your problem, John," ugly Buford breaks back in again. "You're too damn lonely. I told you, you need a woman in your life." Out of the blue, the image of the petite firebrand emerges. Then Gwen emerges followed strongly by an emerging Catherine. I had written about her after her description of her first visit to the *Mii Amo* spa. No strong thunder or dancing lightning – just testosterone lapping against deserted, sandy shores. Catherine still lingers as a castle in the sky. I know she is probably still Bob Dorian's lady. Messing with another man's woman is not good medicine, even if he's not a bonded friend. There is a rubric of trust that courses through the memes of our collective. Or at least, it seems to me, there should be.

That night of Eddie McMahon's funeral, I take the red-eye away from that encounter with death and my past, and back to the high desert land of Northern Arizona. I feel relieved to get out of the congestion, the noise, and the fast pace of city life. My heart still carries the cross of the loner; but it feels lighter now that the grace of the red rock place has come to my aid. But damn, Buford's remark had hit home. Who knows, maybe prophet of Galilee felt like a Lone Ranger? In the final analysis, Sully is probably right: it takes a village. And Lomas Serenas is reaching to be a village. Yet I don't still feel whole there. Nevertheless, the still forest and the whispering Something More continue to be a balm.

People are complex animals, I remind myself. We need space around us, territory with some elbow-room. Don't fence me in. I guess one of the prompts for my snap decision to settle in Sedona was the meditative quality of the rocks. The prompt was largely inaudible because, before Sedona, I wasn't interested in anything meditative. Still, some meditative energy was interested in me. But on the other hand, we need to be close to others. Buford's right.

As my mind is browsing back in the brotherhood of the dorms, a young black stewardess in my section of coach asks, "Is there anything I can do for you?" "No thank you," I manage.

As she moves up the aisle, I savor the swell to her hindquarters. The God/designer certainly did hindquarters well. Yes, Buford's right.

As the American Airlines 757 plane climbs higher into the dark night, I close my eyes. I'm washed out. My head starts to nod, my consciousness drifts off into one of my interior conversations with myself: *Funny, when I started teaching in the city I ate it up: the neighborhood, the packed subways, the endless movies, the bars, the Stadium, and the Garden. Not to forget, the Irish camaraderie, and the Jewish princesses totally tanned on the Jersey Shore. Old Satan could have been my neighbor, but that wouldn't have bothered my young ways. I guess that's normal for that time of passage.*

The plane is bouncing rhythmically. My tired mind rambles in heavy-eyed memories. Buford Edward's taunt about needing "to get laid" comes bouncing back through my mind. Actually I never really cottoned to that burly blond guy from Buffalo back in the dorm days. He was a master of sarcasm. Maybe that's why I didn't like him – I have that weak trait too. It's a trait that thinks itself cute when it sees a weakness in others, and then rises to the verbal lunge, like a fencer, rapier ready to deflate the bigger or imagined better than itself.

Buford had been a winning, handsome skirt chaser, probably another of the jealous reasons I didn't cotton to him. As a graduation present, his father gave him a Mustang convertible. Buford was also your typical thrill-seeker. He was driving over the speed limit on the East River Expressway when he rear-ended a blonde in a Porsche. His face hit the steering wheel of his Mustang. His days as a skirt chaser crashed – what woman searching for the father of her baby wants a man with a crushed-in forehead, flattened nose, a left-eye a little higher than the right, and a smile that only does left- turns. As a sperm provider, Buford ranks with Frankenstein.

So, life has handed him 'the disfigured card.' We all have our *wish they were otherwise feature-cards.* But let us not forget that there is more to us than the cards in our individual hand. We belong to the family of Man. I remember, from the dorm nights, that Buford also has a human heart below his roughness. When men share, even with a few pints of Guinness, signals fly. I know that, but I forget. Buford is human. Unfortunately, since his crash he seems to have given up. He is wide and wobbly. He weighs over 250 pounds, and his mangy beard is a turn-off.

Moreover, it wasn't his disfigured face that bothered me. It was his expression *"get laid"* that wrangled, and re-wrangled through my mind. My imagination brings back the young stewardess with the gift of swell haunches. I had gotten Bufford's gauntlet message. But I don't like it. It is **not** an expression of love, just a piece of language that turns man and women into *its* – things. It's a prelude to violence. I fear these preludes. They seem to be gathering momentum.

I'm startled awake by the bumps of some turbulence. The pilot comes on to apologize and says he is climbing higher and we should reach a calmer altitude in a few minutes. It dawns on me that my psyche is also in turbulence. I use a little of Emily's breath strategy and come back to the fact that Tim Larkin's inquiry about my writing had rubbed open a deep sore spot in my psyche. Why do I pretend that I am going to be a writer? I have never come close to publishing anything. As for being a writer, I am a charlatan, a failure again.

My first morning back home I walk out in the dawn-light. The rocks stand silently offering me their presence, without asking a donation or pledge in return. The awakening that I had grown stale, stagnant, soured in my city existence, and had not been aware of how badly I needed a shakeup was one of my stepping stones out of dullsville.

The thought occurs to me: I guess that's why the famous fathers of the Egyptian desert in early Christianity lived in isolation. They were a loose network of loners, yet united in their pursuit of the spiritual Something More. Yet that isolation too seems a seductive half-truth. It thinks that one could wax poetic and say that the voyage is like a ship of slaves. We row together because we must. I might not even know the dark-skinned man next to me. To be frank, I might not care about him. I want to somehow escape these irons. Unconsciously, yet deliberately, I smile at him. I may need him to get free. And I know he is just like me. In a way I hope he gets free with me. I feel tossed on the horns of the dilemma: risk escaping free or be safe and stay bound.

I don't feel programmed to be a longtime loner. I've got to open up, or else.

Ever since the crash of the financial world, the whole country has been nervous. The Washington politicians are unable to compromise. A financial collapse of America looms as a distinct possibility, as a divided Congress wrangles on over the debt crisis. The repeated scandals in the capital have erased the national confidence that we are still the nation with a global destiny. The belief of Americans in themselves is leaking away.

On the West Side of Manhattan Island, under a dull, sunless sky, a sleek black BMW Z roadster pulls up to the colonnaded front door of New York's Riverdale Country Club. Getting out and handing the keys to a valet parking man, the Executive Director of the Institute of Theoretical Physics is not nervous. In fact, Wyatt Jones feels quite dapper in his tan slacks, ecru Callaway golf shirt, and a white Gatsby touring cap. As usual, he will have his light, Saturday morning breakfast at the Club, and be ready for his 9:00 am tee-time with his regular buddies – guys who are like him, and therefore like him. The gray sky isn't a concern; he's got his day pegged. As he starts toward the dining room, his cell phone rings. He opens, looks, and mumbles, "Oh, god, Mom. Get a life." He closes it with a shake of his head.

After lunch he'll go to his office where he and his old buddy Sam Gold will play an Internet video game. *Porn Girl* challenges their dominance quotients. Sam usually wins, but Wyatt likes the challenge, and believes that eventually he'll win and be the imaginary alpha male. Work is a bore. And in his prurient imagination he is already with Layla, his 6:00 pm romp. The other guys at the office call her "Material Gal." *She isn't much of a physicist,* he concedes to himself, *but she sure knows how make a man feel big and wanted. Hell, everybody wants to feel wanted. Layla certainly does. Yet, something is not right with Layla recently. She breaks down crying for some reason I don't understand. She never did that before, nor do any of the other girls. Of course,* (a dirty smirk tightens his lips) *if I had my druthers, I'd be banging that smarty pants at the Institute. She's got the sweetest derriere. It's a damn shame that it is hidden so much of the time under that drab white lab coat. I don't dare touch the bitch. Billy be damned, she's marooned in her ways. Oh, she's competent, as everybody knows, but obviously naïve about what makes life worth living. Mark my words: she's an ice cube that will never melt. I must buy Layla a nice bauble. Women like those things, especially if they smell expensive. Makes them feel they matter. At least, that's the way I see it.*

In his suppressed, muddled mind there is a silent realization that he is not God's gift to humanity. He knows he's needy. Isn't everybody? When he has to face that skeleton, he blames it on his father, who was also a weak man without convictions. His father's aloofness drove his mother across the river of loneliness into the land of the isolates. *Hell,* he says to the empty corridor as he proceeds toward the dining room, *he didn't even come to my birthing. It was he who taught me that succeeding financially is what matters. People are throwaways. He threw away my mother.*

For her part, Layla knows the guys whisper about her being the boss's item, but she doesn't obsess over that. *They're all doing it. It's what hip people do in this Big Apple,* she repeatedly soothes herself. *I've got a boss who pays me well. Probably more than I'm worth to the Institute. A girl has to do, what she has to do. She has to shore up her safety net with back-ups. If she doesn't look out for herself, no one will.*

Layla Abdul had entered life as the fourth daughter of a six-daughter, lower-middle-class Lebanese family. Her poor, coin-counting, shopkeeper father pandered newspapers, tobacco, and local information. He knew every place in the surrounding neighborhoods of Beirut where women could be purchased just like newspapers. Under the counter he had condoms for sale. They were hot sellers. Good profit. Dumb buyers. The Abdul sisters had few fairy-tale dreams about their futures.

Layla's closest sister, soft-skinned Sabub, third oldest, had surrendered to what she felt was the only destiny open to a poor shopkeeper's daughter. She became an 'escort,' and struck a rich vein in one of her first tricks, and she was off to the races – winning nightly purses. On the late mornings when Sabub slept in, they talked for hours in their pajamas. Subtly, the seed of how to survive in case of need slipped into Layla's working memory bank. She never really understood how she wound up in the University of Beirut studying physics. She surmised that it was her rich maternal uncle, the physicist, who got her in and helped her get through. To her, he smelled like a lecher, but maybe it was his pipe tobacco. She thought of herself as a girl who had prostituted herself by becoming a degreed female. She hated physics. In her mixed-up mind, she was a girl whose derriere needed high-heels, more than she needed to know the laws of thermo-dynamics.

Wyatt Jones, on the other hand, considers himself a success; run-of-the-mill Americans might even think of him as an American *idol*. (Others would say he is the incarnation of the hiding evil. Those thinkers who explain *evil* as passion without direction might have more compassion.)

With help from his family and a little more help from his friends, Wyatt had parlayed a doctorate in physics from the prestigious MIT. And again, with help from crony money and his college connections, he had landed the coveted position of *Director of the New York Institute of Theoretical Physics.* His bullshit attitude walked him into a cushy office.

In truth, Wyatt isn't interested in physics either, but he is a deft administrator, well a manipulator. He knows how to use people. Moreover, he has it all: fat paycheck, soft life, and women to get off on. Layla isn't his only, but she, more than some of the others, lets him have his way. They are in some ways alike, except he likes doggie. She doesn't, but goes along. Neither of them likes physics. Neither is interested in the question of reality. They are both sort of faking life. Wyatt's thinks of Layla as one of those submissive women; she lets him be boss, and do her his way. Wyatt likes pliable women who let him do it his way. Unfortunately, he is careless about protection. Condoms cheat him of what he has every right to. For Wyatt sex isn't a big question; it's a mind-soothing answer.

Tuesday afternoon I go to the barber shop to get cleaned up for the first Friday party at the clubhouse. O'Sullivan, the barber, greets me with the tip of his hand to his forehead, "Sir Malachy." The guy in the chair ahead of me and the barber are arguing about the acquittal of a twenty-five-year-old young woman who is accused of killing her two-year old daughter, dumping the body in the woods, and then going out dancing and partying. "Somewhere the devil is dancing," the guy in the chair quotes. "And her tattoo with the words, *La Bella Vida* (The Good Life). Come on, give me a break, she's been lying through her teeth. Being a mother cramped her style. These kids have gone wild."

"Possibly," the barber responds calmly, "poor girl came from a heavily dysfunctional family. Her defense admitted that she had lied, and that her behavior was irrational. They hinted that she had been molested by both her brother and her father, but there was zip proof. The violence empire media had turned the tale into a three-ring circus."

"Did you hear that they're already talking about a big book contract for her?"

As I listen, trying to put the picture together, thoughts and emotions are pinging around in my brain. As you may recall, I have a daughter about that age. She's a little tough on me sometimes, but she seems to have herself decently together. I have to credit that to her poor dead mother, but I'd heard a lot of stories about her school mates. Some do call it: girls gone wild. It's not easy these days, growing up human. The very air we breathe feels compromised. Whenever I hear some of the statistics on abuse in families, I go into denial, *Can't be.* Gwen's words still echo in my mind: *We're all human. We all want the same things.* Those words have been gathering momentum *sub-rosa.* Although I have to admit that we take drastically different roads to get what we want.

What do we all want? My mind is a stormy ocean of rising white caps and collapsing troughs. When the barber holds up the mirror, I smile wanly, nodding, and decide that a five dollar tip is good enough. I can't really get excited about looking clean-cut and proper, in a world going demented. The Game of Man is a still up-for-grabs.

So on the way home, driving past *The Cave,* I hear the invitation. That's another subtle thing the land of listening rocks seems to do – it calls people to the circle. As I walk in, I spot the macho bartender, and experience a letdown. I was looking forward to talking to Gwen. I find out that she isn't coming in till later. Then I spot an old gray-haired guy at the far end of the bar. I recognize his classic counterculture ponytail, and his gnarled cane resting on the bar just beyond his drink. The sight of him and the thought of having a chat with him is a welcome balm to my day of down encounters. The barber shop jabber had wormed into my mind. As fate had it, there is an empty seat down there next to him.

With one hand tentatively on the empty stool, I ask, "Mind if I join you, Professor Czismali?" He looks directly at me, rapidly scanning the geography of my face. "No. Not at all. Join me. I recognize you. You came to my talk at the Osher Life Long Learning luncheon. I don't forget faces – perhaps our first language, faces."

Daniel Czismali is one of those anthropologists who study people, their origins, and their distinctive characteristics. After his PhD in anthropology from the University of Central Krachow, he studied the Hadza people in the Great Rift Valley of Africa and then the Agta in the Philippine mountains. Both are longtime hunter-gather societies, largely unchanged by modernity. Foragers, they live like our ancestors lived a 150 million plus years ago. He retired to Sedona seven years ago, and still writes and lectures.

His talk at that luncheon I went to was about Man, the chimps, and what made the difference. It was entitled, "Why us and not them." According to current ethnology studies, *H. sapiens* evolved a cooperative temperament that led to pro-social cognitive skills that led to a culture of learning from others. Man's learning traits are not paralleled in any other primate, he said. The professor's examples of the self-centeredness of the other four great African Apes that descended with us from the "Common Ancestor" really whet my appetite. The barber shop conversation, on the other hand, had me primed to wonder if the culture is crawling back to the jungle.

That day at OLLI, the professor made a strong case for early Man's penchant for helping others. He went deeply into the female-male pair-bond pact, and the environment of trust the pact promoted. He presented strong evidence that what made us different is that we started out as small societies of trust. He thinks it started mostly with the women. He did comment that when farming, private possessions, and wealth inequality entered the equation, the happiness indicators plummeted. According to him, we are still trying to face the facts that greed is not good for the species. Sharing is. The violent, aggressive, promiscuous world of our cousins, especially the chimps, seems devoid of trust. "Without trust, extinction," had been his closing statement.

The soccer match on the TV screen behind the bartender brightens with a news flash. I see the professor's eyes narrow and go to the screen. They are announcing that the girl who had just been acquitted is going to be released from jail. I see his forehead wrinkle in question. "Have you been following that story, Professor?"

"A little bit. It's scary. It seems like every other month we have a salacious scandal. I was saddened to see Maria Shriver deceived by her celebrity husband. Many of us Eastern Europeans admired the Kennedy clan. They were the world's Camelot couple. As you probably picked up from my talk, I think fidelity is part of the glue that has kept us together for this long. It's part of our species secret for biological success. I wish I could say *keeps* us together, but somehow or another, I hesitate to. There are signs pointing to the next extinction. Mostly ignored. But despite my negative fears, I am an optimist. Still, a Camelot dreamer, I tend to agree with the great paleontologist, Teilhard de Chardin that there seems to be a direction built into evolution. Perhaps you know that Teilhard did field work in China. He helped in the discovery of Piltdown Man. I met him once at a convention. A deep man. He believed evolution is an unfolding of the cosmos, from primordial particles to greater webs of complexity and consciousness-processing. His writings include a final Omega Point.

"As most open-minded scientists acknowledge, there have been five Great Extinctions. The one sixty-five million years ago that took out the dinosaurs etcetera was one of the more benign ones, if you can call any environmental catastrophe that wipes out millions of species, *benign.* Some days I'm optimistic; other days I think Man may be headed for the dustbin of history."

The bartender spies our empty glasses. "You guys okay?"

Professor Czismali reaches for his cane, and slides off his stool. "Little does me. Age, you know. Nice talking to you," he says, looking me in the eyes. "Keep believing. I see you do. For if we don't believe, we won't make it." He winks at me, and limps toward the door. He didn't know my name. I never told him. Yet I feel he knew me. What's a name, I think, nodding to the bartender that I'll have another, for the road ahead, wondering if I am I kidding myself. As a matter of fact, I still feel like I'm stalling in the road of my life, like a car that has been running close to empty. The professor's mention of the Camelot days reminds me of JFK's inaugural speech: *Ask not what your country can do for you, but what you can do for your country.*

That evening, as the world is getting ready to darken to night, I'm out for my walk. In the sinking sun, the cliff faces are blushing to a soft red umber. The pilgrim traffic on the road to the Chapel, that Sedona skyscraper of belief wedged into the red rocks, has slowed to silent. The planet seems paused. But my monkey mind won't pause. The barber's words, "the violence empire media" had hooked me. I knew what he meant. Violence seemed to be on the uptick. He and I were in the same pew on that one. Somewhere back in my books, I came across the word *ahimsa.* In Sanskrit, *a* is a privative, meaning *not*, and *himsa* means harming. This venerable Sanskrit word is older than the religions of Indus Valley, where 'religion" made one of her earliest debuts. Ahimsa was a constant in the mouth of Gandhi. In English we say "non-violence". Both words point in the opposite direction of violence. Violence is hurting. Kindness is helping. There are many shades violence: war, rape, physical abuse, emotional cruelty, economic exploitation, even sarcasm and innuendo. These are all enticing ideas for me.

Lucky for *H.sapiens*, the scales of Lady *Justitia* might be balanced with random bits of confirming others, especially those close ones destiny has given us. The cup of cold water to the stranger is the cup of kindness. Looking down the street towards Gwen's window, I make the intention to be kind to someone that day.

The next morning, the chariot of the sun is cresting over the red mountains in the east. Tom O'Doolan and I are working our way up the Bear Mountain Trail. It is the most energetic climb I have attempted. It was Tom's wife Maggie who sealed my fate when she said, "Go with him, Malachy. The wild flowers are in full bloom. You'll never see anything so lovely on this side of the pond." She is right; the small, high desert flowers are magnificent—miniatures of color and bashfulness. And that Maggie smelled as fragrant as any flamboyant rose of Tralee might.

After returning from the Bear Mountain ordeal and checking for my email messages, I picked up Michael Tomasello's *Origin of Human Communication.* Good stuff, but getting to be old hat, hardly contestable anymore. Sure, cooperation and helping were the midwives of humanness. Widely agreed. My mood is sour. It hasn't been a good day for the human hive mind: The news reported that one-in-two Americans are financially hovering on the "can't-make-it line." That's hard to swallow. And one of every four women has been abused. I don't read the fine print, just the headlines, which are enough to bring on the worry lines. Yet the vast culture seems to ignore these kinds of facts. I guess I was nursed and cursed to be serious-minded.

Tonight my body feels clay-bone tired, and the soles of my feet hurt, so the jets of hot water in the open-air clubhouse Jacuzzi pool loom like Mary Magdalene's anointing hands. I'd met Tom and Maggie at the special First Friday buffet supper at the clubhouse day before yesterday. Let me tell you those Lomas Serenas gals know how to put together a potluck supper. Maggie O'Doolan's tenderloin of pork roasted with slices of Granny Smith apples and herbed potatoes was to die for. That lady is sure one foxy redheaded cook, and sweet as all that is forbidden. Sally Steven's broccoli-leek casserole was a close second, mostly because I love asparagus tips and garlic, her two secret ingredients.

My inner psyche, however, passed that evening at the clubhouse walking on tender coals. Watching those bonded couples enjoying life and togetherness was a rough trip. Some close couples just send out almost palpable signals about the ingrained joys of a committed relationship. The bored and bitching couples mostly stay home. (Thanks be to God.) For a guy living the lonesome life, the together couples are like a summer rain pelting on the surface of a parched, cracked land that just refuses to open up. I'm beginning to wonder about myself. Maybe there is a loser or loner gene.

I don't think it's a secret that *a close relationship* is the cup of ambrosia most of us want to bring to our lips. Delightful Gwen had said something to that effect my first time in the *Cave*. I knew that somehow I had blown my first time at bat for a new relationship that afternoon. I was stiff as a Taliban judge. Maybe Allie and I could have made it, if I had not been so self-centered. I'm not sure I will ever be ready to get back into the game, though relationship is not a game. (There are few relationship video games that make it.) If we lose the fine art of relating, we'll lose what is credibly the end game for our species.

I was the only singleton in the group that pot luck evening. The sky above must have been ever so stunning, yet I **didn't see** it. I was in the solitary confinement of myself. I'm working on opening up and *seeing* more. I'm not really kidding myself about the fact that I am a little gun-shy of relationship. My failure with Allie flat lined my self-image. Oh, I can sure fantasize about being with a beautiful woman, but in real time I never seem to find the courage to cross that threshold. I've read enough damn books to know that "it is not healthy for man to be alone." Of course, my cop-out is that I just haven't yet met Lady Right – and – Available.

I slide down into the welcoming water of the hot tub, hoping to drown my woebegone wool-gathering. My body lolls. It has its own wants… warmth is one, being touched is another. I emerge from the water, just like the original people did. I see the world above me. *Star Light, Star Bright. First star I see tonight.* The old rhyme chimes in my memory as I lose myself up into the dusky vault of heaven. For a brief moment, I forget myself.

That star there might be the planet Venus, I romanticize. That O'Doolan lass is an Irish Venus. One more Venus is all I need, right? I can't help it. I'm lonesome. I feel like screaming to the out-there emptiness: *Help!* But, of course, the out-there is not empty, I remind myself. It teems with life. I look off into the multicolored flanks of the Mogollan Rim. *Yes you can,* the mountains standing strong on the horizon seem to say after a hushed moment. *Be aware. Remember, John, what Emily said: a drop of the dark mind can spoil a whole pool of the pure, clear water.* And you know that loneliness is 90% perception. There's beauty and connection all around us.

An early waning moon climbs higher into the darkening silence, accompanied by a peace, broken only by an occasional plaintive, courting call of the solitary owl. It sounds like he also is on hold for a soft response. But no response comes. Poor guy. I can commiserate. I know the feeling. It had not been a good afternoon, not a single e-mail from some old friend. Personal communications are getting less and less frequent. It's as if they think I abandoned them. Ironically the flood of come-ons to join LinkedIn, Facebook, Online Matchmakers, and sexy-looking singles keep on coming. Relationship has become a money-making gig. I get spams galore from Christian singles, Asian singles, and, of course, young, lonely girls in the Verde Valley. Most have fetching smiles. If you look at the laugh lines around the eyes, you'll see the craving for security.

I don't in actuality know what it feels like to be female. It must not be easy because they're so sensitive, naturally caring for the wee ones. I think of them as more insecure, but I suspect *insecure* is another word problem. Nevertheless dating is no game – for authentic women. Oh, God, another generalization!

As the stars start stepping forward, my mind floats up and further out into the galaxy. I want to leave behind my frustrations and my inclination to consider myself *the hero of the story.* I smile at a nice star, hazily cognizant that the jets are massaging some of the tight spots in my lower back. My senses are opening up to the world around. The steamy vapors arising from the water seem to settle my mind. I linger in the steaming water, stewing in the challenge of one of my ancient and vexing problem: Who the hell am I?

The mystery of being both animal matter and aspiring spirit still nibbles at my bare butt. Nowadays the savants of so-called classical science, wave the question aside. They stamp it: **dualism,** like some rejected USDA meat. In rebellion, I am currently comfortable with thinking of myself as not just two, body/mind, but even a kaleidoscope of multiple, colored bits of self, constantly being turned and whirled by Life.

I dip my head down into the hot, churning water. My lonesome brain hoping that some gal who looks a movie star will arrive, disrobe, slip in beside me, and reach for *myself*. Of course, she may be just as stressed out as I am. Maybe she just went through a divorce. Who knows, a dip and grab of flesh may be her version of the good life.

But my vagabond mind is waning and waxing. The jet hitting my back feels good. Spreading my feeling hands on the flesh of my chest, I say to myself: These are my physical atoms, the bits of my body. Someday these material molecules will run down and my lungs will stop taking in the pure air of the high country. They will cremate my body and scatter my ash bits into the wind. Who I call 'my Self' will become different. I color code these bits battleship gray. I am embodied. I'm not an angel, not just spirit.

Since no young Hollywood-babe has arrived, my mind prances on. Below the battleship gray, I imagine a multicolored medley of bits: yellow bright as a sunny day, purple as a rainy day, blue as a lonely day, and red as an angry day. I am a web of continually rotating, changing feelings. These are my emo-bits, with moods as real as those carbon particles, which die off every seven years or so. I have no clear notion about what happens to these colorful traces when the chemical molecules shut down. Perhaps at death, these emo-cognitive-firings just falls back into that vast collective layer some call *the collective consciousness.* The collective is a mandala of thinking, willing, feeling, remembering, and the still to be named capacities. Sure that's partially where all this color of my life evolved from. (Gosh, there is so much we don't yet know.)

My feathered friend, hidden in the dark green foliage, hoots again. To my solitary mind, it sounds like his wished-for companion also hasn't shown up yet. Poets say an owl can see into a person. Perhaps he hears my mind and is hectoring me on. Nature knows how to push buttons. Or maybe Mr. Big Eyes is content to just troll the forest for company. Yes, I whisper again to my steam-cleaned mind: I am molecules of matter. I am bits of personal and cultural emoting, and my imagination strains to see the possible.

I stand up, exposing myself. I throw my arms dramatically open to the universe. With fear and wildness, I shout: "But *I am more.* I am *Ruach,* the wind who moves over the deep darkness. *Ruach* now blows all around me, and suffuses my body. I want to feel the Spirit in me, and between the trees. The Eternal Reality winks in the rock faces."

For the first time in my life, I am beginning to feel part of this whole breathing, animate realm. I kind of believe all these wild thoughts, though not fully. Conceivably, this white light of information has been on the planet since before the dawn of man. Like a kind of energy, it can never be extinguished, as the new frontier scientists assert. It can never go poof into nothingness. My Sancho Panza body feels somewhat relieved. The

Quixote dreamer inside me still feels like spurring on to tilt the windmills.

I climb out of the cathartic steam of the blue-hued, tiled tub, mumbling to myself, *Words. Words. Modern life tries to become just a word game. But, the cliffs out there are real – veritable time-space captured in iron loaded rocks. People here say that it is good for my spirit to be present to the animated realities in the world around. They say the ancient people saw "anima" in the west wind, in the coyote, in the venting bowels of the earth. They sensed the deep textures of reality. Like artists, they saw beyond the mere visible. Now our minds distract themselves. They play in malls of fancy clothes, loud cosmetics, and frivolous books that pose as the cardinal bits of reality. But, by damn, I'm giving Emily's way the old college try. Still something, or is it someone, is missing.*

Getting out of the hot water, I wrap myself in my black silk bathrobe, and hurry in to the clubhouse showers. The steam and my ramblings have wiped me out. The cool water of the shower will cleanse my impurities. The back of my mind knows that I am being driven to shape up. The life forces of this special place are herding me on, cowboy style.

On the far side of the planet Gaia, in a windowless room in the bowels of the University of Mumbai, four naked men sit in dense steam. With a small white towel in his lap, each man sits in monk-like silence. They sit a distance from each other. Amit Gusain's brown body glistens with the perspiration of pores letting go of toxins. His body tingles with life. Racquetball gives his body-mind the peak experience of well-being.

According to him we should be talking about the Age of the Whole Body. The Age of the Brain is yesterday's news. In science, snooze you lose. His skin is an information processing center, taking in the message of the steam. Every part of his body has antennas to pick up signals: his cranial neurons, his spinal cord, his gut, his gonads, even his feet. Classical neuroscientists like to wax on about the regions of brain firing. But as far as he is concerned, the whole body receives incoming messages. The memory of Anna stirs a primal center in him that neither his religious background nor modern science can put into *prose*. That mystical realm is for the *poets* and the singing seers. For him, the body as information processing is just a launching pad into the Bigger Reality. What about the cosmos? Anna has explored the cosmos. He wonders if she ever explores the feeling regions of her body. He doubts that she does. She seems to fear the body.

Nonetheless, emotionally, his psyche is tied in tangled knots, his head storming with dark clouds of doubt and regret. Shortly after arriving back in his hometown, he had walked through the brothel district he had walked as a school boy, past the alleyway where he first laid eyes on sweet Adveena. The smell of women-used seemed even worse than he remembered. Back then they were a low caste of comforters. Now, they truly smell dirty; they are the pawns of rich men…and women. Daunted by the Herculean dream of doing something to free these sex slaves he sees everywhere, the quantum guy asks himself why he ever thought he could somehow help. It all seems like a Krishna dream vanishing into the tepid air of the Bhagavad Gita field of battle. Sitting in the silent steam mist, he feels desperately alone.

His beloved mother had passed away while he was making a name for himself in America. That morning he visited their old hovel home. The shadows of her memory had intensified his loneliness. His mother had loved him.

At the same time, the image of the white-skinned woman with the blemish on her neck appears as a palpable phantom in the misty fog in front him. He misses her and regrets that he isn't back with her. He should have asked her to marry him. His bet is that if he had asked, she would have come to yes, after some serious thinking. She is not a woman who likes change. They had a relationship that could be called love, unlike his arranged relationship with wife, whom he is trying to stay away from. But news travels fast in the narrow alleyways of overcrowded Mumbai. He knows he is a prisoner of a culture.

Shortly after he graduated from Stanford, his mother was diagnosed with terminal tuberculosis. She had quietly left the city – family, friends, household, and worldly possessions, and gone to a forest ashram in the hills, where she died alone. Sitting there in the steam room, Amit resolves to visit that ashram the next day. He vaguely believes in what he calls "quantum reincarnation." He knows the material body falls away from the energy of the bits of immaterial information that Western religions call: the soul. The soul or atman does not fall into nothingness. As he understands it, it can't, scientifically. The thought whispers through the steam: If you go to the forest, you may meet the spirit of your mother. She may help you as she did when you were a boy.

The next day on the drive up into the highlands, he sees the droves of poor and needy people, cripples and beggars. They are everywhere, seated, begging, along the roadside, or following a line of skin-and-bones, white cows – those sacred animals, symbols of the earth that gives and asks nothing in return. It's worse than I remembered, he thinks. His mother often spoke about the karma of caring for others. His mind begins flitting back and forth from his mother to Anna. He can't get Anna out of his mind. She is like a wounded goddess on a pedestal in his third-world mind. She's intelligent. At Stanford they told him that his IQ was over 200; hers has to be just as high. She's so beautiful. He often wanted to touch her soft white skin, but never did. He had too much respect for her to tarnish her. He knows that she has suffered even more than ordinary women do. But below her hurt tissue, there is a gentle stream of what his saintly mother would have called "kindness, or compassion." Anna is a woman with heart. He knows that.

Two hours into the lonely journey up the high hills into the dark forest, his mind has all but convinced him that he is making a big mistake. He comes to the conclusion that he should return to New York and propose to Anna. He could certainly get a job at some American university, perhaps Princeton where Wheeler taught. She could retire and they could start a family. Time, Amit feels, is on their side. She is young and beautiful.

The forest ashram is a small community of nuns and lay women, not far from a larger gathering of male sadhus and sannyasis. It is composed of fifty small female huts, with sand-covered floors, and palm fronds for walls and roofs. A communal space sits in the center. The forest is quiet, except for the chatter of the monkeys and the scurrying tails of peacocks. Maybe the big banyan trees have something to say about what they have seen. Glimpses of men and women in cotton clothing can be caught walking meditatively among the trees. He is still processing the place, not experiencing it.

He walks down to the river and sits down next to a large root of an aged banyan tree. He can't help but fix his eyes on the black soot, neatly raked into the white sand of the riverbank, vestiges of earlier funeral pyres. In his mind, he sees his dear mother's body surrounded by flames and her spirit, her Atman, rising to join the all, the Brahman. He sits cross-legged listening for the song of the flowing river that had taken her ashes to join the waters of Mother Ganges. Her heart had to be valiant coming here, away from the distractions of the world, spending her years focused on the quest for *janna*, wisdom.

Hours later, on the drive back to Mumbai, Amit feels the change that is coming to birth in his heart. Sitting under the banyan tree, he had heard two words *drkpp* (courage) and *janna* (knowledge as wisdom). It is possible that his mother had whispered those ancient words to him, but that isn't what seems important. The universe does whisper, that he believes. Somehow those two words had opened his eyes. Perhaps indeed, he has been called home to undertake that Arjuna social task that would require both courage and wisdom. He must be true to his mother's heritage. But what about Anna, he wonders? She needs a relationship. *I do too,* he nearly weeps, feeling worse than the tearful old hermit he saw in the forest. A direction to his two-edged challenge is calling: stand courageous or die on the sterile vine you are on. He knows he must answer. He must stay.

Back across several time zones, on the east side of the Isle of Manhattan, a woman dressed in stylish dark-gray running shoes, black Capris, and a black sports top, looks tuckered out as she turns the key to unlock the door to her small flat. She is one of the New Women: the professionals with a demanding job, childless, and unattached. Today her shoulders have a sag to them, and her chin seems to point downward. Work and life have been stressful and barren of late. Anna Pagani, is just returning from her Saturday morning run. She had hoped the run would help her out of her deepening, black funk. But it hadn't. The funk had stolen in like a dull winter fog soon after her friend Amit left for Mumbai. The dark mood shows no signs of lifting.

It had been another dull morning on the concrete path along the Hudson. She had seen that interesting guy with the German shepherd dog running beside him. A guy she's noticed before – several times – but never figured out how to start a conversation with him. She just wasn't good at that sort of thing. She hadn't really paid much attention to guys in the early years of her career. She'd never had a dog, but even dogs are starting to seem like interesting companions. Lots of gals run with dogs. Some, she guessed, for protection, but others for companionship. *Maybe it's time you stretched to something new*, a voice inside hinted from time to time. (Deep in Anna's anima, a monster lurks that she never lets into the light of consciousness. It is Mr. Devil that hurts young women, and never leaves them alone. Most devils are evil-eyed males, as far as she is concerned.)

She sprinkles some lavender salts into the steamy tub water. She starts undressing, getting ready to soak in some solace in the hot water. A soak used to soothe her in her plateau moods. Recently, she has had more than her share of plateau time. The phone rings. Dressed only in her black briefs and black sports bra, she cautiously walks to the writing desk in the living room of her sixth floor flat. She gets few personal calls. She has no friends, to speak of.

Outside, the morning sky is still sunless, under a dull, moist layer of gray. In the mirror above the writing desk, she appears, tucking a loose strand of dark brown hair over her right ear, exposing her mark. Anna is not the kind of woman who looks at herself in the mirror. She looks at the call machine, hesitating. She doesn't recognize the number; it isn't local. Fear knots her stomach as she debates: *Danger. There are a lot of weird people in the city –psychopaths, murderers, rapists.* Yet a kind of sixth sense, or an unrecognized need for something new in her life, prompts her to pick it up.

"Hello."

"This is the VerdeValley Hospital in Sedona, Arizona. Is Dr. Anna Pagani available?"

Hospital? Why on earth are they calling me? Probably want money. Nevertheless, it could be some kind of emergency. But who do I know? At that moment, it dawns on her that her mother's brother, her Uncle Guido, moved to a place called Sedona, quite a few years ago. *Gosh, I haven't seen him in years and*

*years. Of course I can't blame that on Uncle Guido. I've been
pretty much a nose-to-the-grindstone recluse myself. It seems as
though I've fallen into a rut.*

"Yes, I'm Dr. Anna Pagani."

"Thank you, Dr. Pagani. Your uncle, Guido Cavaggio, has
asked us to call. His lung cancer is finally going to bring his voyage to the end. He's extremely weak. Dr. Favrol, his oncologist
does not think he has much longer. Mr. Cavaggio would like you
to come to Sedona, Arizona, as soon as possible. He'd like to
talk to you. This very morning he said to me, "She's my favorite
niece, and my heir. She's the only one left in this country. We
need to talk before I go to wherever atheists go.""

Oh, poor Uncle Guido. Lung cancer? Heir? Her brow knits
in alarm, and her nemesis spot feels like it is reddening. (It isn't;
it's a nervous memory of hurt, something akin to a phantom
limb.) Confusion and concern flash across her face. An ominous
sensation grips her chest, as she instantly foresees a freight train
of change heading right at her.

"Can you come? Time is of the essence."

Stunned. Terrified. Anna hesitates.

Then she stammers, "Yes, I guess I have to. How do I get
there?"

We will arrange everything.

Early that same afternoon after her foreboding phone call from the hospital in faraway Arizona, Anna calls Layla, the other woman physicist at the Institute for Theoretical Physics. They are not what one would call close friends; in fact, they are mirror opposites – color Anna ice blue, and Layla hot pink. Anna really doesn't have any close friends. Surely you will not be surprised that she is sheepish about asking any man to keep an eye on her apartment and her personal things while she is gone. She doesn't like any crossing into her private life, especially if it smacks of intimacy, men, and trust. She knows that much about herself. After all, the city society is seamy, and there are men with fetishes. Maybe that's why Layla always wears sheer panty hose. Besides, she is not going to be gone for that long. Maybe Layla will even enjoy seeing how one of the staid girls at the office lives. She doesn't think Layla has much of substance in her life.

Anna is familiar with Layla's ways; she knows that the guys call her vulgar names and grope her behind in the lab. Anna can relate to the pain of being treated like a thing, so despite their different mores, Anna, not a judging person by disposition, feels a certain soft-heartedness for Layla. She suspects that everyone has some abusing ghosts. Anna's solitary self knows that she has retreated into her shell of work because of those abusing

ghosts. Many people are like a terrapins who withdraw to protect themselves. Maybe Layla submits herself to men to help
her forget her roots in Middle Eastern poverty. She must also
feel her scientific mediocrity. Sometimes alone in her silent flat,
Anna wonders: *For women, life can be a crap shoot, can't it? We
all have to be so careful.*

Layla is a needy female. She reaches out by talking almost
non-stop, so Anna knows a good deal of the general lines of Layla's prequel: She was a foreign exchange student, an outsider.
She fell in love with an American boy from Minnesota, her first
entanglement in this country. She felt they clicked and were great
together. It helped that he thought that physicists were cool. However, like many mid-western American boys, Peter Perkins felt
that he needed to defend his family and friends against the evil
axis of terrorists, as well as make the world safe for Layla and the
future children they dreamed about. He enlisted, and was shipped
out to Iraq. Eleven months after his arrival, Peter's platoon was
patrolling the streets of a small village, when one of the Humvees
ran across an IED, sending the bodies of six fellow soldiers flying
in all directions. The hellish smell of burning flesh never left his
nostrils. After his return to the States, Peter went downhill rapidly – drinking, brawling, and shouting into the night. One day he
even lashed out at Layla, slapping her across the face. That same
afternoon he shot himself with his sequestered service revolver.
Layla found him dead on the bed they shared.

When Layla came over to Anna's flat, to go over a few simple
routines, Anna was strung out and tense, not so much because
she wasn't used to relating to Layla outside of the Institute, but
because the scenario of going to see her Uncle Guido die was

just too surreal. A couple of family members had died in hospitals in her lifetime, but somehow she was always fortuitously absent at that awesome moment of closing the eyelids. Now she was being asked to meet and talk to her mother's brother, who was in the throes of cancer, on the edge of who knows where or what. She was unprepared for such a personal encounter. She didn't do spiritual, nor did she do death.

As if to make matters more unsettling, Layla fell head over heels for the apartment, especially the location on the Upper East Side – very dignified. "If you are going to sublet this place out for a while," Layla gushed, "please, please put me at the top of the list?" *If they find out about my problem,* she thinks to herself, *nobody will be nice. If the scandal hits, Anna will be next in line to be director. She deserves it. She's a good gal at heart.*

"I have no intentions of subletting anything out," Anna snapped back.

Late that afternoon when a cab pulls up to Anna's front door, the sky is still gray and grumpy. The city is making its nightly noises, with fuming toxins and angry honking. It has been a stormy summer, and now the early autumn days are coming in off the river colder than usual. *The weather is definitely going through menopause*, she remarks to herself, as she lifts her long, dark-stocking legs into the rear seat of the cab. She has always found change unsettling. She prefers the consistency of routines. She suspects lots of people do. And now, she finds herself flying into the dragon's mouth. She has dreamed of dragons. They frighten her.

As the Jet Blue A320s flight to Phoenix thunders into the velvet blackness, Anna, seated in seat 6B, is grateful for the empty seat next to her. Out the window she sees the unending sky and the delicate, faint outline of the rising half-moon. Scientists don't put stock in omens, but she stares at that half-smiling moon. Few people at the Institute would guess it, but below the scientist demeanor, there hides, a *puella aeterna* (Eternal Girl), born and raised in the Bronx by an Italian mother. That same frightened *puella* has the Snow White trait of feminine sensitivity. She feels a caring for Layla. She'd heard the rumors. She tries to stay away from them, but those kinds of toxic messages spread like viruses. People are hinting that Layla is in STD trouble. The innuendo is that it might involve their dapper boss. The mere thought of him tenses her.

Guido's travel agent had arranged a limousine to drive her from Phoenix to Sedona, 100 miles north. Anna's journey was arduous: rush-hour taxi to Kennedy airport, two-hour stopover in Texas, not to mention her uneasiness about what she is doing – it's all so unforeseen. Years back, her solo life in Manhattan had settled into a manageable routine. No one would say she is happy, but she isn't unhappy either. She's normal for this day and age, a card-carrying member of Riesman's *Lonely Crowd*. She's positively not in the market for change. The landscape is sparse as the white limo climbs the grade to the Prescott, high desert plateau; Anna succumbs to sleep, physically, emotionally wrung out.

After two more hours of journeying into the unknown, Anna finds herself sitting, completely discombobulated, by the bedside of her drugged and mostly comatose uncle. He is in an oxygen tent, but appears peaceful. He seems to respond when she squeezes his hand. He says nothing; it is as if his physical person has been holding on until she arrives, and his consciousness rests on the threshold of slipping away to the forever. Anna like most well educated scientists is heavily invested in analytic, linear activity: organize parts in steps, calculate, and size up with language. Left hemispheres specialize in serial processing; the right side tends to get caught up in distracting loops of feelings … like confusion, fear, or loss of control. So it's not surprising that Anna is tighter than a drum and repeatedly looking at the clock, wondering if this agony will ever come to an end. Consciously, she's not into emotion. Her primitive brain stem is inwardly terrorized that she may be sitting in the room with the Demon of Death, dressed in red-and black tights and a turned up tail and a pitchfork, smirking and tapping his foot, just like in the stories she read in her lonely childhood bed. She's a scientist, yet deep within, she is a woman.

Needless to say, Anna's well-trained problem-solving mind is not plugged into what is going on in the stunted right zone of her brain. Unbeknownst to her, part of her muffled Atman is wrestling with the majesty, the complexity, the beauty of death – the mystery of a life's exit. The hemispheres are like embryonic twins; they know one another before words come to complicate. Currently some theorists explain that the right appreciates wholes, sees the big picture, and likes connection rather than separation. Anna hasn't needed to use her right abilities. Her skill of putting *it all together* is retarded. Her condition is not abnormal in this society that enthrones the scientific, and trumps compassion, human relating, and the what-it's-all-about mystery with greed, goodies, and quickies. Regrettably, part of Anna lingers back in her developmental, traumatic time.

A high country nurse tries to soothe her. Claudia is what we all dream of as the Nurse Betty – the cushy bosom and constant pleasant face who acts as a midwife between suffering and redemption. Guido had obviously bared his soul to Claudia before going off to his waiting frontier. But at that terrible time in the smelly room, Anna can't focus on Claudia's words. Still, the nurse's words write themselves indelibly in her heart.

Guido passes away three and a half hours after Anna enters that room which smells antiseptic, lifeless, in a word, inhuman. When the doctor closes Guido's eyelids and the nurse pulls up the white sheet, Anna puts her hands over her eyes. The frightened child within, raised devoid of a wisdom tradition, trembles in her imagination at the scary, unwanted vision of a passageway to the beyond. She had never before mentally accompanied a person to death's door. Her father, Luigi, had died in that accident and his remains sent to Sicily. Mother Gina had gone back to her people, died in her sleep, and was buried in the family plot, wearing her red shoes. Anna had not been able to go to Sicily on the spur of the moment. She sadly remembers her mother's words, when she boarded the plane to return home, "My life in this country has been a life of servitude." At least, Anna had been able to buy her mother a business class ticket to go home.

Ever since high school, Anna wanted to make something of her life. She had seen her domineering father in action, and her mother's sad submission. She knew without fancy words that her mother was a sad vignette of the patriarchal culture. This personal secret was a driving force in her quest to succeed in the man's world. She deemed herself one small step for womankind: a woman accepted as an equal and professionally appreciated. Perhaps, she thought, nowadays this is everywoman's secret.

At this clarion moment, our scientist shudders with a fear that her life is out of her control, right there in this haunting hospital. Death is a life changer, and the specter is stalking around in the lower regions of her right brain. She feels the floor under her shoes seeming to tremble as if a quake is rumbling. She feels she is wandering close to the boundary of primal fear.

Still and all, it had been comforting to see that Uncle Guido seemed happy holding her hand as he slipped into the traumatic tunnel into uncertainty. He appeared to smile when she squeezed his hand. It had been a long time since Anna was emotionally moved by another human being. Still, inside, she is a frightened girl, looking for a hand to grab.

Later she takes a taxi cab to the address the hospital gave her. A young, *café au lait* skinned woman helps her out of the cab and into the house and some clean black silk sheets.

The next morning, the sun nearing high noon, Anna opens her eyes, hazily aware that she is surrounded in a soothing quiet … no honking horns, no blaring sirens, no street arguments. She hunches her shoulders, and draws up her knees like a child. Something's wrong. After a while of holding herself, she turns her eyes to the window; an azure blue of the sky is smiling. It seems so pure. It's not that dirty sky over Manhattan.

The room is spacious, with thick, vermillion earthen walls. She sees the open door of a bathroom, gets up, tends to her bodily needs, and washes her face. The heavy image of death comes back. She brushes her traveler's teeth, hoping to clean away some of the previous day. Seeing a multi-colored, blan- ket-robe hanging on a wooden peg, she cautiously puts it on, wondering, where am I? What am I doing? Her nose catches the aroma of coffee and freshly baked bread. As she steps bare- footed out of her room into an open courtyard, the majestic red mountain formations behind the far wall take her breath away. Astonished, her eyes widen in wonderment, and she bursts out, "Oh my goodness! Look! I've never seen anything like this. Oh- my-god, is this Sedona?"

On the other side of the courtyard, she sees what must be the kitchen, and a woman with light brown skin and dark hair pulled back in a bun. The woman is young, with strong, but calm, features. Apparently a mother, she is reading a story to a younger version of herself with matching dark hair and wide, wondering eyes. As she approaches, she hears, *Changing Woman explained to her husband the Sun, You are in the sky, and I am earth. You are constant in your brightness. I must change with the seasons.*

The scene makes a deep impression on Anna. She stands looking at mother-and-child. It's a scene of caring – an archetypal image. As she enters the kitchen, she says, "Wow! This place is fantastic. I've never seen a place so dramatic." The wide-eyed young girl is kneeling next to her mother, obviously enjoying the story.

"You're in the Red Rock Country, Miss Niece," the woman with the caring aura says. "This is the sacred space of the old people for many, many years. Old people say: God created the Grand Canyon special nice, but she lives in Sedona." Behind the woman is a shelf of brown clay pots and jars, some low, rounded with open moths, others taller and gourd shaped. They are all charred from being in an open fire. The mother smiles sweetly at the child, who understands without words. Both stand. There is a dignity and peace about them both. "Good morning, I'm Kai Begay and this is my daughter, Nascha. We have lived here with your uncle for nearly ten years. We will miss him. He was kind."

At heart, Sedona is a small art colony, in a geological Eden, nestled 4,500 feet above sea level at the base of the Mogollan Rim, the southern edge of the Colorado Plateau. The cliff face of the Rim rises another 3,000 feet to Flagstaff, and the Hopi, Navajo, and Apache lands of the Plateau. The picturesque, little tourist Mecca is surrounded by the Coconino National Forest, almost two million acres of wilderness. Many of the 12,000 *locals* are accomplished or aspiring visual artists. Perhaps as early as the late 1950's, the New Age Aquarians, a metaphysical movement of alternative spirituality, came like famished pilgrims to this place of energy vortexes.

Nearly a half century before, pioneers and settlers hoping to start a new life, had left the East and Midwest, and homesteaded along the Oak Creek Canyon. Carl and Sedona Schnebly were among them. (Sedona, the woman, is another story – another heroine of a thousand aches.) Today, busloads and caravans of visitors delight in the attractiveness of the physical land and the smorgasbord of the New Age practices. Most of all, they hike into beckoning and bestowing hills. Even though many come with stress tightness, hiking and being in nature seems to help restructure their molecules.

Kai gestures gracefully to the sideboard where coffee and pastries are carefully arranged. Anna notices a medium size painting on the adjacent wall. It's of a handsome young woman in a long dark dress, black hair pulled back in a bun, and a child strapped to her back on a wooden carrier. It is beautiful. It's poignant. It's very warm. She turns to the mother. The woman with the chocolate-hued skin and the long thick eyelashes smiles. "He painted it for me, and gave it to me as a gift. I shall always treasure it."

Both women are wondering what the future holds. Yet both honor the silence of not speaking before time and their relationship have worked. Anna pours herself a cup of coffee, and wraps her hands around it. She needs a dash of warmth. She feels out of her element. As the temptation to wander comes, she knits her brows. The gentle mother reads the body language and says, "If you need anything, let us know. Mr. Guido's lawyer has called. We understand. As the people south of the border say, *Esta in su casa. (You are in your house.)*" Anna doesn't understand the words, but she hears the welcome in the mother's voice, and begins to wander. The house feels strange and sterile, as if it has not been much lived in. Everything is clean, tasteful, and expensive.

The house is u-shaped around an open courtyard. *Spanish,* Anna thinks. (Actually it is Pueblo.) The entry hall, parlor, and study-library form the front cross-member, with the dining room, kitchen and housekeeper's quarters along the west arm. Guest suite, master bedroom, and a large, cyan-blue wooden door at the end of the east arm. Right off the bat, she knows she couldn't live here. Never. Too much space. Too much light.

At the end of the eastern hallway, the cyan-blue door is closed. She cautiously touches it. It opens softly to her touch. The high-ceiling space with studio loft windows is flooded with outside light, and rugged rockscape views. A large, maybe 5' x 7,' easel and nearly finished canvas stands tall in the middle of the room, a pallet of paint and some brushes on a stool next to it. The painting is powerful, frightening. It features a large, gray-and-blackened dead tree. Its stark, arms point sharply up into a cool blue hue. Next to it, on the right is a large, rough, carmine boulder; on the left a low, green bush with tiny red berries. *It's a ghost tree,* Anna mumbles, *dead, defying death, and refusing to give-in and topple over. It looks courageous.*

In far corner of the room, a mattress with disheveled sheets assures her that, yes, this room has been lived in. Above the mattress is a woven rug with wavy horizontal bands and exotic designs. The rust, black, red and blue colors are alive, as if trying to say something. On the floor near the mattress is a small book.

Her mind returns to image of the shriveled up man in the oxygen tent. She shutters imagining him curled up in a ball on this mattress. The man in the hospital was only a wraith of the jovial man upon whose knee she had sat while he sang her old Sicilian songs and made her laugh. His lung cancer had reduced him to a ghost of who he had been. She had felt sorry for him. *Perhaps she owed him. Perhaps she should stay in his house – for a while.*

"Mr. Guido, very sick," Kai says from the blue doorway. "Very sad. He not let me clean his special room. Not good for old man to live without wife."

That afternoon Anna agrees to go on a "must-do" jeep tour that the housekeeper recommends as the way to get a feel for the place. Anna had hesitated, wondering if she wants to get a feel for the place. She feels off balance. She'd just as soon go home today to what she knows. Yet she knows she has to stay for a few days at to tie up the loose ends. She owes that much to her uncle. Or does she? She didn't ask for all this change. Okay, well, the place is unique, she has to admit.

Kai's cousin, Angel, drives Anna uptown to the Earth Wisdom Jeep office. The typical Sedona all terrain, open-sided customized jeeps can carry six people in a back raised-platform. Anna, a singleton, is invited to sit upfront with Randy, the driver, who looks to her like the real McCoy – cowboy hat with a band of red feathers, long gray braided ponytail, black John Wayne boots, and a Minnesota drawl. She shakes her head. What am I doing? Something rustles her imagination, which she can feel stepping into a new rhythm.

After introducing himself, Randy launches into his spiel, "This place is change. It has been underwater six or seven times as the ancient Pedregosa Sea rose and receded, depositing layers of limestone. It has been a coast, a desert, a plateau. *Becoming* is this town's maiden name. As you look at the sides of the rising hills, you see colored layers of rock. Below it all is the pre-Cambrian layer of sedimentary rock, dating back 3.8 *billion* years. Yes, I said *billion,* years ago. Mother Earth is a pretty old broad," the cowboy says, laughing at his own attempted pleasantry. "The present city is built on a dark brown layer of Redwall Limestone which we only see at certain deeply-cut places, like sink holes. When you catch a glimpse of the deep brown, you are traveling back to 330 *million* years ago. The red layer that you see to our right near the base of the mountains is called the Hermit Formation. The red is caused by iron-oxide (rust) left by the waters of the receding sea. The golden colored layer higher up is Coconino Sandstone, blown in from distant Saharas. The grayish-blue layer near the top is almost pure limestone fossils of mollusks, snails, and prehistoric shellfish deposited by the ever-changing ocean. It may look like these weathered hills have died and stand in the heavens as monuments to what was. No, these grand formations are changing, works in progress, still becoming. It's evolution and erosion. We older folks understand erosion. I began my life as a bionic man with a knee replacement last year," Randy says with that baritone laugh that hits a chord in Anna. "It's build-up, collapse-down, and build-up again. If you stay here for even a short time, the mystery of life's rhythms seeps into your system."

Gosh, I just wish he would cool it, Anna's mind niggles. Inside she is jittery and anxious. It's more than just jetlag. All this talk of change and the vastness of the world-around her is annoying. It's unhinging. Curiously, Anna feels something stirring in her innards. It is something unfamiliar, something different, yet something that is calling, as if some unearthly being is trying to contact her through the microwaves of space. It's a spooky feeling – as if life, the place, and her gut are whispering: *Be still. See. Hear.* At the same time the image of Kai, the caring mother, stirs in her. Anna has not really cared for anyone. Her existence is her work, her career, and the ladder of achievement. City life has reduced her who dreamed of being someone, to just a scientist in the gray flannel dress.

That night Anna sits out under the short, slanting roof at the rear of the open quadrangle that was Guido's backyard. She is unwittingly struggling with who she is. One would rightfully think that the spectacular light show in the night sky would lapse a cosmologist like her into a trance of forgetting herself, wouldn't you? But Anna's ability to *just be* in the present moment in the big scene is disabled, almost like the bound feet of Chinese girls in older times. In the situation she works in, her mind is one of those proverbial robots, following routines. She is still having a lot of trouble accepting Guido's place as hers. She hasn't come close to deciding if she is going to stay. Why should she? She might close it up, or rent it out, or sell it, and be done with the whole annoying business. Besides there is the problem about what she would do with herself if she didn't have a job to go to. On the phone, the lawyer said Guido had given her "a carte blanche." *Carte-blanche is a ticket to confusion. I don't like confusion. Hell, I want my quiet life back.*

Kai comes out carrying a tray. She pauses. Anna senses that woman is listening to the gentle zephyr of warm air moving in the yard. Anna hadn't noticed it but now she does, guessing that Kai hears something more than she does. Kai senses seem shaper, more alive. She puts a tray of Navajo lamb wrapped in blue corn tortillas and a half-carafe of red wine on the side table next to the lounge. "Mr. Guido's favorite supper." Anna isn't much of a wine drinker, and doesn't usually eat meat. But Kai is so ingenuous, and Anna so bone weary, she takes a few polite bites of the lamb, and a few sips of the local red wine. Neither tastes like home. A full moon floods the silent space with silver light. Randy's readiness to joke and his baritone laugh carried her back to a special day when she rode in the front seat of Amit's Hyundai. Weary, she lapses down memory lane.

Perhaps it was the spring in the air that day, perhaps it was the lush green of the campus, and the electric atmosphere of students on mopeds and motor bikes, but Anna recalls feeling alive and affirmed that day. Amit had invited her to drive down to Princeton University to hear a talk by John Archibald Wheeler, one of the legends of American quantum physics. She wasn't really that interested in the quantum stuff, but she was, without owning up to it even to herself, personally interested in Amit.

Wheeler, over 80, had coined words like *Black Hole* and *Quantum Foam.* His talk was on his *It from Bit* theory. Anna understood only some fuzzy generalities about Quantum Theory. Still she sensed that Amit was excited by it, and interested in Wheeler's hypothesis that the basic stuff of reality is **information**. Wow! What a seismic shift in thinking, she had to admit. Amit seldom talked openly about quantum entanglement because most of the others at the Institute thought it too weird, despite the fact that the math and the experiments were there to back it up. Even Einstein had called it "spooky."

As it turned out that day, Anna thought that Wheeler himself was worth seeing, his voice strong and confident, his pacing energetic. But it was his happy eyes that caught Anna's attention.

She saw the twinkle of a teacher and smile of a scientist proud in his chosen work. She remembers fantasizing about Amit as a gray haired physicist, with the light of a seer in his dark eyes. She conceded that the quantum ideas – or something like them – are going to be the physics of the future. She wondered if she and Amit had a future.

On the trip back up the Jersey Turnpike, Amit seemed subdued, deeply mulling over Wheeler's words. Anna really hadn't understood most of it. To her, quantum theory was a scary game, like going out on a thin limb. It was more scary change. Amit made it sound like a new belief system, like a brave new world. He was silent for miles. Her intuition sensed that something else was gnawing at her friend. What she didn't know at that time was that Amit had received a tempting offer from the University of Mumbai to return home to do research and teach. But she could readily guess that the words of John Wheeler had stirred up a desire in her friend to be a voice on the frontier of information physics. She did know that Amit was a man who wanted to matter, wanted to be helpfully involved with the human quest – and people.

Anna accepted the silence, sitting with her fists lightly curled, her self-manicured fingernails lightly pressing into her palms. Naturally, her feminine mind was running tapes: *Is he angry with me? Did I do something stupid? No, he's just wrestling with some other phantom.* After some time, she got up the courage to break the silence: "So, what are you rolling around in that Indian head of yours, Amit?"

A boyish smile broke over his face, as if he was grateful to be called back to the present. "Wasn't he marvelous? You have to admire a man who appears so personally ordinary. His students love him. And yet he is so extraordinary in his thinking. Wheeler isn't alone in suggesting that reality is *knowledge, information, consciousness...* **Words, words,**" he said, playfully rapping the heel of his right palm on the steering wheel. "We get hung-up on how to talk about these great inscrutables. And reality remains mostly mystery! Words are our stumbling stones. But we have to use them, don't we?" He looked over and smiled, the tensions gone from his face. That was a trait she envied: he could be intense one moment, and play the light fantastic the next.

"I don't know where I stumbled upon the idea," Amit said, palpably comforted to have someone who would let him talk his talk. I know you're probably familiar with the Big Bang theory. If what exploded into reality, was information, as Wheeler suggests – or knowing, or consciousness, or something along those lines, then the Brahman is Eternal Knowing, and each little Atman is a *bit* of knowing." He looked over at her with a grin, obviously pleased with his own brand of theorizing. She knew enough to see that he liked to play the alchemist, throwing some packet of quantum discoveries into a cauldron of venerable Vedic wisdom. He had told her that the Vedas contain some of the oldest recorded discernments of man. The Vedic seers had experienced the Something More that lay behind what met their senses. They crossed the bridge beyond the visible, into the sphere of the invisible – the unseen that is able to be seen by calm minds. They were the pioneers of *Homo religioso,* a term she couldn't get her mind around.

"What does dapper Wyatt say was there when it all went big bang?" Amit asked with a grin, and paused. She knew he thrived on mental jousting.

"I don't know," she answered, after hesitating. "Sometimes I hear about a zero-sized speck, a cosmic egg that exploded into an initial soup of matter and radiation."

"Yes, that's one common set of words. Another starts with a vacuum, with string-like microwaves of sound. But where did the cosmic egg or the microwaves come from?"

"You're getting at **infinite regress**, aren't you?" Anna remembered saying shyly, but confidently.

About this point in her reverie, Anna falls into deep sleep under a starry sky. Walking lightly in her deer skin moccasins, Kai comes out and covers her up with a blanket. Amit is already walking beside Anna in her first dream of the night. She misses him.

The house that Guido willed to his niece is a spacious home surrounding a Spanish-style courtyard, which looks out into the green conifers of the National Forest. The oft-lionized Cathedral Rock formation looms up out of the surrounding green-clad slopes through various windows. This particular morning, Anna sits at the dressing table in the master bathroom. She has never sat in such a luxurious space. Languidly brushing her long, dark hair, she feels like a make-believe princess. She enjoys it, and at the same time is afraid of it. In the mirror, she sees Ted resting on the black silk pillow of the bed.

Back in the Bronx, Billy O'Callan had lived up on the eighth floor in the same walk-up as she did. Every morning he was there at the foot of the stairs, waiting for her, and they walked together the six blocks to PS 13. He was a year younger but always made her laugh. Sometimes in the school yard, Billy inflated his little chest like a fighting rooster and told the bullies to "Back off." When Billy's family had to move, Anna was already scheduled to exile in the Catholic School. That sad morning of leave-taking, Billy, with a mist in his eyes, gave her his little brown teddy bear. "Here, I'm getting too old as a boy to have a teddy. Maybe you'll take care of Ted for me." For years, Anna had placed Ted on her pillow where she could see him as she drifted off. Ted is her totem friend. She had sensed before she left her cozy apartment in Manhattan that she might feel alone in a strange house. She had rightly imagined it as spacious and cold. Ted became a carry-on.

Many years ago she had made a major decision and took out a mortgage on her apartment on the Upper East Side, quivering and questioning. Yes, she had a job – her first job, and as it would turn out, her only job. She never got around to thinking out of the box. She was safe where she was. She had never made such a big financial decision before – all by her lone self. It was small – one bedroom, one bathroom with a wood framed mirror and very small dressing table, one sitting room, and a cramped kitchen. No big deal, she was not the entertaining type. It was in a safe, high-end neighborhood. Nights she would curl up with professional journals, like *Nature, Scientific American,* or *The American Physicist,* and listen to some stereophonic Ravel sonatas. She did have one naughty pleasure – sinful for a bluenose scientist – science fiction. The prospect of life on other planets in the cosmos turned on her juices. Possibilities do that. Now in Guido house, she finds herself alone, and confronted with another big decision. Not a scientific decision.

She hasn't slept well since *the call* which had thrown her quiet routine into turmoil. It has all happened so fast. It's meant changes she strongly doubts that she is ready for, or wants. *Change involves risk. Risk opens the door to hurt.* She knew hurt, like the key knows the lock. *I don't want to have to step through that door any more than I have to.* She is still nowhere close to making the pressing decision: what she is going to do. *Perhaps I should just be sensible and go back to my sweet little burrow and my one neighbor on the sixth floor. I've grown accustomed to seeing old Mrs. Applebaum walking her little dog in the corridor, and mumbling to herself. She's like me, never has any visitors and never complains. Sometimes she frightens me. I can't imagine myself still in that apartment when I'm almost ninety. But it happens in the city.*

Her submerged mind has always, noiselessly, feared the inevitable, unavoidable change – death. Getting old will be a serious change. She isn't old yet, nor is she exactly getting any younger. Chaos is ever possible, even in Newton's mechanical world. Oh, chaos. Her internal chaos escalated when Amit returned to Mumbai, leaving her in a sense stranded in her predictable routines. Maybe "no man is an island," but sometimes one can *feel* like nothing more than a tiny island. Being a tiny, unknown island is not good news, but often unavoidable. That may be why cartoonists love those little islands with one bare coconut tree. They suggest a desperate situation. Amazingly, Amit's altruism endears him to a part of her female heart that lurks inside her staid professional persona. Never you mind that his leaving has exposed her, alone and friendless. For more than a decade, the woman with the blemish and the brown man from the slums had moved comfortably in a shared field with a silent bond. He married; her waiting silently.

It was the death, she knew, of the young Moslem girl he had met by kismet years ago, that had tipped the blindfolded scales and called him back to Mumbai. Adveena had been his first love. Anna had missed that first-love stepping stone. In both her heart and her belly, she felt that void. She busily worked to ignore it. In a quiet sense, she appreciated his concerns; he is another oriented man. She could at least share his happiness. His altruism was one of those crazy reasons that made him special, set apart in her female mind. Her scientific consciousness did not use that unscientific l-word. Yet her female consciousness, softly accepted their unstated connection as *love*. Admittedly, she was clueless in Sedona about her interest in that first stepping stone. Sometimes she brooded that **if** a fairy godmother appeared and gave her a choice, between love or success, which would she choose? She knew the taste of success, but love? Anyways she didn't believe in fairy godmothers.

Little Adveena had been from a dysfunctional single-woman minority family. Her mother was a sex slave. Back then, none of that had mattered to the young brown boy, who knew that religious differences and the prostitution of women were just part of the air around him. They weren't realities in his family, or his life. They were just unhappy facts of life, like tics and malaria. On the happy side, he saw something like a light, something unique in Adveena. His fledgling dreams involved getting a serious education so that someday he could rescue this one special little girl from the poverty of the alleyway, and make her happy. (Eventually, Amit would come to realize that no person can make another happy. All a person can do is contribute to the conditions that allow happiness to come to that other. But such quixotic dreams loomed years down the road when he might be a gray-haired politician, if the species survives.)

Ever since he left India for Stanford, he had carried the guilt that he had abandoned the shy Moslem alley-girl. He eventually lost track of her, as people do. When his younger sister wrote and mentioned that an alley girl, he once knew, named Adveena, had died of HIV, he was shaken to the core. Her death laid bare the memories of the poverty and prostitution he had seen walking to school. At that juncture, he made the Quixotic decision to return to his native land. He had often felt the soft call to help his sick country. Anna knew him. It was inevitable, and now is irrevocable. She herself could never be strong enough to live in a foreign culture. New York is all she knows. She has suffered in the city. She has learned to survive on that island the Dutch stole from the Indians. The numbing of urban living and the powerlessness of being an outsider make sorry bed fellows. It's my only bed, she reminded herself. Teasing her hair a bit in the mirror, she confesses to herself: I don't think I can live anywhere but back in Manhattan.

She ties back her loose hair into a tidy, professional bun, and starts to put on her light touches of makeup – after all these years she is an expert in the under-stated – in the don't stand out physically. One of the new young California secretaries at the Institute wears no makeup. Anna shakes her head, thinking: *She won't make it. You've got to make compromises. Little by little the world is changing, but boys still rule the playground. And the guys expect make-up.* Anna has always tried to fit in. She deeply wants to be accepted, so she keeps the rules. One of her female teachers in college had said, "Keep the rules, and the rules will keep you." Be invisible, and the bullies won't come after you.

Opening her short, white silk dressing gown, she stretches out her left leg pulling on a black nylon stocking, the kind she has worn for all these years. Then she follows with her nice right leg. Standing she sees herself in the mirror – beige bra, matching briefs, showing above the black garter of her NY society stockings. She feels almost satisfied. She has earned the right to be pleased with her body. It has taken a lot of work, a lot of hours at *NY Fitness* and the downtown *Yoga Ashram*. Yet, she doesn't think that her body is all that super. It's not quite up to current expectations, which seem to be getting skinnier and quite expensive. But they are the today expectations, and if a woman wants to avoid the stones of rejection, she'd best keep herself close to the men's expectations.

In the mirror, she sees her uniform, – a below the knees, black skirt and a white silk blouse – both professional-looking, both stylish, both acceptable. (She has an identical gray uniform also.) Anna is careful about her appearance, even if it all gets covered up by a white science lab smock. She's not into flirting; she just does what is expected. At least below the consciousness line, she understands flirting. It's as natural as the mating coos of the windowsill pigeons. Still, she has more or less given up on the prospect of finding a relationship that would bind up the loose ends of her detached life – essentially, she is neither a knower nor a known. She's nobody, a faceless scientist. Maybe relating is just accidental, something that happens by dumb luck. There seem to be as many failures as successes. Is there any kind of science to all of this? Seems important, but not part of my reality.

She slips into her soft black leather pumps – not flat-flats like some of the older secretaries wear, but medium heels. Her mind drifts back to her mother. Gina loved shoes – she often stopped and stared at women's shoes. In high school, Anna joked about her mother's "shoe lust." She knows that her mother had no freedom to choose anything but the most prosaic. Actually, *her mother*, who had lived as a prisoner of her apartment, and the word *choose* were words from two different dictionaries.

When she died in Sicily two years after Luigi, Anna bought, and express-mailed a pair of red alligator leather shoes to the undertaker, and insisted that the protesting undertaker put them on her mother's feet in the gasket. "No, it is not possible!" he shouted into the phone. Anna insisted and won. It was one of the few rebellious things Anna had ever done.

They had only gone back to Sicily once, when Anna was about nine-and-a-half. It was the one time, Anna saw her mother as a full person. It was as if the hillside air had let the girl from the old olive orchard out of confinement. Once back in her own native hills, the quiet Bronx house-prisoner changed back into the attractive young woman the local townspeople remembered – outgoing, good-humored, and kind to everyone. She even sang one night at a family party. Back in her natural habitat, she became an energetic, smiling woman. It was an image Anna would carry buried in the chamber of her heart. Amazing how much our environment molds us, she thought looking down at her shoes. It can freeze us in a mold, *if* we let it.

Her mother had made it through her days as the Bronx house-wife. She had sacrificed her options when she let herself be given in marriage to the hardheaded rich city boy. It had been a while since Anna last recalled that image of her mother – the girl from the hills, happy on the land. Nowadays, there is a lot of talk about possibilities, she mused. For some people there's only what is and has been ... seemingly no future within reach.

Dressed, Anna gives herself a last inspection in the mirror. She is on her way to the lawyer's office to sign the final house papers, hoping that he won't be asking her for some kind of decision. At this time in her life, she doesn't care what Amit and others mean by the "big questions." As far as she is concerned, a huge personal question is staring her in the face. For her, the day-to-day questions easily trump the "big" ones. She has been moving along just fine on automatic pilot, like her mother had. Why did her mother's brother have to go and upset her cart?

Yes, that's me, she smirks at the mirror. *Whoever me is? Is that body really who I am? I don't think I've ever wasted much energy on figuring out who I am. I'm a scientist with a job. I do science, therefore I am. Wow, this house thing is a gauntlet thrown down at my feet. It's making me whacky. Still I do feel some kin loyalty, even if it is thin.* Guido was the last of her mother's side of the family. Still staring at the woman in the mirror, she thinks: *This house gift is just too much. It could ruin everything.* She pauses, and addresses the woman in the mirror: *Perhaps the time has come, and everything needs to be ruined – whatever this everything is.* Inside she feels the tumult of contradictions.

Kai knocks, "Taxi cab here." As she walks out to the red and white cab, she is turning over in her mind stopping at the Hike House. The jeep driver had pointed it out as a good place to buy hiking clothes. She feels an urge for something colorful. Just for this short leave of absence. She wouldn't think of wearing them back in the real world.

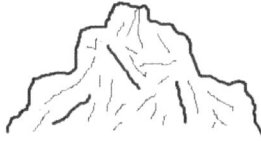

Pierre Bruni's office is in his home across town in the Thunder Mountain Estates. A short bald man with rimless glasses pushed up on his head and halo of white hair around his ears opens the front door. "Bonjour, Dr. Pagani. It's a pleasure to finally meet you. Mr. Cavaggio spoke so warmly about his niece. Come in. My office is in the back."

When Anna steps into the office with floor to ceiling windows on the outside wall, she is stunned again. Everybody in this place wants to bring the world outside inside. Her eye catches a small painting in a prominent niche on the left side wall. She recognizes the style. The left side of the painting features a steep wall of rusty red-orange cliffs. In the center, a slender red rock column stretches high into the bright blue sky. Atop of the rock marvel which has been carved out by eons of wind and water, a small, lone green pine tree stands conspicuous because of it illogical perch. She turns to Mr. Bruni. He smiles. "My honorarium for preparing his last wishes. A more than generous gift. He was a sensitive man. I'm sure it is very valuable. It's a scene in Fay Canyon. There actually is a tree perched on that rock pillar reaching into the blue sky. The wind or a bird must have dropped a seed there years ago. Hard to imagine there being enough dirt to allow a lonesome seed to succeed. The whirling winds must have tried in vain to sweep it away. It's a testimony to life's tenaciousness to survive. Please have a seat."

The furniture is Southwestern, pine wood and dark leather. The right wall is lined with book shelves with what look like art books and unique rocks of many sizes and shapes. "Your uncle and I were friends, even though we only met a couple of years ago. We had a lot in common. I'm an artist of sorts. Who isn't in Sedona? I collect rocks with unique shapes that have an energy that somehow speaks to me. Beauty is in the eye of the beholder who can see the different, the one-of-a-kind. I'm on the board of the Alliance of Local Artists. Each year we have a benefit auction to help our local Food Bank that feeds a lot of needy people. Even here we have the needy. Your uncle had donated a painting, and I went to his house to fetch it. He was such a nice man. He was one-of-kind. Mind if I call him "Guido?"

"Please do, and I'm Anna. He used to call me "Little Annie."

"I know he was sincerely fond of your mother. He said that as a young woman she sang beautifully to the hills. After she was taken away to the city, she sang no more."

Anna nodded, with a beginning mist forming under her eye lashes.

"I suppose you may also know that Guido suffered a similar loss in Paris, where I was raised. He lived on the left-bank, near the Place de Contrescarpe where Hemingway wrote *A Moveable Feast*. Guido liked to say that Sedona is like Paris, a moveable feast of colors, shapes, and interesting people. A place where one can always enjoy some unique face of the Gaia. At first, young Guido was happy in Paris. He had a young mistress, a Russian art model studying at the Sorbonne. (Anna recognizes the Sorbonne. Pierre and Marie Curie taught there.) Yuliya vanished without even a good-bye note. I could tell from his eyes and his thin voice that she had broken his heart. That's when he went away to the South Pacific. I think he wanted to get away from the place that had hurt him. Of course, he was an admirer of Gauguin and his light brown skinned women.

"It was there that he learned that he had lung cancer. He came here ten years ago, hoping the clean, high country air would help him. It did keep him alive for ten years. In the South Pacific, he had been given only one year to live, two at most. But the red rocks have an energy that revitalizes. He loved to go out into nature and paint *en plein aire.*"

Pulling down his glasses from his forehead, the Guido admirer became the Guido lawyer. Reaching into a drawer, he pulled out a brown portfolio fastened with brown ties.

"It's all here. All quite simple. All straight forward. You are his sole heiress. Everything is yours – house, paintings, trust account – no strings attached."

Anna frowned. It was the first time she had heard anything about a trust account.

"The trust is a handsome sum. You are the sole trustee. It's all in these papers. You can take them home and read them. I'm sure you'll find it clear and to your liking. As I said there are no strings attached. You may stay. You may sell it all off.

"He did make one request. If you sell the house or if you decide not to retain his housekeeper, he would like you to help her and her daughter relocate. He suggested a severance pay of about one year's salary. But even this matter is left to your discretion. He was a family man, a generous man, and a kind man. He was a believer of a kind."

Anna's legs felt wobbly as she walked to the cab carrying her portfolio. Her head was pounding, like a mild migraine. As the cab moved through the town, she sat staring at the red mountains that surrounded the town. Then she could wait no longer. She opened the portfolio and quickly found the section on the trust. "Oh, my God!" she exclaimed. The driver looked in the rear view mirror at the breathless woman in the back seat.

She rushes into the house, goes directly to the bedroom, changes into her hiking clothes, leaving her professional clothes in a pile where she stepped out of them. Her spirit just needs to clear her head amid the wise, old rock oracles, high up on the Chapel Trail. She doesn't even pause at the tree where she had seen the pretty, but noisy, blue jay the day before. She needs space *Oh, get me out of here. I can't handle all of this*. She needs to let something sink in. Or perhaps she needs to mentally throw something off a cliff – like those documents. Her confusion borders on panic. She needs a friend to hold her hand. But she has none. Change is again slapping her in the face. She is frightened, and deliriously excited. Fate has handed her a lottery in a silent brown portfolio.

She climbs furiously and reaches her grounding rock spot. Sitting, and breathing as if she realized that she is breathing (perhaps the rock below and her body-openings are instructing her). She takes in a deep breath, feeling her diaphragm lift. Slowly, she calms and looks out into the distance, unable to focus on the details of the world around. For a brief, lost moment, she sees without saying, sees without naming. Her focus is diffuse.

The lawyer's mention of the Sorbonne had unleashed a storm of inner butterflies. For too long she has lived in denial. She is not happy at the Institute. When she was an idealistic coed, barely escaping from the trials of being a teenager, she had ambitious dreams despite her problems. She wanted to contribute something significant like Marie Curie had done. Those dreams have slowly been forced off into metal file cabinets. Perhaps it would have happened anywhere. Female scientists have never had an easy road. Moreover, she felt that Wyatt Jones had it in for her because she wouldn't … It had gotten worse after the award. She'd never had any freedom to pursue her ideas. She'd always be under his thumb. She felt trapped there. But now the trust money was the magic key that could unlock her situation. She could now afford to move on.

On the way back down the trail to Guido's house, a plan begins to come together in her brain. She will quit. She doesn't need their pension money, or recommendations. She could go teach at some university – perhaps Stanford. Amit liked the West Coast. In her imagination, the Pacific Ocean rolls in gentle, feminine. The Atlantic is masculine, cold, and rough. She could get her foot in the door, offering herself at a low salary. The dream of teaching and being free to do her own research makes her lightheaded.

But that night Anna can't sleep. Her mind is a wild mustang, kicking and bucking. Strangely, she feels uncomfortable about leaving Kai and Nascha. Over and over she tells herself that she doesn't owe them anything, other than some money. Guido would understand. He himself seemed to know when it was time to move on. Certainly she'd take care of them financially. Nevertheless as she fights herself in and out of some weird REM sleep, she has the feeling that she is overlooking something.

Even the little tree at the top of the Fay Canyon rock column keeps appearing as if it has a blinking message for her.

Perhaps the message wants to suggest that she is unaware of the freeing up of her a woman who is hiking the red rocks? Is she closed to the messages Nature is sending her? That day in the Earth Wisdom Jeep she overheard someone mention "The Fever." Maybe, just maybe, her life needs a little rise in temperature. She can hardly ignore the fact that the workday treadmill can become her robot-like trap. Another voice in her sleepy head, rebuttals: *That's all you are, who you are trained to be a robot.* Yes, her dreamy mind responds, but now I can reach for the forbidden-to-women brass ring. I'm free. As she crashes into deep sleep, she recalls that her mid-life marker is not that far over the horizon.

The next morning, a bright sun already high in the sky, she awakes, still unable to give up that she is a city dweller, and only a city dweller, but willing to compromise for a while. The trust has changed the picture. She'd stay out her six months leave of absence. She has that right. The red rocks can continue their magic. It would be good for her. It's time to take care of herself. Then, she'll resign, thumbing her nose at Mr. Lech, and start a new journey. She'd stay in touch with Amit. She'd write him later today.

Her first morning in Guido's house, Kai had mentioned that she and Nascha walk mornings early, "It is good to be close to the land. The land knows secrets – secrets that keep you balanced, secrets that make life happy. The mountains, the canyons, the winds, the birds, they are our teachers. My people believe that they teach that we are all one. Many people hike here." Anna had asked her about the Hike House. "People say it is nice place, but I have never been."

Several days later, Anna Googles hikehouse.com on her laptop, now resting on the desk in the unused study. Google shows that the Hike House is right in the center of one of Sedona's main tourist hubs. Tlaquepaque is an upscale Mexican-style village of galleries, shops, and fine restaurants. It is across the way on the other bank of Oak Creek, in the shade of some ancient sycamores and cottonwoods. And across the street from Tlaquepaque is the Center for the New Age with psychic readings, aura photos, tarot readings, chakra balancing, and a host of other metaphysical adventures. Crystal Magic is a popular visitor stop for "essential oils, crystals, and all things spiritual. Hey, you came here to escape the humdrum, do the different. Live for a change," the info clip says. Anna is grinning.

A couple of mornings later, sitting at her dressing table with the day turning happy, she silently dialogues with the changing woman in the mirror, *All my New York running clothes are dark and dour, besides they're getting a little old.* (She is even loosening up with the mirror on the wall.) *I've got to admit there is something magical about this place that lightens my load. It must be the high desert atmosphere, or the mountain air. I think the travel magazine on the plane raved about the Arizona sunshine.* (Her mind flits back to clothes.) *After all, as the biologists report, even the female birds like to pick up new colorful threads. Right now, right here, I don't care if I have to throw them out when I get back home to my own apartment. I don't really intend to let the trust money change me too fast. But for once, I've got some loose change, some discretionary money. I think Uncle Guido would be pleased.*

Life seems to come across as less complex in the mountain peaks at 4,500 above sea level. The head and heart work lighter. Anna makes a serendipitous decision to buy something with a splash of autumn color. Back in college, she heard the expression *Carpe diem (Seize the day).* The Latin had caught in the branches of her mind, but hadn't put down roots – for sure, she hasn't made it part of her lifestyle. The French *Prenez guarde (Be on your guard)* has been more her style. Anyways, there is something impromptu in the pure, clean atmosphere of the high hills. Right from the first morning, she felt a soft difference impinging, even if she couldn't expressly admit it to herself. Here, *feeling* seems to have an edge over *thinking*. But feeling makes her nervous, vulnerable.

As she gets out of the cab, her stiff self feels a little foolish. Her melting self feels giddy. Who says she is an ice cube that will never melt? She hesitates outside the Hike House, questioning whether she should be sensible and go back to Guido's house. Colorful clothes just are not Manhattan. Then she lifts her chin, clenches her left hand, and crosses into the Hike House Energy Café, with its wafts of fresh baked goodies and aromatic coffees. Boosted by the sensuous signals, she goes on into the equipment-clothing section. Smacking her in the face, like a candy store, is the wall of colorful hiking shoes and boots. *Ah, the shoe lust is alive in the Pagani genes. I fear I'm going to splurge – a bit.* The corners of her mouth turn up as she walks into the happy buzz of fit, mostly young, people trying on boots, scanning flat screens, and loudly conversing in the energy café. She isn't consciously seeking lively people, just some hiking clothes, perhaps some information on the different trails. But it's a seductive, bestowing ambiance. Could she enjoy being in the midst of the happy young people? She wonders. (Her deep feminine tissue knows something in her life is missing.)

A cute blonde, named Debra, greets her and waltzes her to a wooden bench in the footwear section, quoting Marilyn Monroe, "All it takes to conquer the world is the right pair of shoes." *Oh, my gosh,* Anna thinks. *My mother would have a meltdown here. So many options: walking shoes, cross trainers, hiking boots. For a footie, this could be shod heaven.* (She smiles, knowing she has just attempted a funny, so unlike her usual self.) *Wait a minute. This isn't my mother's type of footwear. Her roots were the Sicilian hillsides, so were her boots. But she had her young secret dimensions too. She was a strong, knowing woman in a sense, although she felt that her life in America had been a life of being yoked, like an ox, to her daily drudgeries. Like mother, like daughter.*

Anna buys herself a pair of brown and orange hiking cross-trainers, and a pair of burnt umber convertible hiking pants (you can unzip the below-the-knee section, and hike away in bare knees and calves), and a yellow top with red ancient-people symbols. She hasn't forgotten that red and yellow are the colors of the Sicilian flag. She also buys herself a water bottle belt. As scientist, she knows about dehydration. She's lighthearted on her way out of the clothing section. She meets Karen who opens the interactive trail finder and spends fifteen minutes helping her – for free. Anna can't believe how nice and helpful people are. Something in the air, she wonders? The pace is nothing like the rushing, sometimes elbowing crowds of the streets of Manhattan. While she is being reckless, she decides to get herself a smoothie, and just sit and chill out for a few minutes. She's had so much to deal with in the last few weeks.

As she steps out into the open air patio of the Energy Cafe, she scans for a place to sit. Off to the left, two gals, both chicly dressed blondes with assorted shopping bags around their feet, are talking away and hand waving. Their lively hands and fingers remind her of a New York delicatessen, and their aura is just as trendy. There is a third empty seat at their table. She debates with herself for a microsecond about joining them. She knows that she should try to be more social, but takes her strawberry/banana smoothie toward the last open table in the far corner next to the bare wood ladder leaning up the wall. Her mind scans the artifact: it must have some old significance. *Perhaps, it's about climbing to another world*, she thinks, still making peace with Amit's departure. No surprise, she chooses to go to the lone corner seat.

"So Emma, are you going to tell me what your intuitive had to say?" the blonde with the anchor-woman haircut is saying, as Anna moves past them to take her seat.

"Her name is Gypsy, and I think she's distaff. She mentioned her partner at least twice. I could see that look in her eyes. As for her wise words? 'The sooner I make an effort to move on, the happier I'll be.' Daah!"

"Good, I agree. Personally, I don't understand that persuasion. Yet I have to admit we all need a special relationship. Maybe it's my silly hormones, but I prefer men. They're not all like Ron, you know. I never liked him from the beginning. That, you do know. You deserve better, Emma. I suppose we all do, but we settle, don't we?

"You probably married too young, and you're not getting any younger, girlfriend. I saw what happened to my own mother after my father left her for that teenage bimbo. She gave up on men. She ended up a crabby old maid. I felt sorry for her. Hell, it could happen to anyone of us. Relationship is a cross full of splinters laid on soft shoulders. Sometimes we are forced to embrace it, yet we know it leaves scars."

"Your mom was a nice lady, Vicky. It was sad to watch her go downhill, but I can understand. When you've been cheated on by someone you put your trust in, it really hurts … big time goblins that don't go away. I don't know if I can put myself out there again." Emma's voice has a Boston, well-educated, accent. Her bright blonde, silky hair is cut short, asymmetrical, angled close to her jaw, contrasting with her dark eyelashes.

Anna gets caught up into this uninvited conversation. She has been a stranger to girl talk for the past many some years.

Seems like fun to have a friend, but it's a whole new language she doesn't speak. Her mind wonders: *Sounds like Emma's just been through a divorce. Kai's comment about not living alone, doesn't sound as right-on as it did the other day. I must confess that I've been thinking a little about men recently. But maybe I'm just too battered and bruised by my early experiences, or lack of them. To be honest, maybe it's too late for me.*

"Hey, have you been a bad girl? Did they make you sit in that corner, like in kindergarten?" Anna quickly looks over to the woman with the silky blonde hair whose fingers are gesturing and saying, *Come, join us.* "You look like a local. Tell us about this enchanting place. You must hike; looks like you bought new hiking clothes."

"What?" Anna stammers, a little startled, and unsure of what to do. (*Join them,* an inner voice pokes. *They look nice. They won't bite. Open up, Dr. Pagani. You've been shut down too long.*) So she decides to cross over.

"Thanks," Anna answers, slowly getting up from her dunce chair and carrying her smoothie and her Hike House shopping bag to their table. "Hi, I'm Anna Pagani. I'm not a local. I'm actually a New York lifer. I've only been here a short time. Time collapses here. Please don't ask why I came. Too confusing. Too sad. But everyone said hiking is the thing to do, and I'm getting to enjoy it. It's so awe inspiring here. Yes, nature is fun and relaxing, so I bought myself a new outfit. I'm actually excited about the prospect of hiking into beauty, feeling a little more colorful. I've been a runner in the city. But to tell the truth, that gets boring. Same-old, same-old. Don't ask me why, but I am beginning to actually feel a need for hiking here. It's the kind of feeling I don't usually have. Hey, I'm a physicist who hides in the City's concrete jungle, a wasteland in its own right."

"Nice to meet you, city girl. I'm Emma Reynolds, and this is Vicky Connors. She's from Chicago, and I live in LA. We were roommates at Swarthmore, and she talked me into coming here to get away from it all. Have you ever been divorced? It's the pits."

"I've never even been married," Anna divulges, with an unsure, captured giggle. It feels to her like Sedona is getting to her – opening her. She doesn't usually talk to strangers like this. She's amazed that she is exposing little hidden, secret parts of herself. "Back in the Bronx schoolyards, I got a lot of grief from boys about my birthmark," Anna says pointing to the right side of her neck. "I closed up like a touch-me-not mimosa. Just yesterday, looking out the window at these magnificent mountains, I was thinking to myself that I've been hiding. It's easy for a scientist to hide in her work. To tell the truth, I fear I'm afraid of life."

Both women fall speechless for a short moment, surprised that a woman could be so transparent about the abuse she had suffered, as if she was opening the hornets' nest of her feelings. The dyed-blonde from Chicago cagily wades back in: "I don't think you birthmark is that bad. You're an attractive woman."

"Thank you. I think the mark seemed bigger when I was little. I was frightfully white from being inside most of the time. Or maybe I've just made peace with it."

"We're just here for a couple of days. I had some airline miles, and I thought Emma could use a little distraction. Her husband's been cheating on her, the dirt bag. Why can't guys control that thing? She just got fed up and divorced him. So we're doing the town, some retail therapy. We were just over there in that Center for the New Age. I went to a clairvoyant channeler who promised to bring me new psychic energy. Truthfully, I'd have gotten more energy out of a facial. I don't believe in this spirit-energy stuff."

"And I went to a relationship intuitive who told me exactly what I expected, but still don't like to hear," Emma volunteered. "So save your money, City Girl. But, come on, show us your clothes. Clothes are happy things. We all like clothes. I should've saved the fifty dollars I paid Gypsy and bought a Sedona t-shirt: **I did it on the Red Rocks.** Who'd believe it? Me?"

Anna's mind is struck by the words about clothes being "happy things." Just a short time ago in the dressing room, she had looked at herself in the mirror, in her new outfit. And yes, the expression on her face was happy. It kind of surprised her.

Ever since Eddie's funeral, my footsteps fall heavier. I sleep lighter. It's an early autumn Saturday morning. I wake to the sensation that a sickness of unease is seeping into my bones and my spirit. I still can't muscle up the nerve to write. Some mornings I feel manic, thinking that I'm making progress along Joan of Arc's trail, even though the cloud of uncertainty persists. Am I progressing? A little. I guess. I hope. Other mornings, like this morning, a cloak of depression settles upon my shoulders, when I'm alone. It's still dark outside and colder than I feel it should be. No doubt about it, the world and the climate are changing. I'd prefer the more predictable seasons of a couple of years back. My inner weather is laden with these ashen feelings that block out all warm, affirming light. As you know, I worry about mankind's direction. The bad seed of violence seems to be rooting in. It has a chance of winning. I don't know what the odds are.

There's something ironic about being in touch with these inner squalls. Sure, this inner turmoil disturbs me; I have a terrible time trying to concentrate on my breathing when my mind feels stalked by a lack of confidence. At the same time, I've read many wise words that say tribulation can mature a person, like suffering does. I have a sneaking suspicion that there are many demanding professions and madhouse offices that drown out what's actually going on inside a person, especially for us literal types. I suppose there are many normal zombies who don't even suspect they have minds that don't know how to focus. I was going down that headless incline until Emily turned my head.

In a sense it stands to reason, doesn't it? Eons ago, men learned to *just do it* – focus, forget feelings, face acts, and bring home the mastodon meat. Now after ageless seasons of macho change, we men are supposed to be more like women: peaceable and sensitive to our feelings. Some students of human nature like to look back to the chimps, the bonobos, and the early hominids and say, "Hey, we are wired to be this way. We've been this way for nearly 200 million years. Our primate genes are said to be brutish, promiscuous, and grasping." The poet Tennyson called Nature "red in tooth and claw."

Still many new 'frontier scientists' disagree. *It's cooperation, Stupid!* Some even dare to hope that evolution is approaching a new border crossing. Maybe, if I can gather the pluck, someday I'm going to write an essay entitled: *Look forward to the Omega Point. Not backward toward the savannah. What kind of people do we want to be in the time to come?*

For all that tangled and tortuous thinking, I have to admit that, at times, I am comfortable with the inkling that the wilderness is making inroads through the underbrush of my early, inner conditioning. I sense that I am being led like a docile donkey toward finding peace of mind. I'm not fighting my stiff mind as much. But as I have said, at other times I feel I am kidding myself about the power of the place, and I want to throw my hands in the air: *I give up!* Maybe I am too deeply conditioned to change. Yet change seems to want me.

On the other hand, it may be that I'm going down into the quicksand of a culture that is getting sicker and more besotted with each passing decade. The media records of current events certainly support such a dark hypothesis. Still, on the smiley side, pockets of the culture appear to be stepping toward the *humanum*. A remnant, reaching out for hands to hold, appears to be walking more mindfully. They are a modern day, desert-crossing tribe, like the wandering *Hapiru* once were in the Sinai. Nevertheless, I still think, the merchants of greed are bent on sinking us and themselves in that quagmire of materialism.

As I open my sleepy eyes from my mental meandering, I sense that morning is breaking and the forest waking. The birds are chirping their greeting to the sun, and the bats are flitting home to hang in the darkness of their caves. How those blind creatures achieve their sonic sense of direction is another mystery of Nature. I dress quickly, make a small pot of Ethiopian coffee, and head out to my *sanctum sanctorum.* My finger pushes the button. *Voila,* the roof opens.

As I look out at the world the Scrooge in my amygdala is still upset that the talking heads of the media have a kind of witch-doctor influence on our collective psyche. It might also be that, like Martin Buber, I have invested a lot of energy in search of my mother's memory … in search of my first love. "Love" is another Brazilian nut I'm not finding easy to open.

The cool, blue, fresh scent of pines and silver-green cypresses starts to calm the dyspepsia in my psyche. As I've mentioned, when I first came here, flush from the sale of the house in San Francisco, I helped design this glass-house monastery behind my townhouse, with the part of the roof that fronts on the forest retractable. Admittedly a luxury, I was giving noodle to my defense mechanisms. I was fortunate to have the funds. A lot of people aren't so lucky. I was ahead of the worst of the real estate cliff. Sometimes that self-pampering hurts, and I'm a little happy about that. It means I care. Mornings I savor listening to the land stretching awake. Likewise, on soft nights, I can read at my desk, sometimes by moonlight. It all melds into my striving to be attuned to the ambient world, as the charismatic Emily described the Sedona challenge.

Shortly after my wife Allie's death, I woke up to the fact that somewhere along the line, I had slipped beyond the buoys that channeled me through my tender years. The whole enchilada had gone spice-less – my God, my religion, my sense that life is meaningful. For many of my contemporaries, *hoi polloi*, the absence of meaning elicits no more than the *"not a problem"* quick retort – just water off a duck's tail feathers. Even my molecules know that this God-shaped-hole (meaning-shape-hole) in my mind isn't the result of some dramatic epiphany: No knocked-from-my-horse experience, no *Eureka* moment, no red-hot Jezebel. My sense of an-other-oriented, meaningful spice of life had just stealthily hemorrhaged away, back into the sand and fog of the City by the Bay.

The pernicious culture of **me-ism**, random sex, avid consumerism, and benumbed working-for-gain appears to be polluting the collective spirit. Don't laugh. This is serious. When I first came to the red rocks, I was awash in the backwater of individualism, materialism, and senseless chatter. I was also living almost totally in my head. I still tend to judge those who barely have the leisure time to think.

My morning mind, like a lawyer, is pleading with the dawning day: *Hear my side of the story. Understand me.* I'm not the Lone Sailor. It seems like there are more people in my leaky boat than there are Sinai-like wanderers heading for happier homes in the hills. But let's face it; my confusion might just be a "midlife crisis." Nevertheless, the *H. sapiens* species might also be in the throes of a mid-life turning point for all we know.

By the end of my undergraduate studies, I was aware that my boyhood dreams were thinning away. Unmoored and emotionally isolated, after my friends all moved hither and yon, I, an emotional seeker searching for his El Dorado, went west to San Francisco – escaping from my roots, my past, but not my doubts. (I guess I've said all this already, but these kinds of narrative threads keep coming back, and back.) Doubts, as you may know, are like summer dandelions: they're ugly, and a bitch to get rid of. So as you can hear, this Homeric ego is still on the quest for answers, still lusting for certainty.

By day, in San Francisco, Mr. Malachy teaches American history, comparative religions, journal writing. At night and on weekends, I take more classes towards an M.A. in religious studies. I persist in my journey to re-find the possibly-impossible answers to my doubts in some brilliant course, some eye-opening quote, or some piercing professor. High-powered academia surely had to have the answers to these questions that matter. Fundamentally, I was scratching for fresh "proofs for the existence of God." The idea of a benevolent Supreme Being who is the *lapis angularis* who keeps the whole Roman arch from falling to the ground haunted the hallways of my consciousness. To me, this concern is the dough of *Homo sapiens'* bread of life.

My brain persists in panting for proofs; proofs like Aristotle and Aquinas thought through. Several years after I graduated with honors – but no stabilizing answers, my spiritual legs still wobbled. Perhaps the madness to capture *God* in words is a smelly red herring. On cloudy days it feels like a lunacy. On sunny days it feels like the call to come home.

After we were married, Allie and I had hung on to some of the church-going trappings. For a while, we took the children to Mass on Sunday – we didn't want to cheat them of the great boon of *religion.* After all, *Homo sapiens* has also trekked as *Homo religioso,* probably since the birth of that first, dark-skinned, human child in the African savannah. Some scientists say that the unicellular prokaryotes of three billions years ago had an 'intelligence' that the environment brought together to form communities of cells, (of selves). Religions started as communities, and religion is not something man can wash right out of his thinning hair.

Yet, religion wasn't something that Allie and I seriously sat down and talked about. Like many couples, we just presumed that we were both on the same page. Another one of those don't ask, don't tell, scenarios. Of course, I fell into blaming it all on shallow thinking Allie. These days I see the tragicomedy more humanly. She just wasn't a gal into brooding about the ponderous issues of life. These days not many dare that. Life is about getting over the daily dozen hurdles. Sadly, that seems normal. Our inability to dialogue about what mattered to us was one of the silent assassins of our relationship.

And what made matters harder: somehow the messages coming through the wax in my ears, in my Sunday wooden pew, sounded stale. The preacher didn't sound like the wandering prophet who had no place to lay his head, nor that same rabbi who told stories of a smelly Samaritan who stopped and extended kindness to a Jew left near dead by violent thieves. But even to this day, I wonder if I failed my son Matt who has no interest in religion. He has become one of those happy-go-lucky, everyday agnostics, who dream of Steve Jobs and big breakthroughs. My daughter and her boyfriend go to church. I'm not sure why. Bonding, as well as sex, is so crucial at the coming of age stage.

I'm grateful to that visionary from the South. She spanked awake my interest in contemplation, or as the scientists like to call it, right brain attunement. I'm sure that I'm not a Thomas Merton. I'm self-protective and prone to self-justification. I just want to be accepted. I suspect that's what we all want, as Gwen says. Living without certainty feels lonely. Perhaps if I knew the answers, I'd like myself better, and people would like me.

I decide that I need a trip to the *Cave* to imbibe a little of Gwen's hard-scrabble wisdom, promising myself to have only two drinks. I know that despite all my failures, I am trying, at least intending, to develop that attitude of presence to others. Hopefully, that skill can turn out to be my 'Get-out-of-jail' card. If I get my mind on straight, the road ahead will straighten out. I need to get my inner GPS up and running. I don't have a clear vision of what I'm looking for, but as the cutie says: *We can't give up, can we?*

In my mind I see the barmaid's eyes with that girlish spar-kle. The other night, I could see that she had her hair done. She even moved with a more gracefulness. I don't know why but that night the image of Gwen brought back the sweet memory of *the seeker at the library.* On that day back in 2009, I was still without buoys. Perhaps it was her same ginger-blonde hair. I had never been able to erase that girl who hugged me in the library portico from my mind. In that embrace, I felt a common humanity. She had grown into a mythological figure in my heart. We are all questing for something different than the day-to-day distractions.

A couple of nights after our soul-to-soul, library-portico encounter, the news had latched onto the tragedy. They had a 911 audio clip. I heard the panic stricken voice of a woman: *Help! Send Help. People are dying. People can't breathe.* The newscaster explained that terrible tragedy was happening out at the Angel Valley Retreat Center. I knew that's where the seeker who gave me the hug had gone on her vision quest. I was almost sure that I recognized her voice, and my heart knotted up with both love and fear.

For months I watched the news, wondering about her. The media ate up the "inspirational speaker" who proffered "Harmonic Wealth" if you took his retreat. Wealth and sex seem to be paired oxen that struggle forward our sled of memes. The guru of wealth-wisdom was very well-healed. It's said that he may have pocketed $500,000.00 off that week gig in the Sedona wilderness. Sixty-four people had reportedly paid $9,600, plus travel expenses to be "spiritual warriors." They were serious about seeking; they had fasted for 36 hours, alone in the Arizona desert with only a sleeping bag (for an extra $250. He'd sell you a Peruvian poncho). After two days without water, they were crammed into a make-shift sweat lodge. Three died and eighteen were hospitalized with burns, dehydration, breathing problems, kidney failure, and fever.

Some mornings when am hiking, I remember her and her vision quest. It's not every day that a sweet young woman sits on a cold bench, shares her soul, and gives you a hug.

Anna, dressed in her new, colorful hiking outfit, stands by the kitchen window enjoying a mixed bowl of blueberries, raspberries, and sliced banana, Kai's sunrise salad. Outside the delicate, soft-hued, slanted light of morning is filling the world with imagination and promise. It's the fountainhead of a new day. A faint flicker of memory brings Thoreau to her mind. He thought morning the most fecund hour of a person's day. Back in the big city she was a dutiful morning machine. She did what she had to do to fit in, be normal. A woman had to keep her body in shape, and perform at work. That's why she dragged herself out of bed mornings.

Now each morning she feels an almost erotic energy, well, something stirring in her body as she gets ready to go hiking. For her, hiking tastes like a mixed bowl of exertion and solitude, concentration and forgetting, hearing the sounds of silence and feeling the nudges of energy. Yet she doesn't think of Nature as a spiritual experience. She'd heard one of the checkers at the health food store say something to that strain. However, unwittingly, she is silently submitting to and undergoing a change of heart. She'd heard Amit say that Nature is an entangled web of connections. She wasn't ready to put into words what she was enjoying. She was just a girl, finally enjoying the world around her, yet knowing in the back of her mind that someday soon she had to go back to her real life.

As she walks to the beginning of the Chapel Trail, she is humming softly under her breath; *Morning has broken, like the first
morning. Blackbird has spoken, like the first bird. Praise for the
singing, praise for the morning.* (Her roommate in college had
loved Cat Stevens.) The sun is already strong. Up ahead she recognizes the Madonna and nun formations, silhouetted against the
sky. She can smell the fragrant freshness of the conifers and the
berry-laden junipers. Two cottontail bunnies chase one another,
zigzagging across the walkway. She surprisingly suspects that it
is a **he** chasing a **she**.

She had hiked a little of the Chapel Trail one of her first days
after the Hike House visit. It's close to Lomas Serenas, and full
of changes and challenges. Most of the trail changes are at a
level of change she can now deal with. This trail starts down
through a deep wash, strewn with huge boulders and tree trunks,
tumbled down some many-long-years-ago, probably during a
torrential rainstorm. She imagines that a ghost river once ran
through here. She can hardly picture the ferociousness of water
that can bandy about these mammoth chunks of stone. Nature
has her own moments of violent change, it seems.

Soon the trail starts to climb toward the red cliff face to the
north, meandering through the verdant chaparral and manzanita
bushes with their tiny red apples. Along the side of the trail, the
high-country's signature desert prickly-pear cacti flair like silent
knights errant of resilience and survival. Finally, after a healthy
uphill climb, she arrives at a wide and long mesa of sloping red
lava slickrock, and slender, green ocotillos with red-tipped tassels – some as spindly tall as fifteen feet. Her heart is pumping
from the climb, and her lungs pulling in clear drafts of cool,

clean air. The mesa is a sanctuary that invites reflection. This morning, she has gone farther, and feels more into the whole experience.

A flat boulder signals her to sit. To her hand, the red rock is warm with the sun. She sits and can sense the warmth stirring into her lower body. She lingers, savoring the sensation. Her female bottom warms to the invitation. She takes a few swigs of her water, and drinks in the whole valley. She already recognizes the famous formations: Bell Rock, Courthouse Butte, Cathedral Rock, and the Madonna and Child spires. She has heard that Bell is one of the much talked about vortex spots. Even these famed land formations seem to open their arms to her. To her own surprise, she is finding it easy, almost second nature to feel at moments like this, that she is part and parcel of the Sedona hills. Maybe there still is a little of the Sicilian hillside blood in me, she muses. Someone in the Hike House had also used the expression *The Fever.* Anna hadn't given it a second though; fevers are things to be avoided.

She shakes her head in dismay as she recalls the stream of the idle chatter that had been rambling through her head on the trail – chatter about her work, chatter about her boss, chatter about Layla, chatter about not really supposed to be staying this long. She had never before been aware of how much distracting noise there can be in one's mind. She feels that the warm rock under her is sending signals, inviting more deep minded reflection. She unknowingly resists. She isn't ready for it. Yet, some part of her really wants to stay there with her bottom on the warmth of the land. It feels so good.

On her way down, the image of Guido's room comes back, and she remembers the little book on the floor. She had totally forgotten about it. There were very few books in the house. Uncle Guido was obviously, a man who perceived with his own eyes, not a man who read the ideas of others. When she gets home, she goes straight to Guido's study. The room is exactly as it was the first day, the ghost tree still unnerving her. She picks up the book, *Man's Search for Meaning* by Victor Frankel.

She remembers the book. It is a classic she'd read for some undergraduate philosophy course. She thought it quite touching back then. The memory comes back of a man in a Nazi concentration camp. The man is constantly thinking about his wife, who has been sent to a woman's camp. He doesn't even know if she is still alive. Her memory helps him survive. She matters to him.

Inside the book is a faded photograph of a slender young woman in a long black dress, and a black pill-box hat. Except for the Eiffel Tower in the background, the photo reminds her of the cover of another book she read around that time, *Anna Karenina.* She remembers that Russian woman's difficult struggle to fit in to their old-boy rules. On the back, the photo reads: Bonne Noel, Mon Amour. 1948 Yuliya. Anna smiles. *The old fox – no, the young wolf. He had his Parisian lover. He hadn't always been a loner, as he was in his waning years.*

That afternoon, as dusk begins to paint the Sedona sky with warm shades of red and orange, she wanders out into the back quadrangle. She relaxes into the hushed leisure of the lounge. A big yellow and black butterfly flies close to her bare outstretched feet, as if curious, and checking her out. She once read that butterflies spread their wings to attract a mate, or close them to hide in a tiny crack in a tree for protection from hurt.

Out of the right corner of the back wall, a quail family rushes to the cover of the manzanita bushes in the opposite, left corner. Mother leads, half-low-flying, half-scurrying, followed by a line of about nine little balls of feathers. The red-plumed male quickly perches on a rock, overseeing his brood, ready to protect. No one can doubt that he is looking out for his own. It's a cute, primordial scene, and Anna quietly savors watching "her family" in action, inadvertently enjoying that male presence watching over female and children. Without forming it into words, to herself she *sotto voce* welcomes her new friends, as if she is becoming a member of a connected community.

According to Kai, Guido loved to sit outdoors in that very lounge chair. He had clearly put his artistic touch on the garden space. Along the back wall, red boulders of various sizes and heights form a rock garden with colorful wildflowers spaced out in the crevasses between the rocks. Kai had pointed out the red, Indian paint brushes as Guido's favorite flower. Orange mallows, purple verbena, small white daisies with yellow centers and delicate indigo lupines are some of the other names Anna remembers, and feels warm about. The names sound almost musical to her ear. What she enjoys most is the aromas of the vanilla cliff-rose bush, and the clump of rosemary, along with the murmur of the water falls – fragrances and sounds not found in the racket and odors of the city. Just lounging there, Anna can feel her whole body unwinding.

Along the north wall, she spots a new grayish-green plant. Kai had said something about transplanting a new agave plant. *Yeah,* she thinks, *transplanting plants might be easy. It's not so easy to uproot people and hope they make it in a whole new soil.*

Beyond the wall, a welcome evening breeze is cooling the desert sands and rocks. Soon, she remembers, the coyotes will begin calling to one another. Surprisingly she is beginning to feel comfortable, in this home she can't mustard up the courage to accept. She has placed her ice tea and cheese and crackers on the side table, a sawed-off stump of a large tree, which after several hikes, she is fairly sure is a ponderosa pine. She hesitates. It is a moment of questioning respect for her departed kinsman.

Then, almost reverently, she picks up Guido's lone book, and begins to read: *Preface: Don't aim for success...like happiness, success cannot be pursued; it must ensue...as the unintended side effect...of one's dedication to a cause greater than oneself or as the by-product of one's surrender to a person other than oneself.*

Perhaps, Guido and Yuliya had surrendered to one another, her mellow mind muses. She sheepishly suspects they had. What does it really mean to give oneself to another she wonders? Her heart suspects she has never really given herself. In a way to her mother. Almost to Cassie. And possibly never again, now that Amit is no more than a dying ember in her life.

Then in chapter one, Frankel's wife's image enters – *I heard her answering me. I grasped the meaning of the greatest secret,* Frankel writes. *The salvation of man is through love and in love.*

Anna puts the book down and lets her mind drift up into the beginning stars of the night, all seeming so close to one another. Her award paper had contributed to the theory of dark energy and the mysterious future of the universe. A sense of the mystery of the spacious cosmos washes gently over her. Her awareness turns inward. She lays back and into a warm dream: A knight in shining silver armor, with a white banner adorned by a port-wine colored sword, is riding out to find a fix for the Fisher King's wound. (Anna, as you might remember, had devoured the Grail Legends in high school.) The paladin's chest has the swell of a woman's breast, and her long, rebellious hair constantly needs tucking in over her right ear. The Lady Knight and her steed wander for what seems a long time in dreamtime, and finally come to a mountain with a fire-breathing dragon guarding the entrance to a cave, where the young damsel who can make the King whole again is imprisoned. The Knight of the Valiant Breast studies the drawbridge that she must cross – and the doorway she must somehow enter. Her dreaming soul knows it is the **threshold** she is afraid to cross. She feels the urge to turn back.

Anna's material body tosses and turns as if all of her is weighing some frightening possibilities. She awakes, drenched in fear. Hurriedly, she gets out of lounge chair, and scurries to the black sheets of the bedroom.

The next morning after almost ample hours of restorative deep sleep, Anna dawns with the awakening of the great outdoors. Her dream-soul feels a malaise. She feels the urge to escape. Hiking seems to heal her childhood wounds and give her a heightened courage. Karen at the Hike House had used the interactive trail finder and picked out 15 hikes that she thought Anna would enjoy and that matched her physical condition. The next morning she had hiked out to the Mystic Trail, another wilderness adventure that starts near Guido's house.

As she walks out of Lomas Serenas, she hears a series of loud clear whistles. She looks up and sees a brilliant Northern Cardinal, with his distinctive red body and crest, and black face mask. He is perched at the tiny tip top of a green pinyon pine. The sun's low morning rays make his red feathers and head crest all the more seductive. He seems to know it. She stops and stares at the creature who with an unflinching voice is welcoming the sun, and certainly courting a mate. She hears a soft song that seems to be answering. A female responding to a male in need.

It was Karen's opinion that it was safe for a woman to hike alone, and Anna relishes being on her own, freed from having to fit in. They say we all have unique thresholds of need for connection, awakened by early experiences. Somehow or other, the city seems to have hardened rules, established mores, and unspoken codes that boxed one in. And add the fact that here she is disconnected from technology and the pestering prospect of being propositioned by some mercenary marketer. Karen did say that some women feel safer with a dog along, but both Karen and Anna agreed that Sedona felt safe.

For the first time in her life, the normally cooped-up city girl is hearing the call of the wild, a new kind of wind singing in her ears. She doesn't feel as tight as she has usually felt in crowded streets or rooms. As she walks into the early light, still with only the bird song and soft, cool breezes for company, she feels the cares of the world falling away. It's as if her inner armor is melting. For a gal born and bred in the close urban quarters, being out in the embrace of the natural environment becomes liberating, a kind of pristine experience. It isn't something she is deliberately looking for or wanting to achieve. The sense of connection just comes, making her understand Einstein's comment: "Look deep into Nature, and you will understand everything better."

As she walks among the trees, the rocks, the scurrying quails, and scampering cottontails, she lets go of burdens she has scarcely been aware of. She continues to carry her self-doubts, but they feel lighter. At times they seem to take flight like a covey of startled quail. At other stretches of the trail, it's almost as if she is doing a carefree, strip-tease walk – throwing a hat away here, dropping a heavy jacket there, releasing a tension in her shoulders here, and forgetting about the pushing crowds back there. She is like a butterfly in search of new nectars. (If you've never felt like a butterfly, you won't appreciate her lightness of heart.) There are no bullies hiding behind the big rocks near the bends in the trail. No nuns staring at her neck. The diverse people, some old, some young, she meets along the trail all smile. "Good morning, have a good hike." "Another beautiful day in paradise." She hasn't encountered one nasty or harried hiker. Nobody physically bumps into you. She senses at the edge of her mind that *Nature* is trying to release a bottled up part of her – an old part that goes back to her days in the schoolyard. Cautiously she appreciates this new *elan vital*. But she is afraid of it also. She can't stay here. She has a job. She could keep the house and come over for vacations. *Right, you don't take vacations.*

Yet, though Nature is a silent partner in the life that, willy-nilly, wants to emerge for her, she has no clear definition of *Nature*. Presently, without being super-scientific about it all, she is leaning toward some kind of semi-animistic force pulling everything toward beauty – like a psychic gravity. (The beauty pull is called *attraction*, a pull like gravity and the other cosmic pulls.) Perhaps, it's a kind of active, ethereal energy in, above, and around the whole flux of life. A little like the unseen, but spiritually perceived energy of the famous vortexes. Amit would have words for what she is experiencing. He might say she was feeling the web of connections.

But *the place* is more than the wilderness; it is a rare melange of the small town thinking, personal community, and the earth house that also embraces the flora, the fauna, and the human as if they all are one – the natural world and the feeling man. The land and the people seem to be of the same stuff.

Karen, the sweet Hike House trail planner, had told her that Sedona has the best access to the grandeur of the world of any city. By one count, there are 170 official trailheads surrounding the town, and a netting of social trails leading out of the neighborhoods. Part of the lore of the place is the vibrant community that gives off an aura of being intent on finding a fuller life. The locals sense that they live in a special space that, wordlessly, teaches ways of listening to the world around. It occurs to Anna that the hikers trek as individuals, but there is something akin to the "swarm mind" of bees that unites them.

The next morning as the sun peeks over the Mogollan Rim, she sets out to hike the Bell Rock Trail. Kai has warned her that Bell is popular, and by ten in the morning droves of seekers in hiking boots, sneakers, and even go-aheads will be eagerly climbing in search of the magical spot that might put some zip into their normally flat lives. Scientifically speaking, she knows that energy escaping from the bowels of the earth is possible, but she isn't sure about the mind stuff. She finds the whole can of worms about what the "mind" is too confusing to open. Even serious scientists have all kinds of new theories. Can the earth energy really affect people in some non-physical way, she wonders? To her own amazement, she is telling herself to keep an open mind. She's wondering if she'll feel a flow of energy up her legs and in through her clefts.

The Sedona region, physically and mentally, is rather beyond the ordinary words that describe the earthly reality as physicists conceive it. What eludes her is the unexplainable goodness in Nature – and the people. The friendly people she meets on the trails keep coming back to her awareness. They are definitely **not** like the oncoming waves of stolid faces she sees on Fifth Avenue. The trail encounters are genuine engagements, meetings that feel like an embrace. The smiles are open, and there is a friendly timbre to the voices.

Her scientific blinkers are being seduced to open. She hasn't decided if the energy of the place can literally get into the people. Nevertheless, she has to admit that she herself is feeling different here. But is that inkling of the presence of a certain goodness real or imagined? She, the trained scientist, just isn't totally ready to accept an invisible presence as factual. Physics should be, she thinks, the science of the material world. She feels like a chameleon that can't decide what color to put forth at any particular moment.

When she returns to Guido House, she takes a quick rinse in the shower. She feels regenerated; her mind stimulated. She puts on the sleeveless, yellow sundress she purchased in a gallery in Tlaqueplaque the day she went to the Hike House. It had been a spur of the moment purchase. A little out of character, but as she looks at herself in the mirror, her spirit is glad she splurged. Her liquid brown eyes even appear clearer, brighter. Below the surf of her awareness, she senses herself surrendering, day by day, hike by hike. In a way she is like a teenage girl being reeled in by a would-be lover. She no longer feels apart from everything. She is becoming part of everything, even if she doesn't put that into those words. She even imagines that her skin has a prettier glow, because of light within that is being coaxed out of the dark shell it has hidden in for so long. Some mornings she feels like singing *The hills are alive with the sound of music.*

On the way to the kitchen to have some lunch, she meets Kai just about to go into her apartment. "Hi Miss Anna, how was your hike?" Kai asks.

"Oh, I loved it. The air here is so pure; the land so unique; the people so friendly."

"It's as it should be. My people say: *Hozho* – being one with the land – brings harmony. We are happy you are finding balance here. We can see it. Nascha says, 'The light inside Miss Anna gets brighter every day.'"

"Thank you, Kai. How is Nascha?"

"She's just fine. She's inside painting. Come in. She'll enjoy your attention."

Anna is amazed; the space is small yet feels comfortable. Everything is immaculate and well cared for. There is an aura of peace in the quiet of the space. Even the kitty-litter box looks well cared for. In the left corner, Nascha is seated on one of those foot-thick tree stumps, painting. Her wide-eyed smile says, Come see. Anna goes over and looks at her painting – a spotted fawn nibbling the low branches of a green tree. The tree is extremely well done, and just beyond the tree is there is a cute orange-yellow five-pointed flower. Nascha is working on it at that moment. Coming from the right side of the flower are faint, light, subtle strokes of white. Anna guesses they are the wind. "I like what you are painting. I think I even see wind." The girl's wide-eyes sparkle, and an innocent smile beams across her light-chocolate face. She exudes pride. "Yes that is _nilch'I_, the Holy Wind. It is in us and in all things." Anna doesn't quite know what to think. She focuses on a faint white stroke in the belly of the fawn and in the trunk of the tree. Something in her wants respond positively. It's a beautiful thought, one Amit would agree with. But her science chains keep her mouth from going there.

"What's that flower you are working on?"

"It's a squash blossom," Nascha beams "Special to our old people. Mama, says it is a symbol of the cycle of life. A flower blooms, then dies. Mama says the seed falls into the ground and then grows again. Papa Guido gave Mama a squash-blossom necklace for her thirty birthday. Silver and turquoise. She has never worn it since that first night. I know she loves it and sometimes takes it out to look at, especially now that Papa Guido is no longer here." Nascha's face clouds over. Anna intuits that the young girl doesn't quite know what to make of death, any more than she does. "I was not allowed to see Papa Guido after he died in the hospital" Nascha says sadly. "The old people say it is bad luck to look upon a dead one."

Anna's mind returns to the hospital and the demon of death. Per Guido's written will, there was no funeral ceremony, no prayers, no flowers, and no eulogies. His body was cremated. Kai, alone, took his ashes out into the wilderness. Only the Navajo woman knew his written wish about where he wanted his ashes scattered. Anna had been relieved, and miffed, that she had not been included, and thought it was a terrible burden to put on Kai. Yet she knew Kai's strength, and imagined her walking in that chosen sanctum, courageously chanting some Navajo blessing, with tears streaming down her brown cheeks. If Anna were real clever, she might be able to find the place in one of her uncle's paintings. People leave clues despite themselves. But she felt that Guido had wanted to go into the unknown, in a private way, walking alone as he often did.

In the upper left sky of Nascha's painting, the sun is smiling, and soft rays of gentle light stream down onto the fawn, the tree, and the squash-blossom. An irregular shaped slab of red rock leaning against the wall next to Nascha catches Anna's eye. As she starts to look away from the open-center squash blossom, she realizes it is almost as sensual as a Georgia O'Keefe flower – and created by a child, still far from being a finished female. Is one ever finished, a soft voice in her asks? The rock slab leaning on the wall bears white painted letters: *In silence, beauty comes."* Nascha sees her gaze, "Papa Guido painted that for me. He had good eyes. He saw so many things."

A rush of pride rustles in Anna's heart. Her Uncle Guido had done something sweet for this little Navajo spirit in his last years. He had given her a gift more precious than the rock slab, or even a turquoise necklace. He had given her a piece of himself, and an appreciation of seeing what's all around. Some yawning feminine part of her stirs: It dawns, like dawn does, moment by moment, more little light within for more visibility. Her inner spirit is willing to admit that she has not done much for another in her life. She has been too busy avoiding hurt. The shards of hurt are buried in Everyman. Below her firing-mind, she knows that she is, in a sense, a failure. She is not a full human.

As another day gathers over the red rock horizon, the goddess Aurora is seated in the great ambiance on a large red boulder, waiting for her burnished consort to rise into the domicile made of dawn. Indoors, in the house of the hermit painter, the arousing warm water from a showerhead cascades down over the dark brown hair, firm breasts, and intimate secrets of an increasingly mixed-up, yet also increasingly emerging female. Guardedly, she feels in her deep tissue that she is on the frontier of escaping from a grindstone life. But her heart is too timorous to accept it. She wonders, *Who am I anyways?* She wraps her two arms about herself – frightened by the blurry road ahead.

Part of her knows that she has to face the road that beckons. She remembers reading in that space novel about a shower that Ava the Andromeda took with the gentle man from Iowa, and a quote from Christopher Reeve's naturopathic teacher: "To be able to feel the lightest touch is really a gift." She knows she is beginning to feel in Nature. She is feeling the pelt of the water. What alarms her is that her gut doesn't feel ready for all of this change. Her gut is still a disaster zone.

As she towels dry, her mind is anticipating the trail leading up to Doe Mountain. Anna finds herself relishing more and more destinations that open up into vast new spaces. For years, she has, without consciously picking up on it, been felt completely closed up, as if she were in a box. The bullies had reduced her to a frightened object. She slips into her delicate wear, grabs the hairdryer, drops her head, drapes her tresses down, to blow her hair dry. In minutes, she throws her head and her brown locks back, eager to be out on the trail. The trails work like an aphrodisiac. She spies her image in the mirror. An okay-yes-for-today, girlish smile races across her face; she cautiously recognizes the woman in the mirror, yet the woman looks different. It's her, but not the old her.

The trail climbing up Doe Mountain is a little scary – a lot of rocky switchbacks, a lot of moments when you can't see the path ahead, a lot of turns where someone could jump out to hurt you. Fleetingly, she wonders if she should be doing this trail alone. But she quickly recalls that these fears are the ghosts of fears past.

A half-hour later, she reaches the slick-rock chute that is the threshold onto the mesa top. She shimmies up into the freedom of a fresh perspective, and she experiences a surge of joy and liberation. Standing on the flat top mesa with a 360-degree panorama of red hills and green forests, she is vaguely aware of the freshly oxygenated blood coursing through her body. Hiking is good for all of her layers – spirit, mind, body. She makes a circle of the mesa top, stopping to drink in the azure background, and the foreground of land, town, and houses. Finally, she heads back down to the house she can't call home.

That afternoon Kai's prepares a lunch of fruit salad and slices of avocado misted with lemon juice. After lunch, Anna wanders into her uncle's studio, not knowing exactly why, but feeling beckoned, as if the room had a come-hither finger. She sits on the little stool near the *Ghost Tree* canvas. Her eyes wander around the room – a stack of finished paintings, (*How do I handle them? They must be worth a goodly sum.*) The brushes, palettes, and canvases seem to be calling to her: *Pick me up. Handle me. Make me useful.* Her changing woman wonders: Could I too be an artist? Is it in the Pagani gene pool? A worry line contracts her forehead. She shakes her head *no.* She is a physicist. She finds all these subtle suggestions to change disturbing.

Anna stays there a couple of hours, lost in perplexing her life, her future, and her potentials. When she finally wanders out of Guido's space, feeling a little spacey herself, Kai appears. Anna senses that it isn't by accident. Kai knows more than her chants. Kai must have intuited what was happening to the woman immersed in the deep mists of a lone psyche in a new scape.

"Tonight is a special night in Sedona: *The First Friday Art Walk.*" Kai explains that it is a monthly tradition in this celebrated art destination. Several galleries, including the flagship Sedona Art Center host art receptions, with refreshments and free trolley transportation. Anna gets the hint. She respects Kai's remarkable discernment, something one learns from the land. She decides she should go. The off-the-wall fantasy about herself and an art gene may have tickled her inner feathers. And besides, perhaps she might meet someone who can advise her on what to do about her uncle's paintings. And she just might meet someone interesting.

Back in the late '50's, some visionary Sedona artists had a dream of a creative hub where artists could come and work together, inspire one another, and teach the starry-eyed beginners. It would be an artists' haven. They held a benefit dinner for a couple of dollars to raise money for the original "art barn." Practically all the 2,500 locals came. The spirit of creativity surfaced into the warp and woof of the land of ancient changing.

Once inside the Sedona Arts Center, Anna finds herself like the farm girl from Liberal, Kansas in a magical world of colorful paintings, glazed pottery, silver jewelry, ornate glass mirrors, carved earthen sculptures, and striking landscape photography. She feels small and overwhelmed at the diversity of talent. A young woman offers her some vegetable crudities, which she takes on a small plate to calm her nerves.

As she wanders around looking at the paintings, mentally comparing them with Guido's and Nascha's, she comes upon a painting by a Cassandra Gee. A sinking feeling drops in her stomach. Cassandra – Cassie…the name opens a wound in Anna's heart. She had seen a woman in the floral section of the produce department at the food market. She was holding up at arms-length a sprig of oranges flowers. She was surprised at how intensely focused the woman's concentration was. The woman seemed lost in the flowers. Anna's eyes had gone to the sign on the bin near the lady: edible flowers for salads. She discerned that the painter's eye sees beauty that most busy people miss. Nascha had said something about Uncle Guido's ability to see.

A few minutes later at the checkout stand, she found herself standing behind the flower woman and heard the checkout girl say, "Good morning, Cassandra. How's the painting going?" When Cassandra introduced herself, and pleasantly wished her a good afternoon, Anna flashed back a smile. She was beginning to enjoy meeting people.

The painting on the Art Center wall is *Turnips*. Anna thinks the red of the turnip is too deep, too red. The older lady standing next to her in the Art Center remarks, "She has certainly captured the essence of turnip-ness, hasn't she? She's can see beyond what ordinary eyes see. It's a kind of intense-yet-diffuse focus that makes a gifted artist."

As Anna continues strolling around, she notices an impressive couple that she has seen somewhere in Lomas Serenas. The man interests her. He's tall with that straight up and down look, but a touch of sadness in his face. There are even what appear to be some same sex couples. Her aloneness begins to weigh on her. No way does she feel like an artist. She is a dumb scientist and still the outsider. At least some mornings, she feels paid attention to by Nature, her new mother. She leaves the gallery shortly after seeing the tall couple.

The developer of Lomas Serenas had envisioned an environmentally friendly and naturally beautiful enclave, with open green spaces, building guidelines, and no rag-tag mail boxes along the streets. Therefore, next to the tennis courts at the end of the clubhouse parking lot, the square, silver mailboxes of the residents are gathered, tastefully uniform, shaded by a big mesquite tree. It's like a watering hole where the animals all come together – another threshold for the social dimension. Kai had asked Anna to stop and check the mail on her way back from her morning hike. Nascha had an upset stomach. There at the gathering spot, Anna meets Sally and Brad Stevens and Sally's sister Gwen Dyksta on their way home after hiking the Bear Mountain trail. She recognizes the tall couple from the Arts Center reception. She feels somehow drawn to the serious man. At the local level, Sedona is a small, small world.

They all bond. Brad is a scientist. Sally, fetching in her ecru hiking ensemble and gray-and-red hiking boots, is patently a people person, as well as a mover and shaker. She pronto invites Anna to a dinner party at her house two weeks down the road. Gwen mentions that she is thinking of going up to the Grand Canyon the next day, and asks Anna if she'd ever been there.

"The Grand Canyon? Is it that close?"

"Less than two hours if you drive like I do," Gwen responds. (Sally rolls her eyes.) "It's worth it. Come along if you'd like. I always feel the numinous there. (Anna isn't familiar with the word *numinous*.) Lunch on the veranda at the lodge is one of those special places that let your mind walk in space."

Anna smirks to herself. Her specialty is cosmological physics. She has written a peer-reviewed paper on one of the Galilean satellites around the planet Jupiter named after the astronomer Galileo Galilei. Her cognitive mind has indeed done a lot of space walking. She is also well aware that she can have a bright future in the cosmos of material physics. What she doesn't know for sure is whether she still wants that world. She is beginning to wonder. But what does she have as a viable option? Nothing. *Nada* right now. Her uncle's house doesn't feel like an option for her. She realizes that her physical self and her routine mind haven't explored much more than a few Fifth Avenue deli's.

"Wow, I'd love to, Gwen. I saw some paintings at the Art Center. It looks fantastic."

Gwen picks her up at 6:30 the next morning. As they drive up the winding 89A, Anna is surprised at how relaxed she is. She has never before been on a road with so many hairpin switchbacks. Adventures like this usually would have brought on heart palpitations – fears of the uncertain. But she is okay with this bit of doing the different.

Gwen points to the left, "That's the West Fork Trailhead parking lot. It's a spectacular box canyon with a symphony of colors, sounds, and secrets, especially in the fall. Zane Gray wrote about it; the canyon seemed to have called to him. If you get a chance, don't miss it this fall." Then, as they head out of Flagstaff, the San Francisco Peaks looming on the horizon, Gwen explains that those hoary peaks are sacred to the Navajo people. "One of the four corners of their world."

"My uncle had – we have a wonderful Navajo housekeeper."

"Yes, my sister Sally knows her and her wide-eyed daughter. Sally says Kai is one of the most dedicated mothers she has ever seen. I think the Native Americans know many things we have forgotten, or never learned. Insights they learned from the land. Sally and I, on the other hand, grew up with a strict mother – who loved to clean. We called her the Old Dutch Cleanser. I guess that's why I hate to clean, and revel in a messy apartment."

Anna half-giggles. "I'm a little like your mother. My peasant mother was the same. Her whole life was compulsive cleaning, cooking, and laundry. My apartment in Manhattan is small, and I'm a scientist. We like to have our ducks always in a row. No unaccounted for changes. No surprises. So, it's squeaky clean."

"Will you be going back to Manhattan?"

"Oh, don't ask. And right now with this beauty, I can't tell. If you had asked me weeks ago when I first arrived, I'd have said "yes" without batting an eyelash. But, now, gosh, I don't know, something is going on in me – in my mind, and even in my body. I don't know what it is. But, you know, it feels good, feels right. Or as Kai says *"As it should be."* It feels too good to be early menopause. God, I feel…"

"The fever," Gwen says.

Anna doesn't understand, and is uneasy talking about her unclear future. She changes the subject. "Is Sedona your permanent home, Gwen?"

Gwen looks over at the cute city-slicker next to her. She likes her. *Permanent? What's permanent, anymore?* The girl is transparent. She may not have "street smarts," but she wouldn't hurt a fly. It's no wonder that she admires the Navajo earth mother. Stripped of all the overlays of culture, they both, Anna and Kai, are female peas in a pod. Gwen herself is enjoying the female sharing. Something in her is tired of listening to lonely men at the bar. She knows what they think they want, which isn't actually what we all really want. It's merely animal. And her successful younger sister Sally knows every page of her story backwards and forwards, and probably doesn't appreciate it all. So, Gwen's hormones are in the mood to talk to a woman.

"I don't know. I'm happy here. I understand what you said about something working in you that you have no words for. This particular place has a way of getting in your blood. In other places, you can have recently escaped from the disappointment of tryst in the sac, only to find yourself hitch-hiking toward the next disappointment. Seems like one is always on the way out of what was, without even knowing where one wants to go. Here one can have a failed day, and wake up, and look at the mountains, and think, *Still there*. And thank your lucky stars that you still are alive, and safe here.

"Funny thing is I've got this one lonely guy who comes in to the bar from time to time. Drinks vodka tonics. I think he's from San Francisco, and he loves to talk about the pair-bond. He claims it was the secret of our becoming human. He's handsome, a scholar type. Half the time I can't follow his train of thought, but I get a gut feeling that what he's trying to say might just be on target. And as I remember from high school Sunday school:

the Greek word for sin, *harmatia,* means 'missing the target.' I kind of like the guy, though he might be too into his head for me. He seems so sincere. I don't think he's ready for a breathy relationship. Some days I'm tempted to up the charm. I could use a little panting. He's a decent option. There a few bad options loose in this town. Unfortunately, I know that."

"So you're not married. Were you ever married? If you don't mind my asking," Anna asks timidly. She's not sure if she knows enough about marriage to wade into that mysterious maze. Maybe she should stop before she's in deeper than she can handle.

"No, I'm not. Was I almost? More times than I care to remember, city girl. Will I ever? To level with you, I sort of hope so. I've come to the sneaking suspicion that serious relating is **the real** reality show. The problem, if you don't mind my saying so, is that relationship is so damn risky in this culture where infidelity has become almost a locust plague. But as our dear Mexican cook, Dolores, used to say: *El que no se arriesga, no cruce el mar* (The one who doesn't risk himself, doesn't cross the sea).

Anna is struck by Gwen's words: "the real reality show." She hasn't watched many, if any, so-called reality shows. As a scientist in the discipline that tries to explain reality, she's turned off by the shallow use of the word. To her, reality is a weighty word, a scientific word. Still, Gwen's yoking of reality and relationship stirs something up in her insides. Amit and John Wheeler loved to tout: *information.* Anna's mind drops into a kind of mental whirlpool: *information, relationship, entanglements, bits of the all.* Nothing is clear, but she knows there is a something to yoking relationship with what Amit was getting at when he talks about information.

Gwen takes her to the Shoshone Point trail on the South Rim. She chooses it because it showcases the drama of the Canyon with its colorful buttes, mesas, spires, and foaming rapids. Shoshone isn't one of the longer trails, and Gwen figures a gal from Manhattan might not be ready to hike at a 7,300 foot elevation. Gwen herself loves the trail. The Canyon's very presence seems to untie her knots, and she can sense that Anna is also in the process of untying some old tight knots.

The trail, a dirt road, wanders through a cool, dense stand of sweet smelling conifers, and leads out to some cliffs that form a narrow promontory jutting out from the plateau. The 180 degree overview of what looks like the entire Grand Canyon is awe-inspiring, and for Anna almost heart stopping. It feels like they are really high, but actually the canyons are deep all the way to the Colorado River.

"Let's sit for a few minutes," Gwen says, indicating some flat white, granite slabs, back a safe distance from the edge. "This is one of my favorite meditation spots. Here my mind can soar like an eagle and float on the updrafts, leaving behind the troubles and the men woes my mind loves to muck around in. Here I can escape from my routines and ruts. It's as if the grandeur calls me out of myself."

Anna has never officially meditated, but she is on the edge of understanding what Gwen means. She feels a little like she is meditating when her tight mind, begins to loosen up on the hike trails. It is like breaking out of a shell or shedding some robot-like joints. She overheard one of the young coeds in the Hike House use the expression, "the wilderness orgasm." Looking out over the peaceful beauty of the canyon, she does feel an inner surge of pleasurable excitement.

As she sits there, watching Gwen close her eyes and join her finger tips in her lap, Anna looks out into the mystical canyon. Claudia, the bosomy nurse who cared for her uncle those last days, had laughed at him for calling himself an atheist. "He was a passionate man," those were her words. "He was passionate about the presence of goodness in the rocks, the trees, the animals. 'Beauty is God's garment. Everything is joined to everything in harmony,'" she said, quoting him. "He was a Nature mystic."

For lunch, Anna orders the Caesar salad with pan-fried Colorado River trout and a glass of herbal ice tea. Gwen has the Angus beef burger, with a side of cactus strips, and a bottle of Corona beer. Anna eyes the cactus strips, but she is unsure of herself, and too shy to ask for a taste. She never heard of eating cactus. Sane people don't eat cactus in the city. Sounds primitive. The trout tastes fresher than she has ever tasted. She wonders how long ago the dear trout was alive and swimming free. She feels guilty, yet grateful to the trout, as if the trout had some kind of consciousness and even feelings.

The day is still warm; the sun softening in the west. Gwen unlooses her braided hair and runs her hand through her still full blonde mane. Liberated, and unwinding, she says, "Sorry, I talked so much on the way up. I guess I'm slipping down onto a burn-out shelf. I dig those poor guys who come in to have a drink and bare their hearts. They are like strays. They make me feel almost maternal. I suspect there are more ways of being maternal than those Italian paintings of babes at the breast suggest. Loneliness comes in many shades, doesn't it? I've seen a lot of the dark, hurting spectrum. But hey, girl, I haven't been treated to your story. It's your turn." Squeezing a lime into her Corona beer, Gwen is passing the talking stick to Anna.

Anna pauses, her temples tightening, as she debates opening up. She's not used to that. A gentle zephyr of pine scent cools the moment. (Gwen, the experienced barmaid, waits, knowing that the cogs of the city girl's heart are engaging.) "Okay, fair is fair. And I'm here, not yet back there." Anna responds, feeling a stir of sisterhood. She follows suit, and loosens her hair, letting her brown tresses fall on her nervous shoulders.

"I was born in the Bronx of working-class immigrant Italian parents. I was born with this obvious birthmark on my neck. At school, I was bullied a lot and withdrew into a protective curl. I'm just beginning, here in this land of different energy, to admit all of this to myself. Most of my life, I felt deeply disenfranchised. The only road out of the hurt seemed to be excelling at something intellectual, something in the man's world. But my self-image, my *who-am-I?* never escaped that Bronx schoolyard. I dedicated all my energy to achieving. And achieve I did, for what it's all worth. But, in a sense, I didn't exist. I had no real feeling self. I became a sleepwalker of secular science. There are a lot of us in drab white lab coats.

"And then came **that scary call.** Like the zombie I'd become, I responded and found myself in the room with a dying kinsman. I saw the soul of someone of my own bloodline slipping poof away. Going where? I couldn't face that question. I don't handle the airy questions well. But now, that fabled hound of heaven (she wishes she could remember that poet's name) pursues me, out into Nature. It's wonderful. It sort of feels like I'm running away from something, and Nature is opening her arms to embrace me. Once this week out on Mystic Trail, I cried, leaning my head on a ponderosa much older and wiser than I. I let something flow. Tasting the salt of uncertainty, I knew the tears were birthing tears. And I knew there were many more tears still in captivity."

Gwen nods, and reaches across the table to lay her hand on Anna's hand.

"As you certainly must know, the peace of the woods invites one to open up to herself," Anna goes on. "I'm tempted to say that Nature is twisting my arm to face myself. It's like an invitation, but more like a summons to RSVP. The noise of the city, on the other hand, requires a certain sheltering – a closing down or is it a closing up? In college, I found a safe place in physics and the data of the universes. The universes are a trip beyond wild. It often amazes me that people don't stand in awe more. Of course, I didn't have much time for that back then. Nowadays people seem so star-struck with those skinny celebrity gals, who wax their wares, and glow in the footlights of attention."

"I have to agree, girl. Few of us get to grab the brass ring of reality. Few of us get to savor what people call *the real thing*. Yet, something in us dreams. My sister Sally and her husband Brad are working at it. I'm jealous. For all that I am not; I **am** a believer in sledding on."

"We can't count my days with seven-year-old Billy and his Teddy," Anna says, barely aware of her deep need, and deeply appreciating that a woman is listening to her stories. "Oh, eventually back in my curious college years, I got taken to bed. (Anna pauses, lost in the hallways of her youth.) I've tasted the heat of the night, but never the warmth of real love. Recently, a handsome Indian physicist and I are, were close. I can't say he loved me, though I wanted him to. He went to India to make the world safe for wayward girls. Perhaps, I wanted a man to take me seriously, make me feel appreciated. My father didn't. Amit came close, but he didn't cross that invisible line."

Gwen squeezes her hand. "I understand. All of us women want to be accepted as valuable. Maybe that's why we like to wear gold and silver and smell pretty. We want to be chosen and taken to a safe home. We want to be apprised as different but equal. Is that in the constitution?" she asks, as the Native American waiter arrives with the check. Anna insists on paying, but is not clear about why she feels so grateful. Maybe it was just being listened to.

The chain of events and encounters that would change my life had begun back in 2008, that dark cloudy glitch in time of the subprime mortgage crisis. That was the year the stock market tanked and Lehman Brothers filed Chapter 11, the biggest bankruptcy in US history. I didn't own a lot of stock, but emotionally, I was already bankrupt. It's easy to forget that Man has been *Homo economicus,* for only the last ten thousand years when he began to harvest and hoard his own crops. That was the dawn of the wealth class: *It's not ours anymore. It's mine!* That economic/financial collapse at the end of the Bush era totally tipped my scales of justice. Justice had been a Malachy household holy word. It was one of the pillars of the biblical perspective. I was thrown from my horse.

In a matter of months, I sold a house and traded-in a lifestyle. I bought a house here in Sedona, and, willy-nilly, embarked on a new style of life. After a short escrow, I started walking the night streets of Lomas Serenas on my first night here in April of 2009. Ever since Allie's suicide, I hadn't been sleeping well. Nonetheless, the star-winking sky in Sedona seduced me off my feet. I'd never felt so surrounded by the arms of the universe as on that milestone night when the Milky Way washed over me in all her silent acceptance. I was defenseless. I was unknowingly ready to be snared by a canny young backcountry thirty-some year-old from the Volunteer State. She would be a close encounter of the third kind that pointed my life in a new direction. For reasons no one could possibly capture in words, her message lodged deeply into my heart. The wise men like to say that when the student is ready, the teacher will appear. Funny thing is I didn't know I was ready. Now a few years later, I'm somewhere in the back stretch, stretching and striding, and perhaps moving up on something. Sometimes, especially out in the natural wilderness, I feel like *I can beat being a loser. I can stop being a loner.*

Catherine, the realtor's partner, is a frequent interloper into my bucking mind. I dream of her as a manifestation of the mysterious and gynous. Both were energies that seemed to be asking to be the new guide rails to my track ahead. I wasn't even aware of how much I wanted a woman like her by my side. You don't forget a real woman. As I furtively look around for her in the stores and on the trails, don't I even know for sure if she is committed to Bob Dorian. Maybe she is just temporarily living with him. Nor do I clearly know what I want in a relationship. Maybe I just don't have the courage to approach her. Albeit, I'm hoping that when I see my Lady Right, I'll know her. Romance doesn't seem to be part of my make-up. Physical sex, yes. That madness comes with the original equipment.

I awakened one night around that time to the pit-a-pat, pit-a-pat of hail on the acrylic bathroom skylight. Mid-January, the heart of the other rainy season, the one we think of as feminine. I fall back asleep, and awake again around 4:30 am. I've heard the hail before, a friendly harbinger of precipitation – rain, and on rare occasions, snow. Excited, I get up and go barefoot to the window. Snow! It's white everywhere. The world is winter white with softly falling, straight-down, fluffy flakes. The boughs of the white flocked pines are reverently bowed in salute to the white benefactor. I recall the words of the poet: *We are all snowflakes. We look alike, but each is crafted unique. We are small, but together part of one big snowfall. Experiences craft us.* I roast a cup of coffee, and return to the window, hypnotized by the feeling of being captured in the oneness of nature.

By 6:30 the gray fog is lifting and the mosaic of red cliffs, green forests, and silvery, meadows beckons. Dressed in my navy blue pea-coat, knit pea-cap, and Ecco boots, I walk out into the church-like-hush, the snow absorbing the morning sounds and reflecting the dim light off the snow-white earth. Six to eight inches is as good as snow gets in Sedona. A trail of two-toed, upside-down heart shaped tracks reminds me that I'm not alone in this wonder. I am a bit of something bigger. The whoosh and thud of a clump of snow falling from a tree speaks to the transience of us snowflakes. My Hopi contractor talked about the *manifest* and the *manifesting* being one. I didn't understand. Standing in the virgin snow, I understand that the material and the mental are of one cloth.

That evening go out for my walk, tired, but at peace. The snow has mostly melted away except for shaded patches between trees. My memory melts me back to one of those other first night walks: That night the stars are in hiding, behind the clouds. I'm alone. The sky is moonless. The world is so silent it's scary. I don't know a soul in Lomas Serenas. An unfamiliar energy wriggles through my body. I'm in need of breaking out of an old shell. I can almost feel it in my bones. I'd rarely been in the wilds at night. I'm scared silly, yet my innocence feels like shouting "Yes. Yes." But I can't. I'm too taut. I don't trust that what I'm doing is what I should be doing. I'm a teen boy who has jumped off a cliff into a river that he doesn't know if he can handle.

But tonight, a few years later, taking my usual night amble, I know that some mysterious flow is taking me to a shore beyond. I've been reading and thinking a lot about trust. I'm sure many of you would agree that trust may be the keystone that holds the arch of Man from falling in upon itself. Jean Amery, the philosopher of Auschwitz, wrote about the aftershocks of torture and rape. Violence traumatizes one's sense of being a secure self in a social place where one can trust. He was born Hans Maier. After his prison ordeal, he changed his name, hoping to find a self who could trust again. Once a self has been reduced to an object, it is a rough journey to trust others. But the magic of the land seems to be leading me. I feel a kind of trust budding.

As I pass the Stevens' house, I see the soft blue, television light in the window that I suspect to be their bedroom. I imagine them side my side watching their weekly Netflix. I can just see Brad arm outstretched between them cradling one of Sally's hands. They are a nice couple. Now, after all these night walks, I enjoy seeing the lights on in the other houses. I haven't been all that outgoing, but the neighbors have opened their arms to me despite my reclusive ways, and my weakness for solitary wine. Alone in the dark except for the occasional soft hoots of my friend the owl, I feel the hole in my heart. My heart wants somebody special in my life, yet my mind doesn't venture to bring that to my here-and-now consciousness. The quotidian wavelengths are too full of talk. Maybe I lack the pluck to change.

It was on a night like this after the rains that I was so agitated by Professor Czismali's warning about extinctions. His words had fallen upon open soil that already feared that our human culture sinking into savagery. And God didn't seem to care. Some days I wonder whether He has given up on *H. sapiens*. But now my heart is becoming more trusting. Some mornings I walk without wording, just letting the world in –well, at least for short squibs of awareness. I'm quite sure that my readings about the history of cultural evolution and my reflections in the woods are opening some fresh inner eyes. I don't fret as much about "God" or my individual immortality. I feel a certain faint trust that I can make a contribution to Mankind's march ahead. I'll die, eventually. My molecules will fall back into the earth. What the Tennessee hill Buddha and her readings have taught me is that each of us is called to contribute bits of clear and kind mind – to the evolving, collective consciousness of *H. sapiens*. Of course, you may not read that in your local Sunday paper. But I intend to strive toward that vocation. I now believe that if I fail to contribute, I'll pass on unfulfilled. I'll have failed the call to help *Mankind* become more human. That's the only way I can contribute to "God's greater glory." The notion of saving the soul of the planet is a kind of new, ticking beatific vision. I'm nibbling. Not much else out there. The Humpty Dumpty's of the ecclesial worlds are wobbling wounded.

As I reach the south gate of our subdivision, I look down Via de la Valle. Gwen lives down that street in the Sunset condominiums, as does Caitlin Feeney. The call of that street surges. My hormones hope for the silhouette of a woman behind a lace curtain. I know my body/psyche feels drawn to that battle field, where the macho side of the sexual tango wants to be rapacious, while the softer side tilts an ear to be non-harming. Being truly human is challenging, isn't it? I experience a thrust one might call *the bud of trust.* I've given up trying to understand the presence of some higher power. Those details and the words have washed away with the tides of the times. My eyes are opening to perceive the universes, my planet, my species, and my self.

The chariot of my mind races on ranting that the march of Man has been an epic of blasts, break-ups, and make-ups. For billions of years, cosmic forces clashed, then came together in collaboration, and gave birth to our girl, Gaia. Gaia eventually brought forth an offshoot of the primate ancestor. And here we are: *H. sapiens.* Wind blowing in the mind, isn't it? Holy Hannah, this whole mega game we call "evolution" is a tremendous video slide show: hunter-gathers, village chiefdoms, kings and states, armies and empires, Romans and sacking barbarians, the dark times of the middle ages, the rise of science, the explosion of conquest, the shame of slavery, worlds of war and then *Curiosity* touches down on Mars. Yet *Sapiens* continues to wrestle a zigzag trail. Many zag, and blot out their pain with drugs and addictions. I snort at myself; I'm no paragon of strength. Others trust that there is open road ahead. I have weaknesses. I want to be in that brigade of minded kindness that challenges the Dark Side. Siddhartha might nod: *right intention.*

My walk brings me to Zack Taylor's house. There a soft light in the upstairs window. I remember Gwen's words about bad options afoot in this frontier town. I whisper my mantra: *May all creatures, especially women, be freed from the causes of suffering, past, present, and future. May I make a contribution to* ***Ongoing Man*** That's what matters, our real bottom line.

A couple of days after Anna hiked the grandest canyon that the currents of the Colorado River had carved, the weather turned unseasonably hot. Anna hiked early one burnished morning, just as the dawn was spreading out her multihued fingertips. After two hours, the sky was sun bleached, and the russet monoliths glowed like mirrors of time. Her body, moist with honest perspiration, felt alive and luxuriant. It was a dry heat, comfortably different from the muggy heat of the City.

When she walked into the kitchen, Kai was humming one of her Navajo chants. The kitchen wafted of lavender. Kai's lavender bread was becoming one of Anna's fresh new delights. She had never been into the world called *yummy.* Seeing Anna's flushed, moist face, the baking lady smiled broadly. "Indian summer," she said, nodding knowingly, and then mentioning the pool at the Lomas clubhouse.

Anna had never even gone into the clubhouse. She wasn't interested in meeting people whom she would soon be leaving. She did like the Stevens, and would probably go to Sally's party, even though part of her was hemming and hawing about that too. She felt restless. Perhaps, she thought, it's this heat. Perhaps it's the thought of going home and air-conditioning. She didn't like air-conditioning, but it was a fact of New York life she accepted and expected. She decided to walk over to the clubhouse. It was too hot to sit out in the back yard and read; and she was antsy, for reasons she couldn't put her finger on, but sensed. She knew about the late Friday afternoon wine and cheese get-togethers. She didn't like wine; in fact she had a deep seated fear of alcohol. She'd seen girls in college get silly and sloppy when they drank. They made themselves vulnerable. And then there was the Cassie tragedy.

The main room of the clubhouse was a big, high ceiling space with sofas and upholstered chairs arranged around a large stone fireplace. The whole side wall of tall windows looked out at the warm scarlet mountains and the cool blue water of the pool. Anna had never learned to swim, and she certainly wasn't about to buy a swimming suit for a few dips before she went back. But it did look cool and inviting. She watched a slender woman with short black hair climb out of the pool. She looked in very good shape, but Anna was shocked at her scanty red bikini and skimpy halter top. Boy, that gal believes in advertising, Anna thought to herself. She could not imagine being so exposed, and only vaguely understood why women need to attract attention. Sure, she knew the laws of attraction. She wasn't really versed in the rubrics of distraction.

Later, walking home from the clubhouse, she passed an impressive two story house. A red convertible with a *Real Wom* license plate was pulling up the driveway. She recalled Gwen saying something about the "big two-story house." She couldn't remember what she said, but somehow she caught the impression that Gwen had been in that house. Her mind fell into a vivid flashback of their trip home from the canyon: Dusk was beginning to fall between the trees. Anna feels tired. "Watch for the elk. They come out this time of day," Gwen says in a loud voice into the subdued afternoon wind.

Anna remembers, perking up, "Golly, I've never seen an animal in the wild, just in a zoo."

"They're wild, damn straight. Sally took me with her on a guided hike with the Park Service during the mating season last year. The ranger knew the perfect spot downwind on a bluff above a forest meadow where a harem of females in heat had gathered for the rut. It reminded me of a hopping sports bar in Omaha. Talk about rutting. Even before we saw them, we heard the bull elks bugling. That's what they call it. It's a low bellow rising to a high screeching, like a whistle, followed by a series of defying grunts. It's one of the loudest mating calls in the world of us beasts. Those animal guys are defending their trophies – their twenty or so females. (Eat your heart out, Zack, Gwen mumbled silently.)

"We saw a challenger come up to a ruling stud. He let out a fierce bugle and soon the two bulls were butting antlers. The ranger said that sometimes they lock horns, can't get unhooked, and die from fatigue and eventually starvation. Oh, men, so silly-dilly, aren't they? That day the heftier challenger broke one antlers of the incumbent alpha.

"And you probably guessed it, once the challenger was the new man in the meadow, he strutted about, stalking and sniffing behinds. Finally one female in estrus, arched her back, spread her legs, and twitched her hocks, signaling that she was ready, and had chosen him to father her next. He slid his chin, neck, and chest on her back, entered her, and suddenly threw his head and neck back, bellowed, and bounded into her, leaving the ground almost a foot. She staggered, back still arched, pulled away and wandered off to lie down. The ranger explained that the dramatic forest moment we had observed is known as "the copulatory jump."

"Even as I remember the scene, I shudder," Gwen said in a vulnerable voice. "I mean it was all about males fighting for dominance over the rights to *do it* to the gals. Ah, woman as commodity, as *it*. Still, what I found most interesting was the ranger's statement that the females have freedom of choice. They decide who does *it* to them. They control. I snicker every time I think about those big guys armed with antlers who think they are calling the shots."

Walking in the late afternoon heat, Anna recalls feeling wiped out emotionally when she gets to what she insisted on calling "Guido's House." After hiking into the heat and seeing a needy woman in skimpy red bikini, she's bummed, bordering on anger, an emotion rare in her heart. Bikinis, she thought, are for teeny boppers who beg for attention.

Kai had made her a cold vichyssoise soup with some ginger root, a cold ahi tuna salad, and a little wicker basket of lavender fry bread chips. Anna caught the tangy aroma of ginger, which she loved. It seemed to calm the turbulence in her stomach. Her mother used to put pieces of ginger root in many of her tomato sauces. She missed her mother.

She takes a cold shower and slips into her white, to-the-knees nightwear. The silk feels friendly on her refreshed body. She takes her prepared tray out to her 'homecoming spot' in the back courtyard, enjoying the aroma of ginger. The Milky Way is spectacularly on display. Anna's mind knows the names of most of the constellations, but she can't shake the strong conviction of the brown skinned man from Mumbai: *Words, words, we ruin everything with words. They are just labels.* She eats her soup slowly, still seeing the lady in the red bikini. She wonders about herself and her own sex energy. Maybe it is frozen down after all these years. She sits back, and gazes up into the endless mystery of existence that peoples and religions have named and renamed since the beginning of man-time. She is slipping across a line into the zone of the *more pensive.*

Her appreciation, okay, her love for, Amit is ripening. Her heart is opening. She now accepts that he is a sincere man of reflection, who has heard his life's call, and is responding. Naturally, part of her hates his being so damn open and courageous. Back in the concrete jungle, she felt betrayed. Here in the living world, as Kai says, the land brings out a healthy balance. She feels a little less self-centered. In an unspoken sense, she's getting over herself. Her childhood knots are unwinding. Still, she fears that she will not have the courage to make the kind of response that Amit has made.

She wants to go home to the big polished Apple where she didn't feel so many emotions. All these images of animals in heat, women parading their finer parts in bikinis, and bull elks fighting over females are draining her energy. She wishes she had a good science fiction novel to distract her. They probably didn't even sell them in artsy Sedona.

Just as she is about to fall into the rabbit's dream hole, Kai comes out with small dish of homemade ice cream. Anna takes a taste, as much to be polite as needing more calories. "It's delicious." Kai beams with the achievement of having pleased her. Kai likes her.

"Peaches?" Anna asks. Kai nods. "Apples?" Kai smiles yes. And something else?"

"Mangos," Kai responds, with a shy note of pride.

After Kai leaves, Anna feels a warm sensation around her heart. Cassie loved ice cream. When she was in the throes of stress, the girl with calypso would sit on her bed and eat a pint of rocky road right from the container. Of course, she'd go on a save-the-hips diet the next day.

Anna had tasted love when she lived with Cassie; and now she recalls that subtle taste of love living with Kai and Nascha. As her mind wanders, wondering if Cassie might still be alive somewhere out there, a new muse whispers to her: A trust fund for Nascha. The screen of Anna's mind fades. She is walking the cosmological trail. And she is alert in time and space. Yes, yes, I love the little painter-girl. Great idea! Oh, my gosh, I'll call it: The Cassandra Middleton Foundation for the Education of Nascha Begay, funded by Guido Cavaggio; Trustee Kai Begay. She smiles up at the winking firmament: *This is one for you, Uncle Guido.*

(Dear reader, In case you haven't noticed: A metanoia, a transformation, is beginning to unfold. Anna is embarking on a new trail. She has taken baby steps to taking in information <u>with her heart</u>, not only with her head as before.)

It is the beginning of her third month in Sedona, and Anna's body is falling into sync with the circadian rhythm of the environment. Back in the hustle-bustle of New York, it took a persistent clock radio to rouse her. She liked to laze in bed, not fully motivated to get up and face her day. Most days she did take a morning run along the dirty river. She had worked hard to get her body in the expected shape and knew she would have no energy for running after a day at the Institute.

This particular red rock country dawn with the world in shadows, and the coyotes heading home after a night of mating and hunting food in the dark, she feels energized. It isn't about her looks or her career. It's a sense she can't quite pinpoint, but her energy grows stronger each day.

She sips a glass of V-8 juice, nibbles on her mini lavender bagel, and fingers her multivitamin. She scans Karen's Hike House printout on Buddha Beach. Hike #7: Start at Cathedral Rock trailhead, climb up to the wide plateau that girds the central turrets. Turn west on the Templeton Trail which will take you to the backside of Cathedral Rock. The trail down to the riparian creek area is steep with many switchbacks. (Suggest a hiking stick.) Follow the trail as it turns south and east along Oak Creek, under the tall, ghostly white sycamores and deeply furrowed cottonwoods, until the trail opens to a clearing alongside a deep swimming hole. You'll be amazed at the sight across the creek on the far shore. Well worth the effort. You can get across the creek on a line of rocks…hiking stick will help. It's a tradition to handcraft your personal prayer pile. (Do not be surprised if you see some young people enjoying a swim. Suits are optional in the wild.)

When Anna gets down to the bottom of the twisting trail, she finds herself in a new world. She'd never heard the word *riparian*; now her body-mind wordlessly grasps what it feels like, what it means. She guesses it means something like a shoreline or bird marsh. She can already hear the creek waters singing into and over the rocks. The trees are much taller, older, and spaced apart with mottled trunks and heavy canopies, already turning gold. Soon the trail meets the rushing, burbling water and turns south-east, along the creek.

Through the quiet she hears a female voice. A young couple appears, coming toward her – perhaps college age, perhaps young honeymooners. The girl is hanging onto his arm and laughing happily. Both have obviously wet hair. *They've just been swimming,* Anna's mind jumps to the judgment. *And I see no indication of swimsuits or towels. It must have been a spontaneous, impromptu quickie.* Anna feels glad that she hadn't come along earlier. She'd have been embarrassed, and would have turned back.

When she reaches the swimming hole, her eyes jump across the flowing water, slower because of the rocks just upstream. They seem to serve as a partial damn and stepping stones to cross. Hundreds, perhaps a thousand, stacks of rocks fill the opposite shore – some with as few as three stones, others a couple of feet high. It is an impressive, enigmatic sight. She instinctively understands what the piles trying to say, although she has no words to explain. She knows that primeval *Homo* believed he could communicate with the water spirits. The Hike House printout had called them "prayer piles."

A smile creeps across her face as she debates, feeling like a little like a child lost into a fairytale land. Normally, she doesn't pray, but she feels this tug to cross-over and erect her own prayer stack. She wants to ask for guidance: Should she go home to New York when her leave days are up? Or take an extended leave of absence and stay in this land of magical unwinding?

The water swirling and rushing between the stepping rocks that are supposed to be a bridge, convinces her to play it safe. Little Annie has never been a risk taker. She couldn't afford to take risks. By acculturation, she is a creature of safety – and walking on rocks in rushing waters is not in her ordinary, scientific repertoire of being careful. She spies a big, safe rock near the edge on the trail side, and decides to sit.

First, she gathers three stones and makes her modest prayer pile on the back part of the safe rock. *An answer, if you please,* she whispers to the air around her. Downstream a tall, blue bird, with thin legs, carefully high-stepping in the weeds near the shore catches her attention. She has never seen a bird so intent in his hunt for survival. Near her, the water looks deep. *I bet they didn't wear suits,* she titters to herself as she climbs on the front of the red rock. She is enjoying the fantasy of the couple messing around in the pool. *They might have... right there – sacred sex in front of the praying Buddha stones.*

The thought of the young couple triggers a poignant, clear memory of Gwen talking about the elk jump, and about her job.

She is surprised at how clearly she remembers Gwen's words "There's this guy who comes into the bar to talk occasionally. A serious guy, and quite into books and thinking. I guess the first time he came in, I said, 'We all want the same things.' Those words seem to have rattled around in his head for over two years. Imagine, a guy remembering something you said that long ago. Flattering, but spooky.

"Anyways about a month ago, he brought up the subject of sex. He said he agreed that as humans we all basically want the same thing. We want to be connected, want to be part of the group, and want someone close in the group to really take us as someone special, and open up. He believed we are prepped by millions of years in small groups to need one another. 'That's human wanting' he said. 'Of course', he went on, 'we are still animals and have an animal wanting for gene transmission, helped on by bodily pleasure. It's a mighty powerful urge, necessary for the survival of the species. Nevertheless, animals don't *love*. And if we are going to keep on in the right direction, we must not lose the ability to love.'

Gwen had served him another vodka tonic and he went on theorizing on that we need different words for sex at different stages of life. He said sometimes he thinks the four letter *f-word* should apply to teenagers and young adults who don't have all their synapses lined up yet. The nine letter f-word (fornicate) could apply to those politicians and celebrities that are in the news. He thinks it would be a great writing project for someone to create a dictionary of copulation. 'Might be too thick a tome,' he added. 'Like a dictionary of names for God.'

According to Gwen, when he got around to the ying-yang of it all, the guy philosophized that part of what the animal layer of a male wants in sex is in part "dominance/submission." He claimed that's big with the other primates. Then, he asked her what do mature women really want when they go to bed with a man? That raised her eyebrows, and she told him she had no textbook answers for him. To tell the truth, Gwen admitted that she actually didn't know how to put what she feels into words. Perhaps the desire to be a mother is part of the answer. She told him that one can't generalize about why a woman wants someone to hug her and light her fire. So she leaned over, and nodded her head toward the boss's office, and whispered, 'Can't talk sex with the patrons.'

Those were the last words Anna remembers in her streamside reverie. She doesn't move when the replay fades into the riparian silence beyond the serene sound of moving water. There is a feminine feeling of soft wetness in the air, and the peace of being oneself, alone, keeps her sitting motionless like a stone nymph. The local New Agers might say she is approaching an altered state of consciousness; others that Mother Nature is calming her inner child. She hazily wonders what Amit might say. He had a mind that liked to wander into the blue. Remarkably, she now seems to have a desire to understand the entangled world of the quanta he loves to wade into. She knows that *mindfulness* is a new buzz word in some scientific circles. Of course, these "frontier scientists" are coining their own words. Her tongue can't produce many of the words, but as she sits next to the stream flowing into its future, she feels at peace. She sits there with a soft smile, lost in time and space.

Swoosh. A noise above in a tree startles her to alertness. She looks up and catches only the broad white tail of a very big bird leaving its nest in a towering sycamore.

As she hikes back up to the Templeton Trail, she cell-phones her driver, Angel, to tell him that she is running behind schedule and won't be back to the trailhead for about an hour. She feels uniquely at one with it all, surprised that the sexual ruminations hadn't clamped her up. Indeed, she is a babe in the woods when it comes to a sense of what it feels like to be a sexual woman – a qualia of being a female. Amit liked that word, qualia. To be honest, she had **not** enjoyed the elk story. As far as she is concerned, violence and dominance are out if she ever engages in sex again. Down deep, she wants tenderness and caring. She wants "someone close in the group to take me seriously." Those are words she remembers from Gwen's rambling guy at the bar. She kind of agrees with that unknown guy, except for "dominance." Somehow she suspects that the guy himself is not an alpha guy. Whoever he is, he's a gentler type.

When she gets back to Guido's house, she is hungry. She meets Kai preparing an evening meal of romaine salad, angel hair pasta, and a vegetarian chili. Kai has a knack for reading her needs. She is famished.

"Did you see all the cairns?" Kai asks.

"Oh, Kai, it was all so awesome. And just as I was leaving, I heard a noise and looked up to see a big, almost huge, bird lift off from a nest. All I saw was a broad white tail."

"You saw a Golden Eagle, Miss Anna. They are there. Everyone knows, but only special people see them. Something good is going to come into your life."

On her drowsy way to her bedroom, she deliberately takes a route past the blue door.

Kai had said *"Feng-shui"* and something about wind-water. Anna had heard the expression somewhere, but paid no attention to it. Now she was getting the sense that it was about keeping out evils spirits, and Nature was involved. She hoped something good would come into her life. She'd had enough demons in her days. Wyatt Jones was one of them.

Anna hugs her pillow that night, hoping the eagle will bring her an answer.

Several streets over on Quail Run, not far from where Anna is sleeping, a lone light shines into the silver-gray moonlight. The man at the computer lifts his pensive head, and stares over the hushed lap pool and the majestic mesquite. He has been invited by the editor of the Serenas Newsletter to write a piece on his studies about the Blue Zone, a National Geographic funded study.

Several international scientists had been studying a region in the Sardinian mountains with a high concentration of centenarians and drew a boundary in blue ink on a map. They felt certain that there is a high correlation between happiness and longevity. They wanted to find out why.

It was his wife who motivated him to leave the university and move to the red rock country. He loved her and he loved rocks. When he first came across an article on the Blue Zone, he came upon a sentence that knocked his scientific socks off: "The biggest determinant of our personal happiness is where we live." He was educated and had a smart wife; he knew the big five of health: a plant-based diet, regular exercise, adequate sleep, economic security, and people you trusted, like he trusted his wife. The whole mystery of an ecosystem that included a community of others who somehow share a reason to wake up and stand up each morning called to him.

"Good night. Have sweet dreams, Brad," a soft voice said. He turned off the light and followed his wife to bed.

Guido's lawyer recommended that Anna at least talk to a real-estate agent to know more about her options. He gave her the card of Catherine Reilly of Red Rock Realty. He explained that Catherine had also recently experienced the death of someone close to her. Her partner, Bob Dorian, had fallen from a cliff-trail while hiking about four months ago, leaving her as his heir. (Pierre Bruni had drafted Dorian's will just six months ago. He never shared his suspicions with anyone – client/attorney trust, you know – but he had reason to understand why Bob left his company to his constant companion – well, his lover. He also had a sense that Bob, an accomplished hiker, was somehow not himself when he fell. Something was unnerving him.)

After weeks and weeks of procrastination, Anna did what she had been avoiding. She called Red Rock Realty and talked to Catherine, explaining her indecision and confusion. She made it clear that she did not know if she was going or staying, selling or keeping. Catherine seemed understanding and arranged to walk through the Guido house. "It's good to know your options, and women tend to see the whole complex field of problems and emotions. We have difficulty sometimes focusing on the cold facts." She promised to work up some comps and recommend a selling price. On her computer, she checked: no mortgage. The house was free and clear. "Your uncle was a successful painter and seems to have had a clever business sense." Picking up that Anna was getting into hiking, Catherine invited her to go hiking the next morning after an early walk-through. "It's a company tradition," the woman with the kind voice explained.

When Catherine came the following morning for the walk through, Anna let out a loud *Oooh!* Her hand shooting up to her mouth. She wasn't expecting to see a dramatically pregnant woman. Catherine looked like she had swallowed a beach ball. She was in her seventh month and looking radiant. A beautiful sight; but it was just such a surprise to Anna, who remembered Pierre Bruni mentioning a "partner." She didn't think he meant "husband." She felt a little behind the times. The culture doesn't stand still. She thought you should be married, committed, to have a baby.

Catherine caught the surprise on Anna's face. "Yes, it was a surprise to us also. A happy surprise for me, once I got over the initial shock. I think I might name him *Unplanned*. Bob had been careful, most of the time. Sometimes he just got carried away before he had time to get ready. I miss him. I'm glad it will be a boy. I like having a male in my life."

Catherine asked Anna if she had any place she would like to hike.

"How's Fay Canyon for you?" Anna responded.

"Perfect. It's flat and shaded. Bob and I hiked a lot, so my legs are strong, but I'm getting a little slow up hills."

"My uncle painted a scene out there. It would be fun to see."

They did indeed see the tree perched high in the sky, and Anna remembered the lawyer's words: "a testimony to life's drive to survive." She marveled at Catherine stamina and inner resources. She felt an attachment to Catherine. She experienced a female depth and an unspoken, shared past between them, even if she didn't know all the wrinkles. She admired Catherine's courage – going forward alone with the birth. Catherine too was a testimony to life, and Anna understood how hard it is being alone.

Catherine spoke admiringly of Sedona Schnebly who lost her five-year-old daughter, Pearl, when a cattle pony bolted, threw the young rider, and dragged the child to her death. Carl Schnebly had taken Sedona away from the scene of death to Colorado, where death again hounded them. After an infectious anthrax wiped out their cattle, they heard again the romance of the rocks, and returned to the post office district named after Carl's wife.

Anna Pagani, the girl with Manhattan in her blood went to bed that night high on whirling ideas, but even more bewildered about her own future. Catherine had said something about her great grandfather and his *destiny.* She'd also said something about finally feeling like a finished woman. "Women were created to bring forth," the pregnant realtor said, with a smile that the tooth paste manufacturers would love. Anna's heart heard what Catherine said, even if her mind was unsure if it would ever have anything to do with her. She was a single scientist, and would probably only bring forth data.

She fell toward dreams remembering that courageous mother-to-be and the love she emanated. Secretly, Anna wanted to be in love. Who doesn't? She awoke a little later than usual. She knew she had dreamed about the birth of a baby, but she couldn't figure out whose baby, possibly Catherine's – possibly hers. Oh, no! That would change everything.

It's late October again, always my favorite time of year. The peak of fall exuberance stirs in the red rock canyons. It's been over four years since the cute Ms. York shot across my bow. Her charisma and her readings have turned me into a direction of seeing with fresh eyes. I now have a better appreciation of the interconnected world around me. For years I'd wandered in the gray fog of ingrained behaviors and the seductive wiles of the dark side media. Gray can be more dangerous than dark black because it is so sneaky.

Of course, another fertile presence has had a hand in helping me escape from my tunnel vision. Sedona the place has opened my perception to both the bonds that tie everything together, and the space between things. I love to look through the space between the pinyon branches. Space is not empty. The atmosphere teems with microbial life, as well as the nitrogen plants need, and the oxygen plants produce. Daily I walk among the trees, taking in the oxygen they synthesize with the light of the sun. I breathe back to them the carbon dioxide they need. It's the give and take of the ambient world. In the city, I paid no attention to this symbiotic relationship. Few people do. It takes a little training in a blinkered culture.

The noonday sun is cresting, beginning its descent into the west. Physically, I feel fit, almost back to healthy. Hiking in the great outdoor has been a tonic to my body that admittedly, I'd let get flabby, just as I'd let my mind get habitual. Trying to debug my word-wandering mind has helped me get more attuned to the living land my feet walk on and the atmosphere I walk in. After a morning of reading some more of Thomas Merton's *Seven Story Mountain,* I'm doing a walkabout in my favorite canyon, the fabled West Fork. Oak Creek runs through here, sometimes softly and slowly, sometimes surging and singing.

I soft-smile in bemusement. For years I turned the pages of research looking for the ancient answers to the seekers' most pressing questions: *Who am I? Is there any meaning to my life? How long do I have? And what then?* This rational urgency has been my nemesis. These obsessions cut like the two-edged sword. Nevertheless, here in nature's sensuous park, I'm able to stand back and take in not only the community of trees, but the quirky individual trees – some tall and straight, some dumpy and stressed. Their crazy arms stretch out this way and then that way, as if told go east, go west, lean south, or stretch north. Some are dark leafed manzanita; some are pines so pale you'd think somebody bleached their needles. They're all so unique. Standing in the presence of *otherness* alters one's mental and physical chemistry. The alchemy of Nature changes the dross of everyday into the precious that the poets call *the numinous.*

Recently, a neighbor's son back in San Francisco jumped to his death from a high-rise balcony. I'd met him. Ricky was a well-educated, young man with a big-bucks-job. Sadly he lacked a life vision. He knew counter-espionage, but he knew scat about his own mind and inner life. Schools don't teach "whole mind." Four years of high school and four year in college and no course on mental health. In high school he did have a course called "phys-ed" where they ran him around the track and climbed him up gym ropes. The part-time teacher was paid by the number of kids who passed. If you seemed to be trying, you passed. Too bad Rickey never got spanked awake by a mind crusader like Emily York. Ricky was your typical young *L'Etranger* (Camus's *Stranger*), drifting in the murky shoals of wanting and self-pre-occupation. In my mind, the phantasm of that smiling, blond boy sadly blazes as a warning in the dark sky of a shaky planetary culture. A culture that has cataracts.

As I walk silently into the sacred canyon, my consciousness sinks deeper into the muse-mode: *It isn't easy to survive in a narcissistic society that is narrowly focused on getting and has no leisure for answers to the vital questions. Significant sectors of this culture scurry clueless even about the meaningful questions. I was a little, well not really, shocked this morning to read that Spain is now experiencing a boom in "brothel tourism." Young girls from struggling countries are trafficked to Spain and then imprisoned in the sex economy. Some are even tattooed with bar codes. Why, why, why do men harm the harmless? We men are so easily lured into the madness of bringing home bigger paychecks – and there's the mid-leg serpent that supposedly is programmed to spread his seed.*

I stop and shake my head, laughing at my deafening mind that is not listening to the silence. The addictive self-talk slowly begins to subside to near calm. My tense body relaxes, and I resume walking into the canyon, savoring the autumn majesty, and the sacred-like tranquility, similar to the silence in which Merton searched for his answers. My wayward mind relapses

282

into a familiar autobiographical groove, where I am central: *As a wee boy, I knew who I was, or at least thought I did. I was an ordinary Catholic boy, like the other boys and girls in my class. I don't know where they're at now. Wish I did. I've burned so many bridges in my voyage to find myself. It is like the demon in the night has dragged my childhood down into the bogs of materialistic and deterministic scientism. Rickey's suicide has knocked my feet off balance. God is eclipsed, along with my guardian angel. The cairns of my youth are no longer visible: my belief in the power of prayer, my hope for a good-guy mansion in the kingdom to come, and my confident hubris that I am walking the narrow trail are mostly gone like the smoke in the wind. Keep the church commandments, and you will be full. Yeah, full of clouds of smoke.*

I stop for a moment at a bend in the creek where the vermillion canyon walls are powerful. There is peace in the air I breathe in. Zane Gray made this canyon memorable in his 1920's novel *The Call of the Canyon,* where Carley Burch, a society girl from the East, wrapped up in herself, is unable to follow the call of love into this rugged, challenging canyon life. The West is too wild for her. She returns to the party life of the soft City, only to lose her opportunity for a golden relationship. As I recall, it was for want of the needed grit and courage.

As I proceed along the multi-hued cliff walls that line the creek, gurgling with the rising waters from the summer monsoon, an eagle floats peacefully in the up-drafts high above the deep gorge. The trees are singing a symphony of fall colors – scarlet-red, burnt-orange, and golden-yellow, against a backdrop of ponderosas and green conifers – a steamy bordello for the senses. Seldom does Nature lift her skirt as she does every autumn in the Oak Creek Canyon of the Northern Frontier. Mindful of Emily's lingering wisdom, I stop, listen, smell, and touch a big red boulder. The warmth in the sun-kissed rock whispers, *Hello. Glad you are here with me.*

A large, familiar ponderosa trunk, marooned on the near side creek bank and wizened by wind and water, catches my eye. Surely, it fell, unobserved by the human world, in the chaos of an electrical storm. It's one of my oracle sitting places. The arching sun begins to fill the canyon space with an entrancing light, and the canyon genie of reflection takes hold of me. I sit down on the fallen trunk. My mind floats up, like the soaring calm into an altered state of peaceful reflection. The canyon has her way with me. Sitting on the log, I lose my mind in a serenity on the other side of the babbling.

I'll never know how long I was sitting there, pondering. Nor will I know what small crackle of noise called my attention back, prompting me to look up stream, where **lo, wouldn't you know**, there appears an apparition – a woman emerging from the forested world. Wow! So feminine, so sculpted, so enticing. Wild boy, I immediately begin dreaming: destiny.

This woman, who has just stepped out of nowhere, into my life, sparkles with a sylvan energy. Framed by the foliage, the sun shining at her back, she has emerged like a Diana, goddess of the moon and woods. It's as if she stepped off a pedestal in the Capitoline Museum. I doubt that many men have had a magical epiphany like this. But as they say in real estate: *Location, location, location.*

She stops, startled. Frightened. Hesitant. Perhaps leery of men. My quick male scanner sees that she is middle-aged, with tied-back, straight, dark brown hair, a determined step, and obliviously loaded with female energy. Whammo! Forget Archimedes' *Eureka.* Forget Saul's fall on the road to Damascus. This, I feel, is **my** moment of magic. I instantly conclude that she is the one whom I've been madly holding on for. As she restarts toward me, my heart beats faster. It's fate at first sight.

I well know that there's something about a flesh and blood female that can send the thermometer of any beast's resting libido way above normal, even above safe. Maybe most grown-up boys viscerally remember their first female relationship, short seconds after emerging from the amniotic waters. I know I still miss my mother, who died before I crossed the bridge that supposedly crosses the river into the land of maturity. I often imagine her observing my life from that I-know-not-where, up on some cloud. She loved to tell the story of the Samaritan who cared. Mother was a Christian woman.

The tallish woman striding out of the setting sun is dressed in tapered, burnt umber Capris and a yellow and red blouse, very shapely. The aura surrounding her is delicious. Her body lines remind me of the Italian actress, Sophia Loren. Even from a distance, her stride exudes a joy of being here, as if she feels rejuvenated – until she sees me.

She restarts her steps, more slowly. As she approaches nearer, frowning at first, then a smile cautiously moving over her face, she tucks a strand of hair over her ear. Then a tapered finger points down-stream, her lips, silently mouthing, *Look!* In that instant, I catch sight of the port-wine-stain birthmark on the side of her neck. Not easily missed.

I instinctively follow her finger and see a tawny-gray, three-year old (so I guess) doe mule-deer, with her slender, gray neck arched gracefully down to lap up some creek water. What a gentle looking creature! Standing staunchly beside her, a six-point antlered buck stares steadily at us. We are in the rut, the mating season; he is traveling with her, waiting for the signal that it is time for him to do what his loins long to do. In their animal minds, males know the rules of waiting – waiting for her body's signal. His moment of responding will be a matter of instinct. This windfall of encountering a scenario of courtship in the wild is fortuitous, pregnant with possibility. My high-brow collegues would nod: *synchronistic, auspicious, promising.*

With the next approaching step of the beautiful woman emerging from the wildness, the doe raises her head, and crooks a front leg. Instantly, both she and the guarding buck turn and vanish into the copse of trees.

"Wasn't that beautiful?" she whispers in a sweet, excited voice, as she nears me. I stand to meet her.

"It sure was," I respond, excited at the prospect of getting to know this beautiful woman, to whom I instantly feel attracted. Selfishly, my body is stirring, and my mind is fantasizing that *she, like some fairy-godmother from the woods, might have answers to the questions that have been burning in my mind. And, of course, answers to more than my head problems. In a flash, I am a tangle of confusion ... appetites, animal and spiritual.* Her gaze scans to the creek trunk I had been sitting on.

"Would you like to sit? If we sit quietly, the doe may return to finish her drinking."

"Yes, perhaps." She vacillates a moment, then sits. "I'm new at this life of the wild outdoors. I went to the waterfalls at the end of the canyon. A personal first, as we say in the Big Apple." (She immediately wonders, W*hy am I dragging in New York? He seems nice. I guess because that's who I am? A New Yorker.*)

I sense she is uneasy sitting next to a man. I spot a silver bracelet on her left arm. It has an inlaid, red opal cross. "That's a pretty bracelet. Real silver, isn't it"

"Ten bucks," she says with a snorted laugh. "I got it at a Burning Man Festival. Crazy experience. The old, whiskered desert rat seems to make them as his mission in life. He said, 'Wear this, and you'll be part of the Jesus movement.'"

"The Jesus movement?"

"Yes, I'm not sure what that is, but I liked the bracelet and the price was right. It would be a hundred bucks in the City. I'm not a Christian. I'm just a physicist. Not a churchgoer, although sometimes, for brief snatches, I feel drawn – at least here in these red rocks – to the notion of belonging to some kind of group that believes in people and meaning. And please, don't ask me what I was doing at a Burning Man Festival. My friend Amit had talked me into it. He's one of those guys who like to play with the burning questions." *I sure know the type,* my mind grins. My insecurity level begins to rise, but quickly relaxes. *I like this woman with her childlike aura.*

I blurt out, "Moments of beauty are like whispered answers to those burning questions."

Her eyes fly wide-open, her eyebrows arch, and her lips quiver slowly into a frightened question. She stares at me. She seems threatened. Her provocative dark eyes seem to be trying to pierce inside me. After a micro pause, she literally jumps to her feet, smoothing her blouse. I see the hope of us bonding, crashing.

She stammers, "I've got to be going."

There I sit, the bump on the log, watching her comely, bare calves, hurrying back up toward the trail to the parking lot. My fingers nervously move over the roughness on the wizened trunk. Damn, I've blown it again. What is it about me and women? This lucky dead trunk has been spared philosophical quandaries. It didn't mess up with burning questions. Undoubtedly, the tree's animating force has returned to Nature, taking up a new life in a new seed.

Sitting, listening to the whispering flow of the Oak Creek, my mind's eye again sees her surprised eyebrows shooting up.

They were such strong eyebrows, very expressive. I seem to have touched a nerve with my words "those burning questions." Apparently, there are people who are frightened by the idea of weighty questions. They'd rather just keep on riding up and down on the money-go-round. Been almost there, done almost that, but not really. Of course, there are dark sides to relating to strangers. Perhaps a man, or men, hurt her. I suspect that there are things a sensitive woman can ever forget. The whole world of women is sometimes a complete mystery to me. They are us, but not like us.

Oh well, win some, lose some, my mind commiserates. I'll never see her again. She was pale. Probably one of those visitors from "the big City." One of those fly-by-nighters from back East. Maybe she went to an aura-reader here and will go home feeling groovy. She'll get up and go to the office on day two – same old, same old, simple-souled, smiling Susie-q.

C'mon, it's time for you to stop scrupling, I chide myself. Time to get away from yourself, lose yourself in the uplifting sounds and smells of the canyon. Perhaps the canyon will help clear your mind of these clouds of unknowing. (I'd read *The Cloud of Unknowing* in that course on contemplation.) What can I say? At least, I **am** making baby steps along Emily's quest for mindfulness: cleaning the spam and the dark thoughts from my mind. But it's so damn slow.

Still as I start walking deeper into the canyon, from where the goddess appeared, her first childlike smile slips happily back into my memory. Like the madcap I am, I visualize meeting her again. Sometimes you just have a vibe about people and possibilities. I felt foolish, but I had felt somehow she was in my cards.

Buber's writing has taught me that we need to find real-time human bonding before we can encounter the transcendent Something More. Woe is me, the unbounded man, not securely tied to anyone. To my delight, in that fleeting encounter, she came to me like my Lady Destiny.

The canyon is quiet, almost sympathetic, waiting me out. The morning visitors are gone in their buses back to town for their sushi at the top of the Hyatt, or their pizza at Picasso's, or a traditional duck dinner at the Heartline Café. Yes, the place is a movable feast, dawn to dusk. Not really what you would call a disco town. Despite my *lados flacos* (weak flanks), my heart accepts my need to soothe my insecurities, and I feel good about what is churning in my inner self.

On a lark, I decide to take off my hiking boots, and ankle-wade into the shallow part of the creek. Last year I saw a lot of little trout minnows here. Whoa, Nelly. The water is shocking cold. It's actually painful, so I stay only three or four minutes. As I hobble back to the log, carrying my boots, I ask myself, *What are you trying to do? Punish yourself?* I lace up my boots and just listen. The whole idea of listening often comes to my soul of late.

My first years here I'd studied every book on Buber I could get my hands on. I believed that Buber had hit the bull's-eye: relationship with a special human *thou* can open a dialogue with the Transcendent Thou. The crux of the process is meeting the otherness of a here-and-now person. He wrote that life addresses us, comes to meet us. Each destiny must find its own belonging and direction. But it was all, head-stuff, piled upon more head-stuff.

Yet, just recently, my eyes are opening to a step in the relationship process I hadn't taken notice of before. An idea in one of the Tennessee gal's books has been working in the antechamber of my consciousness, like yeast works in dough. It is an anti-concept concept that appeals to my growing interest in the nonverbal brain and contemplation. The idea is that **if** you wake up the ability to see the uniqueness of that slender, twisting pinyon pine over there along the creek, or the beauty of a gray winter morning sky with its sliver of crescent moon and thin rosy fingers of cloud, you are on the trail to being able to make contact with the particular beauty of a flesh-and-scents person. From seeing the beauty of one other being, be it a flower, a bird, a tree, you can glimpse the beauty of the One All. I had to agree with Buber: Nature can be a threshold to the world of relationship.

I'm antsy. I go down to my study. I pick up this morning's *Serenas Newsletter*, and spot Brad Stevens' article. I like Brad. He can be a little stiff, but he's sincere. I read: *The science is mounting. The place of your life makes your life. But place is not mountains or oceans or wind-cleaned islands. Place is people. Without the other nearby grapes on the vine, the pinot grape withers and dies. If the grape has a cluster of family and friends, the vine thrives. In a healthy ecosystem, the grape becomes juicy and willingly shares its nourishment. Living in a community that comes together face-to-face and cares for the neighbor, especially the elders, the suffering, and the aloners. That is the Grail of happiness and long life.*

My forest friend, the wide-eyed owl, announces his presence. I feel the urge to have a stinger, but resist. I'd like to know Brad better, but really I'd like know that woman of the canyon wild, even better. Brad is right: it is people who make our lives worth getting up for each morning.

The next day I'm walking down the trail toward home, tired and distracted, after a long afternoon of wandering the wilderness up Wilson Mountain. My mind is rushing on ahead of me: I was seriously shaken up by that woman of the woods whom I scared away yesterday with my remark about the "burning questions." I must have breathed out a kind of fiery dragon breath. That's understandable since my psychic demons have long pursued me, like Odyssey's sirens pursued him, luring him on to shipwreck. She appeared so alluring and so winsome. I obviously touched a raw nerve. I've whispered *I'm sorry a hundred times.* Me and my big mouth.

Nonetheless, lately, I have been aware that I need to get out of my fear. I have been a coward about facing my addiction to the rational brain. Creature of habit that I am, I retreat to my study, open the roof, and boot up my PC. But, I remember *The Cloud of Unknowing* advising: "go after experience rather than knowledge." Certainly, the world-here-around abounds in experience.

It is the soft end of the afternoon; the cicadas are still thrumming, the quails calling, the wind whispering in the trees. An impulse to map my life into a kind of position statement is still pestering the grooves of my brain. A kind of personal vision statement, that's what you need, auto-mind presses. Luckily, my emerging-self butts in, insisting this is <u>not</u> what the cute, blonde Spider Woman would advocate – too mental, too apt to turn to cold stone, too individualistic. Literal-thinker that I am, I itch to retake the quest for clarity. Clarity or unknowing? Yes, that seems to be the question.

The magic jinni of the high country raises a voice. I stop, pause, and decide not go to my ivory tower, not to open my computer. *No, I'm not going to try to cast this feeling into* **words**. I've already walked that ill-fated treadmill of aching for clarity. It's a near illusion, a quest that must fail. Change is always afoot.

When I get home, I'll just sit on the back deck *en plein air*, and try to just be with myself. I seldom take a *time-in* to just enjoy being in my own skin. One of Emily's books used that term, *time-in*, to describe a quieting moment of inward reflection. I give it a try.

Sure enough, my mustang mind is soon kicking up its heels: *Granted, you believe there is a force, a power – a presence that humans have long called "God." But don't waste your time trying to prove or explain the mystery in words. Perhaps there is a happy hunting ground or some sort of fairy-tale place where this bit of knowing I think of as* **me** *goes after the cremator's fire burns the pyre. Again don't waste your breathe. It's mystery! Right now, there are only two things that you need to put into action.*

For starters, you need to try to perceive <u>yourself in the world around you</u>. Slow down and listen to the voices of the planet, the plants, and the winds. Slow food for the soul. You need to open your inner eyes to the uniqueness of particular other being. It's going to be hard as hell for you because it will mean getting out

*of your word-bound head. You may not be able to. You learned to
live in your left-headedness at your mother's knee.*

Finally home, I unlock the door of my home, and step across
the threshold into my aloneness. Restless, I plop down in my
easy chair on the upper back deck. The deceiver whispers in my
ear, *Pour yourself a stiff drink. It will relax you.* I can almost
taste the vodka tonic, but I resist, at least till after another try at
a *time-in*. I know that self-control has got to be part of my pro-
gram. Dusk is dressing the Western sky in soft shawls of orange
and red. The evening star winks in agreement. Alone in the mel-
lowness, the hoot owl sings softly, coaxing the night.

My mind wanders back to this morning at the Osher Lifelong
Learning Institute. I had seen Aubrey Mills walking across the
campus. There is something about that man that tantalizes me.
The guy is brilliant and super learned, but he never talks about
his own philosophy of life, even in his classes. He's not about
himself. He just seems to walk through life guided by some inner
GPS, which seems to be about *giving*, about others.

I inhale in some night air, clean and clear, and reach for my
Kindle. I snap on my Kindle Aladdin's light, and bring up Lynne
McTaggart's *The Bond*, the fifth of Miss York's recommendations. I scroll to Chapter 7, Born to Give. Near the end she
reviews the experiments of Daniel Bateson which suggest that
when we move beyond our individual self and consider the other's perspective, we become "capable to the most extraordinary
good." The evidence shows that helping other promotes health
and even longevity. She cites a case of a social depressive misfit
who was inspired by the kindness of one health care worker. In
her words, "One tiny act of selflessness cleared his path." She

concludes the chapter with a University of Arizona psychologist: *'we help when we have lost our sense of individuality and step temporarily into a space of oneness."*

I click of the light off, and close my Kindle. I feel simultaneously upbeat and anxious. My gut, call it aboriginal, reaches out to grab this truth. Another part of my gut questions if I can hold on for the struggle. Two images flash across the secret screen of my ruminations: Aubrey Mills and the woman of the canyon with the blemish on her throat. My heart seem to breathe, *I can be more than I am.*

I sit, expecting my wise forest friend to concur. The forest does not give its hoot, but I know it is with me.

Whether Anna Pagani likes it or not, Wyatt Jones is still a thorny-horny presence in her life. She doesn't consider herself knowledgeable about men, but her boss seems like the bottom of the barrel of monkeys. In her mind, the bottom of the barrel is a kind of crowded men's club of hurtful guys. She considers any unkindness a type of violence. Anna has always sensed that he is frustrated by her refusals of his advances. He doesn't even treat his mother nice. She overheard him on the phone one day when he had called her to his office. He was rude to his mother. Anna surmises that she doesn't know the half of it.

The New Jersey sky had been a hazy blue, and the temperature mild and hardly noteworthy in Weehawken, New Jersey, the day Ruth Jones gave birth to a five pound boy named Wyatt. Her husband Tom Jones was the medical examiner in the Bergen County morgue. As a chemist, he helped ascertain the causes of death – a complex skein of possibilities. It was a demanding, boring job of routine tests. It suited his aloof disposition. People die every day; their last words spoken long before they reach the table in his morgue. Tom was one of those freethinkers who have no theories about the soul or the afterlife. When Ruth goes to the hospital to give birth to their first and only child, he stays at work. She is disappointed, of course, but resigned to her lot.

Ruth Jones is neither tall nor petite. Five-four, 130 pounds, with mousy blonde hair, she is what one would call *ordinary*, in most senses of the word, although some people think of her as sweet. When she graduated from high school, she went to work in the Walgreens drug store as a stock girl. She had no money to go to college, and her grades were mediocre. There she met the tall, taciturn chemist. To her, he was a knight in shining armor – successful, reliable, and employed. She often worried about her future – or lack of it. She sensed that Tom was a man who could provide for her. After their marriage by the Justice of the Peace in the Weehawken town hall, Tom insisted that she not work. She became a dutiful housewife – cooking, cleaning, darning socks, and ironing. She had never learned any relationship skills. She did not know how to speak up for herself. Schools seldom teach those soft skills.

Ruth's family had not been churchgoers. Her husband had been raised a Presbyterian, but he never went. She had tried for her son's sake, but when Wyatt turned nine, he told her that he would no longer be going to church with her. Ruth, of course, didn't believe she should force anyone to do anything.

But after Tom passed away, at the urging of her neighbor, Sue Scanlan, she starts going to the Unity Church. She enjoys the upbeat atmosphere of singing hymns and sermons about patience, justice, and a positive attitude. For her, those Sunday mornings are little islands of humanness in an empty life. The moment when they all hold hands and sing, "Let there be peace and let it begin with me" becomes her high time of the week... her favorite minute. At that social moment, she feels part of something bigger. Most of the rest of the week she just feels like an empty marker.

When Wyatt goes away to college, a silent dream begins to sprout. Vicariously, she is finally going to have a life. She had never been good at science in high school, but she, like many Westerners, is in awe of scientists. They are the wise Greeks of the twentieth century. Her Wyatt is off on the road to becoming a somebody, a road she herself could never travel. She doesn't understand why he chose physics, but she's secretly silly about it. Sadly, the wind of circumstance soon blows out her embryonic flame of hope.

In the beginning of the summer vacation of his second year at MIT, Wyatt brings home his roommate, Sam Gold, a self-described nihilist, deeply committed to scientific materialism. As she goes about her household cleaning, Ruth eavesdrops on the boys' conversations. Sam's dogmatic pronouncements frighten her. He is against conservatives, against liberals, against religions, against moralizers, against anything or persons or government decision that might crimp his freedom. He doesn't seem to believe in anything positive.

A bleak sadness comes over her as she realizes that Wyatt is swallowing Sam's stuff, hook-line-and-sinker. Sam's spilled seeds are finding a needy soil. She isn't the brightest of mothers, but she suddenly knows in her female insides that Wyatt will never mature into the man she envisioned. Women can read the tea leaves: men without vision go nowhere. She will never enjoy that hibiscus she had dreamed of: being a someone because she is connected to someone who is someone to those someones who seem important in the world of the anyones. Her lot seems fate to remain luckless.

One Sunday the summer after Tom passed away, sitting on a stone bench outside the Unity House, she mentions her sadness to Sue Scanlan. Her neighbor tells her that her son is her cross that she must bear up under, just as Jesus's mother had. For the moment, Ruth sees no option but to accept the inevitable: her life is doomed to be a vacant land that she has to struggle across alone. In bed, nights, she curls up in a fetal position, feeling that she is in a holding pen where she has no power to change things, including her isolation. Even her son shows her no pity.

One recent Saturday had been a double-bogey day for Wyatt Jones; he couldn't buy an eight foot putt. And shit, he had women problems. His mother was becoming a pain in his butt, calling, looking for sympathy. Layla had begged off again saying she wasn't feeling good. He swirls his glass of single malt Headlands scotch, looking into the amber liquid for consolation. In the background of his midtown penthouse, the strains of Barbara Streisand mellow out with *One Night Only*. He likes Barbara. On the floor a Playboy magazine with a nearly naked woman on the cover catches his eye. The porn model reminds him of someone, perhaps Madonna. He doesn't particularly like Italian girls, too many hang-ups. He likes Jewish females. To him, they have fewer of those hated inhibitions. Inhibitions are unnatural, and definitely un-American.

The Layla problem is getting to him. She appears to be seriously sick, and getting sicker by the week, it seems. *I'm sorry she's sick*, his mind bristles. *She's a sweet gal, and she has that cute dimple on her right cheek. It makes her look exotic, like a regular Lebanese belly dancer. But I don't think I should be blamed for her condition. Sure, she tries to please, probably because in some ways we are alike. But let's face it, it's the woman's job to protect herself,* he says to the amber genii in the scotch.

He isn't stupid, he assures himself. He has picked up on the innuendos his buddies are chipping his way. But hey, his buddies are masters of the gotcha. One-upmanship is an arena sport for the faux-alphas in the dominance game.

He suspects that Layla is occasionally in contact with that Pagani bitch. The bitch is probably interested in what is going on back at the Institute. After all, she'll be a front runner. A mean expression gathers his facial features. A rising wave of anger often arises these days when he thinks of smarty-pants rejecting him. Twice he invited her out to dinner and she has feigned some excuse or other. Bitch. To a man with some pride, that's no casual slighting. Like any lion king, he expects a woman to respect and fear him. Naturally, he likes women who fear him; they are supposed to.

Nevertheless, though his subconscious mind isn't admitting it, right now, he also fears the bitch. She is the only logical one who could take his chair at the head of the Institute of Theoretical Physics. The other scientists, even the super brains, would make terrible administrators. They're all ostriches with their heads buried in the sands of science. Pretty buns Pagani is a different story. She is more than an intelligent, nose-to-the-grindstone star-gazer. She has some Bronx neighborhood smarts; she probably was kicked around. He suspects she is attached to the Institute. She has little else in her life.

He remembers with bitterness that it is she who parlayed her theorem into that award. Her work did contribute to the theory that the universe is expanding faster than previously thought. In truth, Wyatt doesn't give a damn if the world burns up – after he's had his jollies. He's not going to have any kids. Like his

father, he'd find a kid a drag. Wyatt was even pissed Pagani
didn't make a little fuss about her silly success. If she'd smiled
sweetly at him, as CEO he'd have thrown a party for her, hoping. But she didn't. Why should he make a big deal of her? He
is convinced that women in general lack self-confidence. Still he
strongly suspects that she is just playing her cards for the board.
She is a clever bitch, but he'd somehow outsmart her.

He gets up and goes to the bar to refresh his scotch. Outside a heavy late fall fog has rolled in from the Atlantic. The
night is dark and gray, and looks unkind. He tightens his lips
and runs his fingers through his chestnut brown hair as his
mind returns to putting together a game plan. Even though
he lusts for her behind and longs for a hot fling with her, he
has to get rid of her. Women are dime a dozen. He knows he
has to be ruthless; it is suicide to have a placement standing
in the wings. He has to cover his ass. He has to look out for
himself – that's the American way. He'd screw her, one way
or another.

He has picked up the vibe from Layla that Pagani-ass might
be enjoying the great outdoor life. Good, maybe she'll make
things easy for him and just stay there. Roger, one of his buddies, said it is beautiful there. Rog had played golf there. The
course was nothing special, not very challenging, but the views
from the fairways were off the charts.

One down stroke for Rog: most of the women are with part-
ners of some leaning. That is no problem for Wyatt. He likes the
challenge of getting into a woman's panties, even lesbians. He
likes competition. He likes winning. He likes coming. He shakes
his head, and looks into his scotch. What am I thinking, I'm not

going there. The bitch doesn't know how to have fun. She's certainly not into golfing. She has her head in the stars.

He is toying with having his secretary send her a letter reminding her that her accumulated unused vacation time amounts to only about three months. In addition, one month leave of absence for a death in the immediate family is the industry standard. She would forfeit her job if she stayed longer, without his granting her an extension to six months. He could, but she'll have to ask him.

But pushing her might backfire, he concedes to himself. It seems too soon. He has to think this out more carefully, and wait for his opportunity. He'd keep Layla happy. He needs that girl.

As a subdivision of a hundred and fifty lots, about half built-out, Lomas Serenas tries to keep alive a sort of community spirit. Brad and Sally Stevens are two spark plugs at bringing people together. It helps them that they have one of the most authentic southwestern back yards in the neighborhood to entertain in. A senatorial, branching mesquite tree stands as an Acropolis. The tree has an aura of *Come, sit under my sweet pods and talk.*

They had hiked the trail to Gibraltar Rock earlier that morning. Brad is looking out his study window. Sally is doing her morning laps. He knows her strong body well. The first time he met her she was up a ladder in the Whole Foods of Berkeley storing extra boxes of Almond Flax Cereal into the high storage area. He returns to scanning the *Blue Zones* website for the recent blogs and twitters. He spent his life with the hard science of rocks, but now he feels attracted to the soft sciences of longevity and happiness. For him they are twins of a sort. His fraternal twin Barry had died at age of 14. No one had ever been able to tell him why. They had been buddies, but different. Barry was shy, retiring; Brad liked people in friendly way. He liked cooking for people, and his new science cheered him on. Longevity seemed tied to social structure.

That night Sally meets me at the door, dressed in a short, white cocktail dress. A confirmed activist, she swims *au naturel* mornings in their lap pool, and hikes with her husband almost daily. She is involved in several non-profit organizations in town. She has a heart of gold, and strong, beautifully-white, athletic legs, worthy of any man's second glance.

I have picked up threads of Sally's saga from Gwen. The impression I've put together is that some guy she used to run cross country with left her at the altar. The hitch was about his making big bucks in a big city versus living a life-style closer to nature. Money won, Sally lost, and cried the nights away for several months. She worries about her size, but she works out compulsively.

As I'm walking toward the backyard, her sister, Gwen Dykstra, emerges from the kitchen with a platter of shrimp surrounded by a red moat of cocktail sauce. My reptile-mammal brain raises its head: *I bet that sauce is spicy. Just as I bet Gwen is.* She stops and leans me her cheek for a friendly peck. One afternoon at the bar she had called me "the handsome scholar." I think my chest inflates remembering her compliment. I always wanted to be a real scholar. Sometimes I still think that I should woo this gal from Minnesota. She's been through the toils of relating. In a way she's everyman's dream – a female who lets him talk and listens like a mother. I'm sure the sex would be satisfying. Still, there's something missing in the chemistry between us. Somehow, her inner light within is still dim. Or maybe the fire in my belly has gone to embers.

The backyard is crowded, and alive with folks-a-relating. The air is cheerful with the scents of salads, spices, and freshly baked breads. Brad is flipping meats and fish on the freestanding barbecue island. The smell of hot flesh hangs invitingly in the air.

Being a backwoods hunter, Brad loves to cook venison, elk, and quail. To his right is an open bar with all kinds of beers, wines, and whiskeys. Brad did well as a geologist and university professor, and is generous and broad-minded when it comes to the Lomas community. He winks at me, and gives me a come-hither nod of his head. I walk over to him, and get a welcoming bear-hug. He's one of the many men in Sedona who hug. Hugging both men and women is a high country trait. "Get yourself a drink, John. You're going to love this elk I'm grilling. It's fresh. UPS overnight. You got to love those guys."

He puts the back of his hand to his mouth as if clueing me in on top secret information. I feel privileged. I have shamefully few male confidants. "It's better than the venison. Elks are grazers. They eat grasses. They were a plains animal, until the hunters drove them into the high forests. Deer are browsers. They nibble on woody bush forbs and brambles. So grab some of this elk while it lasts. Most people don't know the difference."

As I am taking my first sip of white wine, reminding myself to go easy, I look out toward the mystic mesquite, with its lush bean pods. Maybe you don't know it, but the early occupants of the area made a kind of tortilla with the flour of the ground beans, rich in protein and nutriments. As the wine warms me, I see the tree as nurturing.

And **lo , who'd believe it!** The marked goddess of the canyon appears again, looking absolutely lovely in her bright yellow dress.

Shit! A stab of alarm, sharply tinged with jealousy, slashes into my mind...a tsunami of emotion. She's talking to Zach Taylor, the poster boy of free love. Why do people invite that loser to their gatherings? I guess it's because he's as handsome as hell – eye candy for lost women. Everyone has got to know that he's a lecherous playboy, living off his dead daddy's money. I guess some women are just conditioned to being treated like recyclables. I don't give a tinker's hoot, if he's a good guitar player and published poet, or not. Damn it, he broke that sweet, young Caitlin Feeney's heart. I've heard the story a couple of times at the *Cave*.

They were a popular singer/strummer combo. She thought he cared for her. It's not easy being an immigrant lass from the Emerald Isle. Life is simpler there. Luckily, she woke up to his other women. He is the switch-master of his own private merry-go-round. It's even imaginable that he has bedded down Gwen too. He takes no prisoners. Male deceit and betrayal are just more devious shades of violence, aren't they? Women seem to have too much shame to talk about their mistakes. It usually takes two to make a consensual mistake, but my take is that the flock of the weaker sex who consciously deceive and betray is considerably small than the raptor males.

Shit, I don't know, but I don't think "the weaker sex" is the right wording. I don't think women are inclined to use men, although I do think men easily fall into using women – as well as one another. At least that's the impression I get from evil empire's mouthpieces. Is the *weak* possibly the *stronger*? Sure, we all want to be to feel that we are *special* to someone. But some men even think that forcible or cajoled entry makes them matter more…at least in the small arena of their own minds. Make no mistake, we all want to matter. Thank God, my mother nourished me with the royal jelly of love.

The woman with the red-wine birthmark appears to sense the searing energy of my roaring mind and gaze, she turns. (John doesn't realize yet – nor really does Anna – the reaction his warm, brown, accepting, canyon eyes had aroused in her.) Our eyes meet. (He has no way of knowing that her mind is flashing back to that moment in the canyon, when she experienced him as a troubled, Rodin-like-thinker, lost in serious thought. And that perception of a man tantalized in his own life had evoked an unexpected response in her – something like, *he needs me.* Under the spell of the canyon's magic, something stirred to life in her dormant place – some womanly instincts, that came with the pristine feminine fluids. At that moment, those maternal feelings began flowing and coming on line. She didn't know it but she was opening up as a woman.)

In an almost prescient moment, I catch the vibe that the enchantress-of-the-canyon isn't enjoying being with the tall, sexy guy with the wavy black hair and the roving eye. Nevertheless, she seems stalled in hesitation, as if she doesn't know what she wants to do – almost like a doe frozen in the headlights of a car on a dark country road. Then I see her lift her chin slightly, but resolutely, as if mustering up some courage. She says a few parting brief words to the cowboy-crooner. As she turns without a handshake or other sign of disconnection, and starts walking toward me, my toes tap a little leprechaun dance. It is a moment of male ego and a moment of an exciting possibility walking toward me. *Maybe she's got a sixth sense about people who can hurt you. And maybe my newly-honed efforts to be not harming are peeking through the thick layers of the competitive schooling of my youth.* It's moments like this that weave a life!

As she approaches, I can feel a teenage-like-grin spreading across my trembling face. Without words to explain, my inner man savvies that I really want this *particular* woman. If you must, call it chemistry or telepathy. I perceive it as destiny dawning. Please don't ask me why I have the intuition that this desire is more than the carnal rascal that hangs below my belly-button. The feeling that this is my moment of fate fills the air around me, and moves like osmosis into me. But the scruple lingers that I might just be stalled in that Pacific bar-room boy who fell for the Sunset redhead. Is it only **that** boy who is excited, or someone maturing in the beauty of the land?

For all I know, this shapely woman might be high on something, like Allie was on Irish coffee when our ships collided. A couple of the other people in the group seem "prepped" to be social. (Only later, will I realize that the lady with the red mark is simply high on the courage of walking out of a prison she has languished in for years. She is doing something she has never done before. She is deliberately walking toward a man. She is high on being challenged to change – after so many stalled years. She's high on making her own choices.) The red rocks are talking, and the natural woman within is walking.

"Hello, I think we've met," she says with a smile that I can see is both trying to be courageous, and tentatively reaching across an unfamiliar between. She is stretching beyond herself. I feel complimented. She too seems to be interested in an encounter. I feel thrilled. "I'm Anna Pagani, the niece of Guido Cavaggio, a neighbor who died a couple of weeks ago. I'm staying in his house for a while, so I'm a neighbor *pro tem.*"

"Oh yes, the hermit painter. Sorry to hear about his passing on. I've heard that his paintings are prized, and that he was a kind man to his household. I never met the man. We solitaries seldom meet. I have met Kai, his housekeeper and her wonderfully polite daughter. They walk the trails around here, seems like every morning. They're a wonder to see. I've heard that the indigenous peoples have a bond with the earth, and believe in the interconnection of all Nature. Seeing Kai and Nascha walking and talking in Nature is like seeing poetry in real time. It's people like them that make this place so special. Or perhaps, is it visa-versa?"

"You are right. Kai is special in my eyes too. Perhaps, the Navajo are special. I don't know. My uncle, the artist, seemed to have had an eye for the special. And he and Kai seemed to have had a relationship beyond the narrow boundaries of what our culture usually thinks of as a male-female relationship, if you know what I mean. But outside his little 'family' of Kai and Nascha, he had little contact with the world of people. He kept to himself.

"Uncle Guido took a walk in nature most every morning; some days with little Nascha. Then he worked in his studio most of the day, and rested in his lounge chair in the evening. I knew him only when I was a child. He was the singing uncle who bounced his sister's daughter on his knee and seemed to be happy entertaining little, no-count me. He and I had a relationship, better than I had with my father. But I didn't trust grown men. At that tender time of my life, I only wanted friends my own age. You, I recognize as the *pondering man* of the canyon."

"John Malachy," I say, debating whether to extend my hand or not.

"Glad to officially meet you, John Malachy," she responds, extending her long fingered hand and looking me in the eye. She has matured in just these couple of weeks.

"I apologize for running off the other day. I've been quite thin-skinned and jumpy since I lost my colleague/boyfriend a few months before being called here. To tell you the truth, I didn't even realize how lost and lonely I am, till I started hiking the wilderness. My apologies, you unnerved me with that reference to 'the big burning questions.' My Indian friend, Amit, used to love to talk about 'the quantum answers to the transcendental questions," always true to his Hindu heritage. As he sees it, the stuff of reality is bits of interrelated information. Bits connected by knowing other bits. He likes to say things like, 'The Brahman and the Atman are one. I am a bit of the Ultimate All.' I didn't really lend a serious ear to him back then, but now out in the wilderness, I'm beginning to recall, and occasionally hear his words in the singing winds. It's as if this place is saying what Amit loved to say. Here, for the first time, I find myself pausing to reflect on his way of seeing the world. Not open to the average multi-tasker. Sorry, that may seem like silly-girl-talk to you. To tell the truth, it even feels a little silly to hear myself say those kinds of things."

"No, please. I understand, though I won't try to explain more in words. I hear you."

We sit out under the magic of the mesquite, and talk into the falling shadows of the high desert. Both of us are unsure of ourselves. Her openness is transparent and understandable. She's in a new environment, knowing hardly anyone, not knowing if she is staying or going. And she seems to be uncovering dormant aspects of herself. I tip of my cap to my gang of three – Buber, Tennessee, and Gwen. They have opened my eyes. I've been trying, hit-and-miss, to inch up that steep hill of being *other-oriented*. As every salmon know, it's getting harder and harder to swim upstream.

Loving to have her as an audience, I fall back into my rambling, "Yes, I'm with you. I'm trying to learn to be mindfully-aware of the rooted individualism that is so *me-oriented*. It seems almost too deeply rooted to eradicate. But, I'm struggling to swim up that surging stream. Change doesn't come easily. The cultural pull to be self-invested pollutes the water we swim in. It is impossible to not to drink in, difficult to flip out of. Self-seeking seems to be a North American nurtured trait."

You are talking too much, my inner Jiminy Cricket signals. Nervous, I go to the bar for another glass of white wine. I'm high on this moment of direction. She says she's fine. I agree. Not about the wine, but how fine it is to be with her. She seems to be really listening to me, listening to the me who is more tangled than his struggling words. There is a light emerging in her eyes that encourages me to talk on. I've long had the idea that talking is the second best way we connect.

Of course, I want her to know me, the man who wants to know her. I'm a man who doesn't feel known by anyone. I restart, "I remember me back in my twenties. I loved to babble on about me, my great experiences, and show people how educated I am. I seldom listened. I still tend to fixate on myself, and my struggles. I never learned to be a man who turns toward others. But as my friend Gwen at the local pub likes to say, 'We can't give up.'"

I can see that the demure woman with her dark hair tied back in a bun is vacillating between being stiff-souled and timid, or on the other hand, opening up and sharing some of her silent, but obvious, loneliness. Somehow, lost in those almost timeless moments underneath the silent bean pods, the hope that we can be soul mates ripens. I seem to understand her. And for her part, it's as if she experimenting with a new persona, like I have been trying to do for the last couple of years. My hunch is that she is starting to go through "the change" – the Sedona change. I can relate to that. At first, it's a kind of shock to the system. The fever hits, and the chrysalis begins to open.

The light that flickers in her warm, but cautious eyes, some-times frightened, sometimes excited, eclipses the mark on her neck. She is her beautiful self – no abused mark disfigures who she is. She seems to accept the crimson culprit that had made her the victim. Ah, cruelty, a twisted trait the benumbed world accepts as part of the modern package. I am having more and more trouble accepting this cultural blindness – especially cru-elty toward women. I doubt that in a small band of hunter-gath-ers there was room for cruelty, especially toward the needy.

The back-current of my mind flows at browser-speed into re-hashing how we, as a species, have become so insensitive, so inhuman. From all that I read, it wasn't that way in the begin-ning, and for most of our evolving history. For millennia, we were bands of men, women, and children who were aware that we needed one another to survive. We contributed to the group. We snuggled one another. In the land of the wooly beasts, no group survived without helping one another. We had to. That's partially who we still are.

Several times, as Anna and I are conversing out on a bench under the mesquite tree, I catch Zach Taylor watching us, maybe her. Naturally, I feel a rush of both jealous anger and petty triumph. What man doesn't want to be the alpha-guy with the beautiful girl? Yet in theory, as a man softened by the winds of the canyons and the fears of the bears I remember that there is some *natural* goodness in most every being. I have heard that lover-boy sometimes donates his guitar and poetry talents to help local fund raisers.

So I try bringing in a calm visualization to suppress my toxic feelings. Visualization is a strategy that I have taken up, thanks to Miss York. Calm scenes, from nature especially for me, can mentally diffuse an ugly reaction. Images of beauty can mine-sweep the road ahead of life's IED's (Improvised explosive devices). De-stressing images are another way to arrive to what Emily liked to call **clear kind blue mind**– a serene sky with no dirty clouds. I'm beginning to tentatively play with Emily's words: **body, heart, mind,** and **the full bits a-firing**. Her readings and the stillness of nature are leading me like lighthouses in the dark. I've come to the shore of wanting to castaway the ongoing inner talking, which is often biting at others. I have come to believe that the heart is a sister organ of the brain and a big brother to giddy gonads.

I'm starting to see more and more that it is **words, words** that lead us wayward. We can't lasso-in our many wild parts into a calm corral of answers. In the subjective bits of our toes, our knees, our genitals, our hearts, our vocal chords, our amygdala, right up to our PFC's (prefrontal cortexes) we potentially are receiving and sending light. But, as Emily liked to repeat, "A drop of the dark can put out the light within." Of course the mind thinks in the head and the heart feels within the body. Emily's stuff isn't slam-dunk easy, but it feels like a right way to try to go.

"Is he a friend of yours?" Anna asks, seeing my furrowing forehead, and realizing that I am off on Zack. There's a slight tension in her voice. She seems to fear him. "Not really," I answer, proudly keeping my uncharitable digs and ugly comments to myself. "Good," she says, very softly. "I didn't particularly feel comfortable with him. He reminds me of someone back at work who has that certain woman hunger in his eyes."

My heart skips a beat. I believe that she has just shared a **bit** of herself. A seed of relationship has fallen into the soil of possibility. I sense that some man back at work is a lecher like Zach. My hunch is that she carries a fear of men.

Gwen comes by and winks. I feel lost. I can't be sure who she is winking at – Anna or me. I am busily explaining Emily's visualization technique to Anna. I am truthfully surprised at how open to serious talk this woman-physicist is. I have little in-depth experience with women, so Anna's interest draws me on. From what she said about her life in the city, and her surprising reaction in canyon, I expected her to be more closed.

It was the only piece of clothing in the closet. Anna had seen the multicolored garment hanging in the guest bedroom closet one of those first mornings. It was truly festive and cool looking, but she had hesitated to touch it. It wasn't hers, and she wasn't comfortable with colorful clothes. But that night after she returns from the Stevens' backyard soiree, she is in an uncommonly positive mood. She had enjoyed talking to someone serious…personally serious. She couldn't put a finger on why. She hadn't done that in forever. She'd had two glasses of red wine, unheard of for her. Perhaps *(A hint of a smile))* she was nervous, like on a date. The last time she had talked openly, soul to soul with another human, was with her apartment mate Cassie. Even Amit stayed close to the surface most of the time. She had come to expect that of the men who came into contact with her.

Staring at the colorful challenge in the closet, she is still having a hard time accepting that this is her house, and that the dress belongs to her. Then, of a sudden, she doesn't care why, but she reaches for the tantalizing hangar that holds the brightly colored garment. The urge to be desirable, to be feminine, starts to rise from her first chakra, heading for her heart chakra. (Of course, Anna doesn't think in terms of chakras.)

She pulls out the orange, purple, yellow, red floral garment, and extends it at arms' length. It looms as the forbidden apple that did Eve in. The label is still attached to the back of the collar: *Balinese Sarongs.* As she holds the hanger in her outstretched arm, still torn in debate, the word *Bali* floats in her mind. Her memory runs wild and exotic. She had seen the movie *South Pacific* in college. She recalls a near naked, young female, happily singing in a waterfall. Her young, deep tissue knew that she envied the freedom of that pretty unencumbered girl. Anna, on the other hand, sometimes feels that she was born encumbered.

She has seen a certain painting in the stack in Uncle Guido's studio room. In the background there are high, pointed, purple mountains, with a few wisps of smoke, suggesting a volcano. On the lower slopes are terraces of green, flooded fields. They look like rice paddies to her. In the foreground, an enchanting young girl with dark hair, beautiful features, and golden-bronze skin, holds a baby. The girl is dressed in a colorful sarong very similar to the one she holds suspended before her. *That must be Bali.* She frowns, wondering whose baby it is. Could it be Uncle Guido's love-child?

Then, a silent feeling of euphoria nudging her, her face brightens. She decides to put on the sarong, thinking, *Uncle Guido wouldn't mind. He had his fun. I'll leave it in the closet when I leave. Perhaps he'd be happy to see me do something lighted-hearted and spontaneous, for a change.*

She strips to her birthday suit, and wraps herself in the sensual sarong. Dressed only in the soft silk, she goes out into the back yard, pulls the lounge chair further out into the open space. Feeling like a Balinese princess, she reclines and looks up into the fiery stars and hovering galaxies, aware of a small tongue of fire in her heart.

The Milky Way actually looks milky. She remains silent for several minutes; her mind is sinking into a reflective current of thoughts, not yet words. In reality her heart is comparing Amit and John. Amit liked to talk about the "uni-verse – the all is one." John had used the word "context – the context of one's life." She subtly knows both men share the same insights. She knows that most people think of the stars as individuals, but Amit thinks of them as heavenly bits of the one Cosmic All. John thinks of them as part of the context of his life. In a sense, she admits, the stars and planets are all connected by strong forces pulling them together and pushing them apart. And in a way, we are all made of stardust – the original bits.

Shifting her eyes to the red iron mountain outlined in the night sky, she has to agree that in a sense the planet earth is just one small bit of the one cosmic dance. She is aware that in John's mind mountains, trees, and stars are all part of the setting of who he is. She recalls him saying that he is coming to see the light: to his evolving mindset, the question is becoming not, "Who am I?" but "Who are **we**?"

Like a night chill, a feeling of aloneness falls around her. The memory of her brief conversation with the hungry-eyed Zach carries her mind back to Wyatt Jones. *There are certainly two types of relationships,* she muses: *Those that tear you down, and those that build you up. I'm beginning to see a glimmer of light too. What's missing in my life is one of those building-up types. Too long have I tasted the bitter cup of being an outsider.* She tugs the loose-fitting sarong tighter around her body. Her mind slips toward a kind of peace at the prospect of hiking to a vortex in the morning with John. She agrees that the vortexes can be thought of as openings releasing some earth energy into the cosmic dance. Then she recalls that she hasn't danced since college.

A creation of erosion, Kachina Woman is a geological hoodoo, a strangely shaped, slender spire of red rock, pointing up into the heavens near the entrance into Boynton Canyon, in the Red Rock-Secret Canyon Wilderness. She guards the canyon that is one of the sacred resting sites of the bones of the early ancestral people. Enchantment, a luxury resort, sits at the mouth of the canyon. Vista Trail hikes up to the top of an adjoining hillock, between the hoodoo and the shoulder of the mountain range. A 30 foot knoll stands on one side and the mountain on the other; a small mesa rests between them. The spot is said to be where both male-and-female emanating energy is strongest. Kachina Woman looks after the People of the Land of the Seven Canyons. The swirling energy of the inner Earth is reputed to facilitate mind and body healing. The New Age shamans call it the "heart chakra of all heart chakras." This small, intimate mesa is considered one of the rare male & female vortexes – both electric and magnetic energy. Anna, the scientist and curious temporary visitor, had asked about the fabled openings that emit energy from deep in the intersecting ley lines of the earth. I had invited her to hike the Vista Trail.

I pick her up in my red jeep. When we reach the turn-off for Boynton Canyon Road, out of the wild Arizona blue, a teen-boy impulse hits me, and I pull over to the shoulder of the forest road. "Say, why don't you try driving? This is a straight stretch with almost no traffic, and I have AAA roadside insurance," I add, trying to add a touch of lightness.

She looks at me, stunned. Panic rushes across her face. An inner moment stirs in her still young-girl insides. Then the corners of her mouth begin to turn upward, and her dark eyes widen, excitement dawning. I can witness on the screen of her pupils the debate waging in those dark, usually controlled, pools of light. She is probably saying to herself, *I'm most likely going back to where I belong. But it would be nice to drive myself when I am here. There's a yellow jeep in Guido's garage.* I can almost hear the synapses of her mind opening and closing. I know I have hit pay dirt. My heart cheers and my toes tap. The first fingers of my left hand are crossed.

"You know, don't you, that I've never driven a car before?"

"Most city girls haven't. It's easy, and I'll be right here, helping you. If I say STOP, take your feet off both pedals. We'll roll a few yards and come to a stop. If you have any notion that you want to learn to drive, a lonely road like this is as good a place as any."

She pauses. I am half expecting, "No, I can't" (she probably is too). After a moment, she looks at me, her brow furrowing, "Do you really think I can?"

My face brightens. Actually I do believe she can do it, a kind of sixth-sense that this competent lady has what it takes to learn new things – to change.

"It's no problem, and I'll be right here. If needed, I can reach the brake pedal with my left foot. You concentrate on steering. This early in the day, there aren't many 'visitors' out on the road.

(I am tempted to say: *They're still in bed, making love to one another in their cozy casitas.* The animal in my loins is stirring awake – again.) *"You can do it."*

Another pause of hesitation, her mouth screwing up in decision. (John doesn't know it, but the decision is as much about him as the challenge of driving a car. She isn't used to people believing in her, outside a science lab. Is she ready to let a man be nice to her?)

"Yes. Okay," she says slowly. "I want to learn to drive, to be able to go where I want to go, when I want to go. In case I stay here, which I'm sure I can't. She looks me straight in the eyes, as if wanting to know me. I hope that our relationship has been hooked.

She opens the door, gets out, and comes over to the driver's side. After some brief explanations of the pedals, levers, and knobs, I say, "Just believe. You can do what you put your mind to." Again she peers into me, wrinkling her delicate, girly nose almost conspiratorially. I even imagine that the birthmark on the side of her neck has a smile. She gets in, throws back her shoulders, blows out some pent-up breath, and turns on the ignition key, lightly toeing the gas pedal. We get off to a slow crawl and continue that way for about a half-mile. Then a touch of relaxation spreads across her face, and the speed picks up. (A somewhat French *film noir* begins to play on the screen in the backroom of my mind. Anna and I are in a bedroom like an Enchantment casita, but more Parisian, like I'd seen in some Hemingway movie. She's dressed only in a black bra and black panties. I'm looking into the dark, soft pools of her eyes, hoping to find myself.)

An oncoming car causes Anna to tense up. My eyes see the car; my mind knows the emotion she must be feeling. "You're alright. You're doing fine." The car passes in its lane. Anna's face releases a smile. She did it! Very softly, she says, *Thanks,* giving me a quick, light tap on my left thigh. (*Wow,* she sheepishly thinks. *What's getting into me?*)

Near the entrance to the resort parking lot, I give her the hand signal to slow down, and finally say, "Pull over to the side." She gently applies the brake, as we approach the gatehouse. "I don't imagine you have a license?"

She shakes her head with the giddy smile of a teenager, pushing that wild strand of her hair back over her ear. Her cheeks flush with victory. She has achieved something new. It is as if she has broken an old mold and opened a new phase of life. I feel my heart skip a tender beat. Here I am, seated with an obviously attractive, intelligent, vulnerable woman caught in a whirl of change. Change she is unprepared for, but beginning to open up to. And what does a White Knight like me relish more than the damsel in distress?

The hike up to the little mesa at the top is not a long climb and only mildly steep. The path is narrow. I lead she follows mostly in silence. We have both recently absorbed some of the language of the land – the silence of the rocks of the ages. As we near the top, she exclaims. "Look, a ghost tree! My uncle Guido painted one of those, but it wasn't so twisted."

"It's a dead juniper," I explain. "It could be a thousand years old. They say it is twisted like that because it grew so near a vortex. The vortex energy pushed and pulled it, so they say." She looks at me quizzically, as if to ask: Are you pulling my leg?

In the final big step onto the hillock mesa, I stop and offer her a helping hand. She seems to be questioning herself. Her dark eyebrows knit a little for a moment. Then she extends her hand to me with a cautious smile. Her hand feels soft and small, feminine. More wonderful than anything I've touched since Amy slipped into the frigid zone. At that moment, we exchange what I feel is a current of synergy, a connection, a silent bond.

When we straighten up on the mesa top, we both take in and release cleansing breaths. We can see the commercial resort, built at the mouth of the holy canyon – controversial, yet tastefully, sensitively created. Off to the right, we can see the crimson cliffs of the sacred box canyon that stretches several miles under a cloudless azure sky. We are looking at Sedona's six-star resort, Enchantment. I know that first hand because that is where Patsy Sullivan, from the Downtown Travel Agency, booked me into this handful of transformative years ago. At that time, they were running a Film Festival Special: reduced rates for the casitas and continuous shuttles into the town for the film times. I was thrilled with my casita – basically two rooms, sitting and sleeping, with views to wow, and a kitchenette, bar, and frig, and of course, room-service. They made you feel royally welcome. Enchantment speaks the body language of a successful vacation spot – a bouquet of native wildflowers on the coffee table, a bottle of Champagne in an ice bucket, and a monogrammed bathrobe. But at the time, I was headless horseman riding out of anhedonia.

The first day there, I met Mitzi Stein on the shuttle to the films. She was a buxom blonde in expensive clothes, and recently divorced. She had one of the bigger, more dollars casitas up the hill with a hot tub on a private deck that looked up into the starry heavens. I might have told you that. After the second day, she invited me to come up to her casita "for a drink and a soak." I know that my frivolous mind could just see her dropping her robe and playfully stepping naked down into the steamy water. She had a nice body. And we know how quickly the male imagination can lift off like a rocket. But, thanks be to God, I wasn't ready for a fling with a recent, needy divorcee. My childhood Catholicism had rooted deep. My soul wasn't ready for recreational sex. One part of me craved it; a deeper part knew it could harm both of us. Nevertheless, now, up here on the vortex, with a woman whose substance I sense, I feel ready, and able to be tender.

Anna and I sit down on an inviting flat rock on this male-female Kachina energy vortex, looking out toward the resort and the canyon of ancestral secrets. I can sense that she is bouncing between relaxing and pulling back into her shell. Then she lets out an *Oooh!* Her hand flies to her mouth. I follow the line of her gaze. A guy with a white Gatsby golf hat is getting out of one of the golf carts at the front door. I turn to her and catch a wild terror burning in her eyes. "Are you all right?" She doesn't respond, just stares at the man who has just alighted from the golf cart. The guy in the white cap walks in the front door. She remains frozen silent for a while. I can vicariously hear her heart trumping.

Then she opens, "This is obviously a spirit place. I feel an energy coming over me. And yes, it's about time I exorcised the damn demon. Do you mind if I tell you a sad story? One I've never told to anyone. I suddenly feel the need, here and now, to release this hurt, this wound. This beautiful place seems to call me to finally let it go. Maybe it **is** the vortex energy. I'm sure this sacred canyon has heard a lot of stories like mine. I tremble with the urgency to unload this bottled-up evil ghost. This place seems to shout: *Let it go.*"

I smile, nod, and reach over to offer her a hand to hold. She squeezes my hand. I can feel both her fear and her gratitude. Once again, a surge of connection. Maybe there is something to the vortex mythos. Beginning slowly, and then more courageously, she tells me about her flat mate, Cassie, and the sicko who had dumped her on the couch, and the miscarriage, and the loss of a singular friendship. She brushes away the tears that slide down her soft cheeks. At that moment, I hear a radiance in her. She has suffered, and has withdrawn into a self-protective safe haven of work and an isolated life. Seated together on the flat rock overlooking the hallowed canyon, a man and a woman are reaching across *the between* of female and male. She is giving a part of herself to me. She is trusting me with a long-hurting secret. I know at that moment that I desire this flesh-and-soul woman as my destiny – my one. There's no gainsaying: Love is mostly about trust.

I am so happy that I don't catch the confusion within her. Inside her heart of hearts, our deepening bond of friendship is making her return to New York all the more confusing. After all, she has little reason to believe that she can enter into an intimate relationship with a man. She hasn't been with a man since her junior year in college – the year before she and Cassie moved in together. The year after that coed relationship with a man had left her empty.

After the hike, as we pull out of the trailhead parking lot, she looks at me with that little girl grin, and I let her drive the same stretch of road, and then take back over. As she climbs back into the passenger seat, she smiles prettily. *I'm enjoying this,* her smile says, and there is no sign of the lip-mouth tension that I'd noticed in the Steven's back yard. On the way into town, I talk about the resort, and my cozy stay in the casita (leaving out any mention of Mitzi Stein). I start to tell her about the five star *Yavapi Restaurant,* leading up to inviting her for a supper.

"Sounds wonderful. My treat," she bursts in. "You've already treated me. And I owe you for the driving lesson. That was fun. How about tomorrow night?"

Later, I will remember thinking at that moment, *You're fun to be with.*

Her forehead furrowing, she asks, "Do you mind if I ask if you believe that the vortex really twisted that juniper?"

I pause, pursing my lips, feeling a tightening in my chest. I'm not eager to get started on my beliefs with her. She has come to the present plateau of her life by a totally different road from mine. An evolving relationship needs time and space.

"I mean, do you believe in vortexes?"

"I suppose the answer has to be "yes" and "no. Or better, I guess I should say, I don't disbelieve in the possibility that there is an energy in the earth that can escape in certain special places. There are other spots in the world, like Glastonbury, that make the same claims. It's just that in my life I have spent buckets of energy on beliefs. I'm trying to simplify. I don't have the time nor the inclination to get involved with small beliefs like vortexes." Anna just nods her head. We are approaching the old painter's house, and she doesn't seem ready to pursue the belief question either.

The next dawning morning I am sitting on my back deck, oblivious to the early mating calls of the mourning doves and the crispness of late fall. I'm spooning in my traditional Malachy morning bowl of Irish rolled oats, sesame seeds, and almond milk, just like my grandfather did. My mind is roiling after a night of wrestling with beliefs. I like Anna. I like her a lot. Sure and be golly, the limbic region of my brain is firing hints of sex. It habitually does. But I want more than what the reptile and the elk want. I want a genuine man and woman connection. I know I have to make haste slowly. She seems a little like that timid turtle, who could easily be spooked back into her hiding shell.

Washed out from wondering if she likes me, I set my bowl on the side table and try to concentrate on my breath. Soon, my tired mind wanders out into the pine trees and blue sky, lapsing into one of my signature inner colloquies: *Damn it, to me, those big questions still seem crucial, certainly important, although they can quickly fall into the bogs of wordy words. I've wasted a lot of my life bogged down in words and concepts. My mind is like quicksand. Thanks to Tennessee blonde, I'm on the border of understanding that too much rationality closes one off from the sensuous world around and the feelings of others – to say nothing of one's own feelings. Even as I dabble in the new physics, I get entangled trying to decide which word is best. I would have enjoyed talking to Anna's friend, Amit. It's not whether the* **primal stuff** *is bits of information, bits of knowledge, bits of consciousness, bits of energy, or bits of matter, it's the bottom line: we are each a bit of the One Bit – of the whole All. This talk about Ultimate Reality and law of the conservation of consciousness, (meaning something akin to recycling and reincarnation,) is all red herring. I have to confess that I have a painful propensity to think that I'm the hot-shit mind who will come upon the new Rosetta Stone to decode the age-old mysteries.*

However, just possibly, I think I am seeing one answer that works. Nothing new. Smacks of the Galilean's answer: do kind things for others – give a cup of cold water. At the same time, we need to take a page from the Buddha: one has to have a kind mind – that **clear kind blue mind** *– before one's kind acts can rise above the prevailing riptide of self-seeking. Somehow meeting Anna has loosened some of my tight psychic knots.*

I hear my friend the wise old owl hoot, signing off after a long, solitary night, alone in the blackness. I get up to go in and get dressed to go out for a mind-emptying walk in the woods. I reiterate to myself what is now one of the wordy planks of my personal life mission statement: *It's not about getting my lily white butt into the pearly gates. It's about contributing to the building up the mystery – the mystery of the universes, the mystery of life, the mystery of human consciousness, and what the future will be, if mankind and the biosphere are to have a future. Hopefully, random acts of kindness can build up the mind of future-man, one random act at a time.*

That same morning, the day after hiking up to the Kachina vortex, Anna awakes about eight o'clock, late by her new, normal body clock. But what is normal anymore? She feels bodily languid and mentally confused. It had been a fitful night. From the rumpled state of the mannish black sheets on her bed come vague whiffs of her dream time. The realization grows in her mind: she is coming out of "the return of the phantom of the schoolyard." It has to be a signal to her that the tectonic plates of her life are shifting. That nightmare has always been basically the same – boys taunting her, calling her "witch" and "devil's child." But it has been sometime since the horror of the night ordeal has returned to upset her so physically. She thought her life was stabilizing. Back in the beginning of her apartment days, the phantoms came on nights when she had spent a lot of reclusive hours, home alone – as if the phantoms were connected to isolation issues, relationship issues. Even then she was competent and functional during the day, in fact, eminently so. But in those long, dark night hours with only a science fiction novel or some scientific journal, the black clouds moved into the vacuum. She had gone to a woman therapist who prescribed some drugs that made her feel spacey and lethargic the next day at work. After a couple of weeks, she threw the capsules down the toilet. She had been raised by a mother who knew hard knocks and lonely times. She, the daughter of a caged bird, had circled her wagons, put on her black stockings, and walked or taxied to her work station at the prestigious research facility.

After years of math work and experimental equations, she had put together a new equation for Callisto's rotation beyond Jupiter's radiation belt. Her research had helped the Institute win a big award three years ago. Yes, she was strong by day – committed, competent, and cooperative. And she was strong in resisting her boss, Wyatt the dapper man. She knew he wanted to have his way with her. Even his bodily gestures and poses announced: *predator.* Layla let slip some sordid details at the water cooler. Instinctively Anna feared him and all men with little direction to their animal drives. She had never forgotten the predator who knocked up her drugged roommate. A ghost now released.

In the back of her mind, there floats a pleasant feeling. She realizes that her heart hadn't felt her customary, baseline dread when she was with John yesterday. He had made her feel listened to. Yet even he emits that scary scent of a man. And her limbic brain is sending warning signals that he has to have those same, potentially explosive animal drives that turn nice boys into bullies. They seem to come with the gonads. Still, he had listened to her. He seemed to have a respect for her. Still, like a puma in the wild would, she reminds herself to tread carefully, always on alert to sniff danger.

Anna shakes her head and runs her fingers though her long tangled hair. Despite her female fears, a look of happiness crinkles around her eyes, *Yes, she had enjoyed her day with a man who seems to be trying to get out from under his rock of heavy questions. Funny how this girl who grew-up in the bus-barns of anti-clericalism, feels drawn to two serious, almost religious minded guys –Amit, and now John. When Gwen had winked at her in the Stevens' backyard, she knew a whole lot more about the man she was talking with. He is the guy who goes into The Cave and bares his soul wounds, even about sex. He's lonely and looking for something more.*

Shaking her head again and grinning, she rolls over onto her right side: *What are you thinking, woman? You hardly know this man, and you know that men can hurt a girl. In Everyman, there is a potential bully, disguised like the wolf in little Red Riding Hood.*

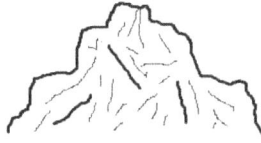

Anna and I get to the *Yavapi Restaurant* early. I want to make sure we'd get a window table since I remember seeing the moon rising over Kachina woman. Anna looks absolutely stunning in a long white, calf-length dress with her left shoulder bare and a modest cleavage. She tells me with sincere pride that she had found the dress at the Twice Nice Thrift Store, which supports a safe house for abused women. Kai had told her about it. Her voice lilts with happiness as she half-whirls. I can tell that to her, it isn't how beautiful she looks; it is whom she has helped. For my part, it is an uplifting moment. I am the observer, witnessing the mystery of a person long imprisoned in the tower of herself, opening up to others. Oh, God, I pray, spare humans from their self-preoccupied dungeons. She is wearing no jewelry except her ironic Jesus bracelet and an unpretentious small silver wrist-watch with a thin black leather band. A purple wildflower tucked over her right ear, just above her birthmark, seems to explain the delicate scent I had noticed on the drive out. Or maybe it is just the scent of a woman my senses were delighting in.

When we get to the hostess station, Aubrey and Rosemary Mills are seated, waiting. Aubrey rises to greet us. "Good evening, John. We're waiting for Paul and Tanya. It's their anniversary, and we are going to celebrate, as friends do. Is this lovely lady the physicist, Sally Stevens was raving about at the board meeting yesterday?" Anna flushes, but smiles. She obviously feels good about herself. She can't remember being appreciated like this.

Rosemary has risen to stand at her husband's side, linking her arm in his. "Aubrey and Rosemary Mills, allow me to introduce Dr. Anna Pagani, who yes, is a physicist, and a very special woman." She hears the sincerity in his voice. Her heart hears that "*a special woman*" for the first time in her life.

"Nice to meet you doctor. Sally Stevens said you were charming," the tall gray-haired man with a twinkle in his eyes says. "Maybe you'll teach a course at OLLI. I don't think we've ever had a course in quantum physics. I hear it's very profound, almost religious."

I see the hostess holding menus to her chest. "Wish Paul and Tanya a happy anniversary for us," I say nodding to the hostess, and gesturing to Anna to go first. "Glad you're going to co-facilitate that course with Paul," Aubrey calls out as we start to follow the hostess.

The personal presence of Aubrey, at that moment of my own evolving feelings, throws open the floodgates of my mind to the cultural barriers, long ago absorbed as personal restraints. Something clicks in my mind. *Eureka*, I finally know the answer of answers.

With her tall curvy body and lush dark hair, Anna turns a sea of male heads as we flow behind the receptionist to our window table. In high heels, she's a Roman goddess. I'd wager that few, if any, of her coveting admirers were troubled by her bright crimson birthmark. And I've got to suspect she might be enjoying a little gender attention. It's obvious from her cautious body language that she isn't used to being seen as a person in a beautiful body. Naturally, here in our society, no one dares whisper aloud: *God, look at that ugly mark on her neck.*

The room is coming alive with the chatter of conversations and the clatter of silverware. Champagne corks are popping and waiters are rattling off the evening's specials. From the dancing sparkle in her eyes, I am thrilled to see that Anna is experiencing something novel and exciting. She is a bud opening. And as my grandfather was wont to say: It warms the cockles of mi heart, to see her coming alive. It's a shot-in-the-arm one's doesn't often get. I credit the land and the startle experience of finding oneself called out of old routine habits to face a changing life and death. To me, she is the Snow White, long asleep, wakening up to the magic of the red mountains.

Having sipped a little of her glass of red wine, Anna seems genuinely relaxed. "Oh, John, this is so much fun. I haven't been out to a place like this in years – if ever. Or perhaps I haven't felt so much like a woman treated as a woman – if ever. Yet, friend John, and I feel you are my friend, pardon my frankness. I'm not sure I can live here in old Guido's house. So, don't get your hopes up, mister man. Maybe the folk saying is true: one can't take the City out of the Bronx girl. But I tell you what, mister trusting man, tonight, I'm here, now, this night, and I feel alive. Let's *carpe diem*," she says with her enchanting coed's smile.

At that moment, Reggie our waiter arrives with a litany of specials, and pencil poised. "What would please Mr. Malachy tonight?" the Sicilian lovely asks, with a devil-may-care lilt in her voice. "Do they serve a big, red Maine lobster? You are being treated, sir. Go for it. I don't get many opportunities to repay people who have been nice to me."

"I think I'll have the buffalo tenderloin, if mi lady doesn't mind" I respond. "I like buffalo – good healthy red meat. It's always cooked perfectly here. You shouldn't overcook buffalo. Actually, I don't eat much red meat anymore. I'm trying to live healthier, but every once in a while it feels good to do something a tad naughty."

"Oh. And what does naughty boy recommend for a lady who doesn't eat "red meat?""

"If mi lady permits, I might suggest the trout almondine. The trout here is fresh daily, from a trout farm up on the east side of Oak Creek, not that far from where we first met."

Anna's mind rushes back to that encounter: She was jazzed with the hiking, the doe drinking, and John's soft baritone voice reminding her of Amit. His warm brown eyes fell like wet rain through her body. But his phrase *the big questions* had scared her. She has long wanted to avoid life's scary questions. She isn't ready. Most of the world around her has ways of avoiding them: just keep running, keep buying, and, of course, keep having sex. Amit liked to talk about the key questions that quantum physics had answers for. Amit would have liked John, and John would like Amit. They're both conscientious men, she confesses, surprised at what she is thinking, or feeling. That admission stirs in her female viscera: *Do I want these thoughts? Can I handle...?*

Then her mind almost returns to the present moment. What she would really like to eat is something like Mama's manicotti, the comfort food of her childhood. She knew it put pounds on her hips, but it had helped her get through the stress of her school-yard days. The school yard is another one of those places you can never completely take the girl out of. On the upper floors of her consciousness, she is having a grand time, yet she knows she is a little over her head. Anything along the lines of Mama's manicotti would be not fitting in to this marvelous adventure.

Reggie brings her trout in a covered silver tray. He opens it with pride. It looks natural like one of those wild trout she had seen in magazines, leaping free of its engulfing world. She turns her head to the side as Reggie removes the head and de-bones her catch-of-the day.

Moments later she says, "John Malachy, you are indeed a good guide. This trout truly melts in my mouth." (*Why did I say, guide,* she thinks.) The meal progresses: John's buffalo is cooked to tender perfection. They talk of hiking, Sedona's small town feeling of friendliness, and, of course, the restorative energy of the ancestral red hills. But neither broaches the stirring change going on within each of them.

"Aubrey seemed like a nice man. He has a warm smile," Anna says.

"Ooh, he's better than nice. In my book, he, and people like him, are the true celebrities of society. They are people who are renowned for doing something significant for the common good. My mother would have called them "saints." Your friend from Mumbai would probably call them "avatars." That's Sanskrit for a divine being who has come down to show us the way forward by their kindness to mankind. Perhaps they can save us from the disaster. Aubrey is a generous man, dedicated to his wife, his family, his friends, and education. **And he's dying**, I say, my voice dampening. There's nothing the doctors can do. It's just a short matter of time."

"Oh, I'm sorry, John. Sounds like he's a good friend."

"Aubrey is one of those rare people who make everyone feel like he's their friend. And he genuinely is. He makes everyone feel that they are important. He's been the president of OLLI – the local Osher Lifelong Learning Institute for the last several years. OLLI is a big nation-wide community learning movement. All volunteers. Each one doing his own thing. It takes a special grace to keep that gang of live-wires, who think they have something to teach the world, all pulling together. He has a keen mind too. He volunteer-teaches about three classes a semester. He likes history, but teaches all kinds of courses. He taught one on Hinduism a few of semesters ago." (Anna's mind flies to Amit, the Brahman, and the Atman.)

"He seemed happy that you are going to co-facilitate with Paul. Who's Paul?"

"Paul's a hiking buddy. Well educated and a voracious reader. Like Aubrey, he's a man of service – involved in a lot of civic things. They both shame me."

"What's your course on?"

"It's not my course. Paul designed it. OLLI seminars are supposed to be interactive. Not teachers, facilitators. It's the facilitator's job to get people mixing it up – discussing, dialoguing, encountering one another. Stir up the hive mind. Paul has put together some readings on communication and collaboration. When I mentioned on one of our hikes that I had just finished David Brook's book, *The Social Animal,* he replied that he was going to facilitate a course, using Brooks, Tomasello, and Buber. He asked me to co-facilitate."

"Sounds like pretty heady stuff."

"It is. That's the silly irony of it. I'm trying to get out of my head, into my senses and direct experience, out of my lock-step thinking. I've spent too much of my life, turning over stones looking for answers to what I confess to calling 'the big soul-searing questions.' They are big indeed – big mysteries! Too big for words, concepts, and books. Too big for dogmas and religions that like to hang, like bats, in the dark past. Sometimes I fear that mankind's boat is sinking. But here surrounded by the red rocks, I feel that I am hiking toward a place of balance. There are **many** smoking questions, and at least **one** answer that might save us from wasting our lives."

"What's the one answer?" Anna asks cautiously, yet with sincere interest in her voice. She recalls Amit and his whelming quantum answers.

"You met **one answer** at the hostess stand: Aubrey Mills is a living manifestation of one of the true answers: building up the *humanum*. Building up Man – body/mind/spirit. Contributing, like a stream contributes to the river. Contributing one's little, private mind to the big ongoing mind of *Homo sapiens*. You could say that Aubrey is a builder-up of social capital. Or as Martin Buber put it: he is responding to the everyday people in his own back yard. If we contribute to our particular web of connections, the other questions will take care of themselves, even without the right words. There may be many other words to wrap the answer in, but right now, *kindness to others* works for me. Or love.

"Aubrey is going to die soon, but the mind of man will evolve on, richer for his having lived a life of caring. We all die. He has answered his call, one small step for mankind."

When I get home after our dinner in the moonlight, there is no way on earth that I am going to count a few sheep and go off to the land of dancing stars. Having babbled so much about my secret demons, I'm drained. I'm not proud of talking about myself. I'm just lonely, and addicted to myself. At the same time, I am super-stoked by the open possibility of a relationship, my unheralded Holy Grail. Yet, I feel threatened by her words, *I'm not sure I can live here. Don't get your hopes up, Mister Man.*

I don't think I could live in New York. Not after Sedona. But maybe for her, I'd try. Do I have the courage to try for someone else? Good question.

I send an intention into the ley lines of the cosmos: *May she stay. May we become a couple.*

Painfully, I accept that I am a living contradiction: Parched for relationship, I hide from my testosterone needs in Buber books and quantum theories. Unsure of self as a loving person, I hide out like a Dark Age monk in the library, pouring over science releases, or buying them to annotate. I'm a cultural misfit. I don't seem to really have the courage to just be.

Still weak, I make myself a stinger with white crème de menthe and brandy, and head to my study – my comfort zone, my Boy Scout tent. I feel the need for both: comfort and protection. I can't find a way to avoid the soothing image of the wonderful woman who now stands center stage in my mind. She also seems to need courage. We are soul mates in a sense.

I suppose we all have moments like this, weak and alone, lonesome and fragile. I step inside my safe zone with a sense of familiarity and relief. I hit the button, and the back eight feet of the glass roof slides open to the beautiful talking galaxies, and the world that I perceive. The world that perceives me. Tonight I don't feel as alone as I have since I turned my back on the comforting myths of my boyhood. My fear of failing is fading.

Over the years, I've been a mental gadfly. I may have a touch of OCD (obsessive compulsive disorder). All my books are religiously grouped in sections, mostly reflecting my journey: Dick and Jane, the Hardy Boys, the Baltimore Catechism, the Gospels, the Fathers of the Desert, Zen and the Chop-Wood-Carry-Water traditions, Krishnamurti, Martin Buber, the neuroscientists, the quantum gang, and now Emily's mindfulness books – both the spiritual and the scientific.

Outside it has rained. A light night rain has just stopped falling between the pinyon pines and the junipers which stand like silent sentinels in the darkness around my little, monkish sanctuary. The night air falls around me. Ah, the forest smells rinsed and soft, as if its hurtful toxins have been washed away. The wide world around my refuge is motionless: the cicadas have stopped thrumming and the coyotes haven't yet started calling to one another. I do cherish the velvet stillness of the high country nights, although they tempt one to lapse into depressed feelings when one feels so alone.

To occupy my mind and distract the monkey in my head from continuously returning to Anna in her white showcase dress, I go to the Buber section of my books, and pick out *The Way of Man* and *The Letters of Martin Buber,* searching for a couple of soul-food passages that might fit the moment and my mood. Plainly the unheard, but clamorous voices in the inner cavern of my psyche are debating one of my new existential dilemmas: if you get involved with a woman, you'll never stick to your quest for answers to your life long preoccupations. All that invested effort will be go down the drain. You may never intellectually contribute to the species as a knowing bit. Isn't that what you are about, John Malachy?

I'm drawn to Martin Buber because he was a man who walked his talk. A journey I myself seem to be having a problem keeping on with. Unlike me, he got off to a rough start in the delicate arena of relating. When he was three-years-old, his beautiful, blue-eyed mother disappeared. (Years later it was learned that she had gone off to Russia and married a soldier.) His distraught father sent wee Mordecai to live with his highly educated and orthodox Jewish grandparents in Austria. There, along the Danube, young Mordecai discovered the love of learning.

When he was twenty-one, he met Paula Winkler at a summer Germanics seminar. Paula, a Munich Catholic by upbringing, is described by her biographers as a wild elfin, tough, and intelligent, who had lived in an artist's colony. Martin, the orthodox Jewish boy-scholar, made a mighty choice and married her the next year. Their first child arrived a year later. They were together as the bonded-pair until her death 58 years later. Her biographers say she was his strength. They were an acorn of two, that nucleus community of the *humanum.* After her death, Martin worked on alone for almost a decade. He staunchly championed a bi-national state for the "Holy Land," firm in the face of Ben Gurion. In *The Way of Man,* I find highlighted: *Everyone should carefully observe what his heart draws him to, and then choose this way with all his strength."*

A couple of Buber's letters stand out in my memory, so I page through the early letters, and find highlighted: *But when I found you, I found my soul. You came and gave me my soul.* That passage had struck me when I first read it. Now I think I understand it. Tonight, with the moon racing in and out of clouds, I have hope. Like the journey that begins with one step, the journey to *the land of the love of mankind* can best **begin** with the love of one particular person. Especially now when mankind teeters like Humpty Dumpty on the precarious edge of the great wall of survival, we need a destiny to hang onto. We were once a group, then we lost our old-way of surviving, and became separate little, individual islands. Now that the planet seems to be reaching another threshold, the challenge is to fuse the long past of togetherness with the modern mind set of "Hey, I'm it. I'm *the hero* of my great narrative." Many fear that if mankind has a great fall, all the King's knights will not be able to put him together again.

Paula, who converted to Zionism, was Martin's *one.* He was her *Thou.* She was the comfort zone that gave him the strength to live a life that brought him to be nominated for both the Nobel Prize for literature, and the Nobel Prize for peace. Both championed by the second Secretary General of the United Nations, Dag Hammarskjold. The morning before Secretary Hammarskjold's plane, on a peace mission, crashed in the Congo, he was translating Martin's classic, *I and Thou,* into Swedish. His notes were found on the nightstand next to his bed.

The tiny pinpricks of light winking between the clouds in the moist sky above me are too sweet to ignore. I feel the need for companionship, so I sit down at my desk and light a scented candle. I read in the quiet light and comforting glow of the beeswax. As I page though my underlined and asterisks sections, I come to what I'm looking for: *It is from one person to another that the heavenly bread of self is passed.* And pages later: *Man did not exist before having a fellow being. Man becomes an I through a You.* And then I have to laugh at myself, the lapsed Catholic reading questions from the Talmud. In a letter to Paula two years after they were married, Martin wrote: *...one must tie the whole riddle of the universe to a single person...In the Talmud it says: 'He who meditates on four things, for him it would have been better had he not come into the world; these four are: what is above, what is below, what was before, and what will be after.' I would prefer to say: Meditate on all mysteries,* __*but in one person who is yours,*__ (bold print and underlining mine). I think Buber would say: your destiny is given to you by your journey. Bingo! I pause for a moment of reflection. Buber's words continue: *and you lie upon the heart of the universe. For everything is in everyone, and only love can extract it.*

Inside my being, a river of excitement is on the rise and gathering strength. I feel that my mental cataracts are falling off. I realize with a new confidence that **I want** what Buber says all men want: to be a *Thou* to an *Other.* That's the Sisyphus-like challenge. The opposite scenario – the pull to treat the other as an *it* – is deeply scripted in the media culture – the fourth estate of our hive mind. I feel my chest tightening. Something in me is arising. I repeat my new intention: *May she stay. May we become as one.*

I blow out the candle, and sit in a darkness that feels like light, not the light from above, but from within. I'm scared, but recalling Anna's smile, there's a flicker in the tunnel. My mind wanders back to a sentence in Brad Stevens' article: *People who can articulate their life purpose in one sentence have the best chance of being happy.* I can do that thanks to those words of Buber.

I finally got to bed that night of our dinner, seeing only her in the canyon moonlight of my imagination. I fell into a deep sleep, planning to go back more carefully into my notes on Buber's *I and Thou* in the morning. The art of relationship stormed high on the peaks of my mind, besides I knew Paul wanted me to be able to inject some relationship nuggets to stimulate the discussion in his upcoming seminar on "Cooperation and Collaboration." But in truth, I knew I had to keep waylaying my mind, knowing that I would be caught in repeating loops of Anna memories. I fell asleep wondering how much time I had, if any time, wondering how soon would she be leaving to go back to that grimy New York. She had made it clear at dinner that she was undecided, despite all the canyon magic. For once, I felt proud of myself, I had been smart enough to know that I had to wait. I shouldn't push her river.

As she slips into the black silk sheets of Guido's master bed that same night, Anna Pagani semi-consciously mumbles, *These sad sheets have to go*. Unknown to the darkness watching around her, and even to the world emerging within her, she is opening like a legendary morning glory to a new light in her heart. The light has been there from the beginning, but it has been hidden under bushel basket of hurt. A brave, new untried world is poised to dawn for her. Tender had been the night of the Boynton Canyon dinner – not because of the stunning show of the moon standing behind the Kachina hoodoo, where they had sat together and shared, days before; not because of the trout almondine that melted in her mouth; nor because they had been in a bright, happy social space, new to her, where islands of people sounded like a caravan of people coming to meet one another. No, it was he… that lost seeker. Or was she simply discovering her buried desire for a male companion in her life? Her father had not been a man for her when she was dragged to a school she didn't want to go to … a place without any friends. He had failed to stand up for her. He had been unable to muster up the courage she needed. Her Changing Woman within quietly knows that destiny is setting before her a summons to courage – a summons to relate to a man.

The man had listened to her Cassie sadness – a secret locked in the dungeon of her heart for way too many years. She was surprised that she opened up that page of her hurts, but she had seen that devil's golf cap that made her tremble deep inside – reminding her of the presence of evil. At the same time she had sensed an emerging power of balance in John's spirit. So, she had finally found the courage to let that black cat out of the bag. Subliminally, she is aware that she feels safe with him. She smiles, surprised that she opened that Pandora's box after all these years. Her face brightens as she recalls the warmth of his touch, holding her hand. Being touched like that is special. She remembers Commander Andromeda.

But a relationship? A man-woman relationship? Wow! Yes, she'll need courage!

John, she senses, needs to thicken his courage too. He needs somebody walking with him. He is a flawed healer, her drowsy mind muses, continuing her unstoppable self-monologue. He's a healer because, like Amit, he cares about the world's wounds. In a world going blind to its own wounds, he cares about others. (We all journey somewhat flawed, don't we?)

My heart feels his smothered wounds, his perceived personal failures. For the second time in my life, I heard another person's pain. These feelings are a pleasant surprise. I'm beginning to feel. He laid his troubles before me, not weakly, but candidly, approaching guilelessly…perhaps like a little boy does with his mother. He isn't asking for sympathy. He seems to be saying, I want to be honest and open with you. You should know a little bit more about me, because you have a right to know who is walking toward you.

In his mind's eye, he has partially failed as a teacher, as a husband, and worst of all as a father. Not totally, but somewhat.

Matter-of-factly, with no self-serving feeling, he laid bare those tender feelings. He opened up and trusted me, whom, in a sense, he hardly knows. Still, I get the definite sense that he sees something in me that he recognizes... he appreciates. Some energy in me seems to resonate with him. It's more than my body, though I catch that he appreciates that too. (Her face registers pleasure.) We women, once we stop and open our eyes and ears, and calm our multi-tasking, catch the vibes. We are like Spider Woman. We know how to listen patiently to the tiniest fly.

Maybe his flaws give him insight into me. Seldom before have I thought of myself as empathic. *Never before have I felt so trusted as a person,* she admits to herself. *I've probably never looked upon a man as a fragile person, just like I am fragile. They've always been the tough guys who laughed at me, or lechers who want nothing more than to grab my rear end.* (She recalls the guy at the Sevens' party.). *I had no doubts about what Mr. wavy-hair was after. His eyes, his body moves were all about animal pleasure. John's eyes, on the other hand, were sincerely accepting, even admiring some light in me.*

After tossing and turning, Anna gets out of bed, grabs her Bali sarong, and goes to the kitchen where Kai always has a tea kettle of water ready to heat, and an assortment of tea bags. She opens one chamomile and one valerian, smirking at her scientific approach to tea and sleep. She is, after all, a scientist. And in a confused fashion, she vaguely intends to return to her bench and office. In a corner of her mind, she is also vaguely aware that she is both running away from some feelings about a sexual relationship, and seriously in need of some sleep if she is to function rationally. Of course, she wants to be rational about the decision staring her in the face. Relating looms as a high stakes challenge.

The night is warm. And she feels a warmth in her heart and belly. In her short, silk white nightie and her colorful sarong, she steps outside into Guido's Eden, and languidly flows herself onto the lounge-chair. Her mind wants to canter, but her physical self is accepting what is – she's emotionally drained. She smiles up into the universe where the stars and the constellations steal the show. She collapses into the arms of Morpheus.

Sometime later, she finds herself drifting back to the shore people call *reality*. Again she begins going over the same mine-field: I'm not totally sure of anything anymore. Mister John appears to be different – strong in some ways, and yet needy. Time will tell. He has his problems too. His words about needing the courage to fail, the courage to live without dogmas, to live in mystery felt okay when he was opening up. In some subtle way, the high country is both opening my physical eyes to the beauty of nature, but also opening my inner eyes to the hollow-ness of my life without any solid touch of connection to another. In a sense, I too have failed. As a child, I internalized the school yard bullies' victimization. Attempting to be gentle on myself, as John advises, I remind myself that I was young and had no mentor. Now my eyes seem to be opening to that culture of antagonism which paralyzed my emotions. I let those bully boys write my story.

I like John. He is a sincere searcher. He reads a lot about relationship. I sense that he wants a person in his life. He wants me. That relationship thinker Buber seems to be one of his go-to men. Even if something serious, like whatever my mystery is dreaming of, doesn't work out, his friendship will be a help on the journey I now feel called to set out on. Destiny calls. Walking beside a fellow pilgrim is a happy-making walk.

A large, midnight black corvid, flapping and croaking, alights on the courtyard tile roof. She does not know if it is a crow or a raven, nor does she know anything about messengers. Her methodical mind sinks back into her concerns: Is John really a man I can live with? Contribute to? Or am I so molded in my ways that I won't be up to sharing the journey with another – a man. But, yes, without words to explain it, I feel that I have something to offer him. He is too roughshod on himself. He seems to have a touch of what a professor back in college called "an inferiority complex." I feel a budding intuition opening up to the influence of this new unknown presence in my firmament. My inner message-sender signals: a woman of flesh can be comforting and confirming to a man in need. Helping another – be it child or woman or man – is a woman's rightful destiny.

She takes a sip of her neglected, now tepid, sleepy time tea, her mind rambling on: Besides, I hear my own chaos with. My inner signs are rebelling at my isolation: *You need to be connected. You have been out in the cold too long.* She puts down the tea, tucks her legs underneath her, and wraps her arms around herself against the lonely night air. *I can tell that he is attracted to me – both physically and, I dare say, spiritually.* Not really clear about what words like those mean. The image of Amit hitting the steering wheel with the butt of his hand and emoting "Words, words" flashes across her back mind for the hundredth time. *But Mother Nature seems to be throwing open some of the shutters of my mind. A new way of seeing reality is extending my toe into new waters. John seems to be tapping into a side of me that has been submerged for years. He's made me feel like Snow White awakening.*

She winks at the ebony, night bird, gets ups, and shuffles into bed, hoping the tea will silence her prancing mind. But she finds herself still wrestling with her decision. *I've been a successful scientist. But have I been a real woman? Can I be a caring woman? Watching Uncle Guido go into who-knows-where must have amplified the call of this place. That call has been the kind of storm that brings up the mud from the bottom of the pond – the ugly mud that nourishes the beautiful lily and allows it to open up. To my own wild surprise, I suddenly want something more. More than the routine of the work bench, more than sad nights with some sci-fi novel. John used an aphorism: "The world is not comprehensible, but it is embraceable, through embracing one of its beings."* She rolls over, looking for her little brown Teddy, *I don't think you are enough anymore,* she whispers as the tea struggles to pull her away.

Below the surface of her mind, images of their night together keep drifting by. They had walked through the casitas, and he had talked of how memorable his nights there had been. Her brain wants to continue the narrative of their day, but her mind is approaching exhaustion. Thoughts keep coming in and fading out.

Back in college, she'd heard of "crossing the Rubicon." It was Cesar's daring choice to change his life. Hiking in nature has led her to the edge of a kind of personal Rubicon, and sub-liminally she is already ankle deep in that river ... and struggling to gather the courage to go on. Her wild mind finds herself on the drawbridge of decision.

Yes. For the first time in her life she feels *wanted*. Not as a bit of behind, but for who she is. She feels appreciated. Oh, it feels good to have finally got to this bridge to somewhere new! A Rubicon to be crossed! It's like grabbing the tiller of one's life – a tiller that has been foolishly locked on "Damn the torpedoes, same steam ahead." For a long, un-clocked time, she stares at the black screens of her eyelids, languidly letting her inner dialogue wander under the guiding signals of some Invisible Energy, that both her male friends, Amit and John, seem to understand, but she doesn't.

Thank you, her emerging-self drowsily whispers into the cosmos, whose vastness she has measured and mapped, but never felt close to. The canyons and the trees now feel closer. She is opening up to some kind of Presence that Uncle Guido felt in this land of wide space and timelessness. John feels it too, and Amit would love it here. Maybe someday he'll come to visit us here. *Us?!?*

The last image before she falls into sleep is in one of those casitas. John is there; she is wearing a short silk nighty and no undergarment – her female secret is partially visible, but she is not afraid, not threatened. Her dream self feels no need to hide her treasure.

The next morning, Anna awakes with a softhearted smile. She has been to the night mountain and has heard an answer to her burning question. It is not chiseled into stone, but it glows like the bush of possibility. She feels as if a good fairy has visited her in the night cave, and touched her life with the sparkling wand of direction. Rubbing her eyes alive, she remembers the jeep driver's words that 'change is Sedona's maiden name.' Outside her window, she can hear the plaintive *woo-oo-oo-oo* of a pair of gray doves relating, the *cow-cow-cow* call of an unmated young male quail broadcasting his need, and the hi-pitched back and forth songs of a pair of red cardinals. She remembers the ebony messenger on the courtyard roof.

Time to get up. Time to be out into the Presence, she exults to the vermillion walls, as she stands up, stretches, admiring the rosy-fingered dawn in the eastern sky out the bedroom window. She dresses, grabs a banana, and heads out to hike the Chapel Trail. Her morning hikes give her new zest. She passes a young woman about her own age, jogging with a large black dog next to her, well-trained and under strict voice control. She has seen a lot of women with dogs. She wonders if the dogs might be their stand-ins for a human companion. She's heard it said that dependable male companions don't come along that regularly. She smirks. Several times in the past, jogging along the Hudson, she had considered settling for a dog. Not now. Fate has lifted her relationship sights.

She returns an hour later to her house. After some corn polenta that Kai had left ready in the frying pan, and a bowl of mixed berries, she takes her cup of Ethiopian coffee to her studio – *Yes, it is now **her** studio. She has mentally crossed a bridge across the river. It is a chancy move. Cesar knew it was a make-it or break-it choice.* As a child of eight, she had been denied choice and dragged to a school chosen by others for her, without her consent. Today she feels strong. She has made a choice; she has chosen her a new trail for her life.

She passes Kai dusting in the living room with a swifter-duster and Nascha following along with a floor mop. "Good morning, Miss Anna," wide-eyed Nascha says politely. Kai smiles and winks. They are girl-friends now – uncomplicated females experiencing no inequality of status. They share the meme that goes back to the birth of humanity in an African savannah. Anna recalls Kai's sage words about it not being good to live alone. It always reminds her of something she heard way back in Catholic School. As she recalls it, God is musing about Adam, to the effect: *It's not good for man to be alone. I will make him a suitable helper.*

She sits down at the desk and picks up the phone. She knows the number.

"Institute for Theoretical Physics, how may I direct your call?"

"Dr. Abdul, please."

"Hello, this is Dr. Abdul," a tired sounding voice answers.

"Layla, Anna Pagani here. How are you? You sound down."

"Oh, Anna, I am. I'm sick, but let's not talk about that. Everything is fine at your apartment. I checked Sunday."

"That's what I'm calling about. Are you still interested in subletting the apartment? I'm going to stay here for at least a year. Maybe for good. Who knows anymore? It's freeing me of a lot of old, meaningless baggage I have been witlessly carrying. And you know what? I didn't even know I was it dragging around. Now my eyes are opening. Don't mention anything to Mr. Jones (Anna catches a garbled mumble from Layla. She thinks it might have been *bastard,* but she isn't sure. She smiles, flashing back to the word the gal in the Hike House used: *dirt bag.*) I'll write a request for a year's leave of absence. If he won't give me that, I'll quit. I want a life, Layla. I lived without a relationship. That's no life."

"Good for you. Oh, to have a real relationship. Wow! Yes, I'd love to rent your classy apartment for a year. Maybe I can heal there. I'm sure you won't miss Mr. A-hole."

"You've got that right, girl. How does a thousand a month sound?"

"Wow, that's a steal. Thank you, thank you, Anna. I have often suspected that below your professionalism there breathes a soft woman. I want you to know that I really appreciate this. It's the kindest thing that has happened in my life. Wow, the East Side. Here I come. I'll walk in there with a new attitude, and my highest heels. Love you."

Anna sits for a few minutes after hanging up from Layla. Sad. She is worrying that the office rumors might not be off the mark. Layla sounded like she is in serious trouble. Anna knows that she could have asked twice as much for the rent, but she feels good doing a kind deed for a woman in need. It's all rubbing off on her. She is available to be engaged by life.

Anna's mind begins to fill with harsh, toxic thoughts about the man in New York whom she considers one of the manifestations of the dark side of evil. The guy who thinks of women as just flesh, with clefts for men's animal pleasure. But some words of her new guide/friend, John, on reaching **clear, kind blue mind** come back. So she valiantly tries to visualize the doe deer in the West Fork. Her new mentor (she smiles knowing that to her he is more than a Merlin) says that visualization is a way to reach calm, to reach beyond the harsh chatter. She's ready for the possibility of calm. She's not sure she ever had it. In this storm of decisions, she sees calm as an island in paradise. Her visualization works for about 30 seconds.

Then she opens the drawer and finds the telephone directory, looking for a number she doesn't know. Luckily there is only one Malachy in Sedona. A little nervous, but actually excited and confident, she dials.

"Good morning. John Malachy speaking," the strong baritone voices answers.

"Good morning, John. How's the book coming? Anna Pagani calling."

"Yes, I recognize your voice. Nice to hear. And the book, oh, like everything Malachy, it's *in process.*"

"Say, Mister Man, I want to go to the Department of Motor Vehicles to get a learner's permit. Can you spare some time to drive me there?"

A smile peels like mountain thunder across John Malachy's face. His mantra-prayer has been answered. He winks at the phone, nodding to some unknown Reality. *She's staying! Lucky day,* his toes dance. *Destiny dawns. Our hearts are made for you, and will not rest until the rest in you, Relationship!*

"Most certainly," he says. "What works for you? I'm flexible."

"You interested in a hike early tomorrow morning? We could pick up the form and the instruction book afterwards."

"Sounds super. Have you ever hiked the Eagles' Nest Trail? It's on the way to the DMV. It climbs to the sky. You can see tomorrow from there."

"Perfect."

"I'll pick you up at seven. By the way, I'll bring a book to read, and you can fill in the forms right there, and get a permit, then and there. Maybe you'll want to drive a little on the way back into town. There's an easy stretch before we get back into town traffic."

Again, a happy smile breaks across the firmament. This time at her end of the line. "Thanks, John. You're an angel." To herself, giddily, *He likes me. He thinks I'm special. I'm a real presence to him. I could just feel it. Such a gift.*

The next morning, Anna sits in her dressing room slowly, dreamingly, brushing her long dark hair. A happy expression plays in the corners of her lips. She is looking forward to the day – the hike, the driving, and her new man friend. She looks directly into the liquid brown eyes of the woman in the mirror, something she has rarely done. She finds herself comfortable looking at the smiling woman who seems to be a newly emerging self. She's obviously a newly freed prisoner. She wonders what a pupa feels like when the chrysalis opens and the new butterfly see the first light of the future.

She had once read an article by some neuroscientist on "The Autobiographical Self." At the time, she only read it because she thought it was the kind of article Amit would like. Perhaps, she thought, they could become closer discussing an article like that. This morning she would like to share her new budding possibilities with him. He is still a hole in her heart, one of those potholes that never gets filled –the kind that stay in the middle of the road you continually go back to. But a relationship with Amit, her emerging self admits, is a chimera. Amit is history. John is possibility. As John says, "The present is all we have."

In her mind, she pictures Amit back with Shakti, that's what his culture, and a flighty woman, would expect. He's probably not personally happy. He has no *I-Thou* relationship like John talked about. The gallant brown man is living the lonely story of a Quixote tilting at the windmills of abuse, but having no real mutual close relationship to make his steps quicken. Unlike the Man from La Mancha he has no scullery Dulcinea to sing about. He may be just heroically wasting his life chasing a whimsy windmill. She feels her brow knitting, remembering John rambling on about a close, trusting relationship being Man's unique road to survival. She somehow knows he wasn't lecturing her. He is just a man who gets himself tangled up in words and ideas. Still, she is secretly wants to lean on his shoulder. He has a vision. Her life has lacked that way of seeing. Not the word trips, but the saving grace of a real flesh and blood relationship.

Anna has never thought of herself as having a story. Now, on the far side of the Rubicon, she feels like yes, like a fresh page of her book is opening up – a page filled with possibilities.

She remembers Catherine. She's due soon. She'll visit her in the hospital. Someday, in the not too distant future, she might even read stories to a daughter of her own, like Kai does for Nascha. It's not too late, she tells herself. Perhaps what I thought was my secret desire has been an illusion all along. Perhaps I don't have to be a success in the man's world. Maybe my destiny is to be Caring Woman. She winks at the woman in the mirror, whispering: "Mirror, mirror on the wall: It's a treat to finally meet you, after all."

It is the next day that **her call comes**. My mind exults; my toes dance. She is giving me her signal. The well of possibility is bursting open. I am elated and boyish, as well as all shook up in my nervous insides. God, am I really ready for **this**?

I am no longer that wet-behind-the-ears young man sitting at the North Bay Buena Vista bar. I am well aware that relationship is no walk in the park. I know how fragile, even explosive, relationships can be, especially mature adult relationships – two freight trains of emotional baggage and ingrained habits streaming toward one another, dead on. The thought crosses my mind several times during the day that, like her, this fool has been hiding on the scary sidelines of being related. Buber's writings had come to mind that morning because intellectually, I agree with him that we can best, maybe only, achieve wholeness **in relationship**. But stupidly, somewhere back in the mists of Avalon, my ship-of-self had chosen to dally in the doldrums of books and New Age searching. Getting to that shore called *love* is more easily dreamed about, than landed upon.

As you can well imagine, ever since Anna's telephone call, her face, her voice, her carriage, her scent keep coming to me, as I try desperately to get my mind around Buber's two basic attitudes – an Other as *Thou,* unique, intrinsically valuable, and other as *it,* someone who can be of use. (In Buber's German

Du is usually translated in English as *Thou.* But *Du* is a warm, Romeo-to-Juliet word. Mother to daughter word. Grandmother to granddaughter word It says You, my special one.) Love is another one of those cosmic-large mysteries, too grand for passing words. With my male *hubris,* I have regularly shied away from terms like *chemistry, fate, made in heaven.* Yet this blessed morning, I can't shake the feeling that *she's the one. She is being given to my caring.*

I give up on serious study around five that afternoon, pour myself a glass of white wine, and go out on the back deck overlooking my study, to reflect and take stock.

In autumn, in the valley sacred to the early peoples, five o'clock is a pensive time of day. It's the hour when the gardeners with their leaf-blowers, the contractors with their dump trucks, and the hum of incoming tourist vans have slacked to a nearly awesome stillness. Even the trees mostly pause, and stand in mountain pose. The sun starts dropping lower in the western sky, bathing the cliff-faces with a fresh, reddish-orange luminescence. Now and again, a brownish doe with a yearling daughter or two, up from their high-sun, shade-tree afternoon siesta, will browse by on their way to their night scrape up in the hills. A kind of mystical time of change, both still, and slowly moving.

In my brief life, I've spent a lot of energy trying to understand myself and what makes us as humans keep pushing the rock of our life up the hill. As foxy Gwen said that first afternoon in the *Cave,* "We all want the same things." Naturally, I'm biologically driven to want bodily intimacy, just like the birds and the bees, the deer and the antelope, the high-minded politicians and the Magdalenes. If anything is DNA natural, it is the chemistry to bring forth something new for the species. For the chimps and the bonobos, a female rump in estrus is a *red alert*, a call to must-do action. For many men, including myself, a young feminine body of child-bearing age can arouse a maelstrom of desire. Nothing wrong with animal passion! As Buber said: evil is passion without direction. I don't deny my sexual attraction to Anna. She has the strong womanliness of a goddess, along with the vulnerable psyche of a child-bride. She's totally woman.

Plainly, I have reason to fear my own weaknesses. I've failed a number of times too many in the past. And despite my recent efforts to be more mindful and less toxic of mind, as the little spitfire tried to teach me, I've got some mental self-regulation muscles to buff up. She deserves a dependable companion, if this dream of mine is to come to blossom.

Yes but, my mind clamors, *get over your cowardliness.* Relationship is a many-tiered venture. Get smart: her **call** signaled more than just a learning permit. She is opening a door, inviting you into her life, and asking to come into yours. That call has to have been a torrent of trepidation, reaching out, with a cloud of tenuousness overhead. Stepping across any threshold takes courage. Clearly there's much more depth to this woman than meets the eye. She has to sense that I feel attracted to her. She probably doesn't realize how stoked I am about our Lady Luck brief-relationship. As far as I'm concerned that meeting in the canyon was no accident. I'm not sure if I still believe in accidents. At the same time, she has to fear that in the inner lair of everyman, there's a lion who can eat her up.

I can't stop reminding myself that even during our time together in the restaurant her debating mind had been wavering, undecided. After all, she has traveled a lonely road, although, for women especially, perhaps that is not the road less traveled. I don't think her father was much a male presence in her early years. I know that the boys in the schoolyard had made her wary of men. I've picked up the impression she has never been made to feel *special for who she is* in the embrace of a man. For damn sure, genuine connection does not come easily, especially in this fast moving, self-absorbed culture that encircles and presses in on our not-so-simple selves.

For me, the big philosophical, burning questions are no longer job one. The dormant, emerging man within wants the wounded woman like Cupid wanted Psyche. Perhaps even after my painful arrows of failure, I too am desire in a boy's mind, like Cupid. But life, evolution, natural selection have fortuitously navigated me to these red rocks where I now stand in the midst of Man's long journey, still insecure, still timorous. But, bolstered by the energy or wisdom of these iron-laced rocks, I feel bravely, still unsurely, more informed. I think I am ready to risk failure, just as the changing elements of the Rim land did and do. Those surging seas, whirling dust storms, and volcanic eruptions were *"life"* encountering change. Human relating asks for change. It is a two-edge sword: it cuts manic for the moment, and then, it can leave dark scars in the psyche: Am I succeeding? Am I getting what I need out of this want-a-be relationship? Will this relationship contributed to my well-being? – All about me. The voice within seldom asks: Is this one step for mankind? More love in the world? Am I contributing to the good of others? Nevertheless, the question hangs: To whom shall we turn, you my canyon woman, seem to me, to hold my winning lottery ticket. I believe I can help you live a fuller life, as you will help me.

Night is falling. The wind in the trees is quietly yawning, adieu. The darkness is coming on with the laden whispers of the pines and junipers growing stronger. I finish my second glass of white wine, and turn the glass upside down, still absorbed in her. There is a lot of deep female goodness in her, smothered under a harsh blanket of bully abuse. Amazing how many ways we come up with to hurt others, when all the while we are sending out signals: *Please don't hurt **me**.*

As I watch, the wilderness slows towards its resting mode, more bits of Buber-think slip through my mind: *Standpoint. Other as other. Granting distance. Recognizing uniqueness. Reaching across the between. Affirming and confirming. Mutuality.* I know a mountain of theory, a mountain of erudite words, but am I ready to cut the mustard? Do I have the courage to be committed to another person, knowing that she too has her people scars; scars that linger, and never fully erase.

A little gray fox moves through the underbrush, out seeking survival. Again I can't help remembering that his genes go back to the Pliocene (3.5 billion years ago), and he is faithful to his partner. I softly wonder why are some species loyal to their sexual mates? What a nice word, loyalty, I say to myself. A white comet streaks across a patch of the cosmic darkness. It reminds me of the transience of life and possibilities.

Yes, I say to myself. This may be your golden opportunity. Shape up! The bell tolls.

This romance of a woman and a man sings like a William Tell arrow shot to split the apple and bring about the release of a prisoner. The under-song rings like truth, even if some of the surface is studded with fiction. Sending heavenward chants about relationship, we can raise the Hymn of Man's Journey. We sing just a few short notes in the symphony of ***The All and the Bits***. But be assured that each of these notes matters.

In truth, we all do deeply want the same things, though we travel different roads in their quest. Exciting, isn't it, to accept that each of our stories is a vignette of the great mystery unfolding? Yet we are crucial notes that make the beat go on. Some will think this slice of life is *pie-in-the-sky*. It's not. The stakes are for real. Others who have heard this tale of hurts and failures will stamp their feet in joy that Anna and John have come upon the potential and the possibility to bond in love. All men have potentials. Many other bits of the remnant will clap, like the spectators in the stadiums of Roman gladiators, cheering on our protagonists as they march toward the light ahead. We, the chorus, share the dream that their odyssey will bring *Homo sapiens* along on the road that is, as far as our hearts can see, his Omega Point.

It is our inductive leap; no, it's our belief, that it would sadden the heart of Ultimate Reality if the Man who walked out of the savannah witlessly blew his chances of survival. Once upon a time, the big dinosaurs pounded the trails of this planet, only to wander into the bogs of nevermore. Now Man appears to be the drum major of evolution – not so much big, but fortuitously endowed. Dino had not evolved *free will.* As far as we know, he was a victim of circumstances. Whatever, whatever… humankind has a choice! A lot is at stake for Anna, but she has made the choice *to turn toward relationship.* Every time Man turns toward love and relationship, he pushes the Sisyphus stone nearer the top of the hill. Anna and John see a future on the horizon. Together they can be part of the remnant that will bring *Homo sapiens* to the next level of person to person relating.

So as the wise owl hoots in the forest, I want to end by saying that Anna's demure smiles and inner resilience have been like a soft rain falling on my hard, parched soul. Now, I feel empowered to write. I take out a fresh writer's notebook, and begin to bravely write: The Book of Malachy. The Romance of the Red Rocks Country. Believe and love, for survival is at stake …

At that moment, across the green spaces of Lomas Serenas, in the house that the hermit painter built, the once *little Sicilian outsider* is snuggling into some new white, sateen cotton sheets that Kai purchased that very morning in West Sedona. Anna's distant recollection of her mother grumbling, "We all want the same things" floats in the mists of her mind. She didn't understand what everyone wanted on that gray, noisy Bronx morning. Now the taste of the joy of connection is on her tongue. She finally feels special. That's what John had called her: "a special woman." She feels she can matter in his life. Anna lets herself go into the sleep of the just…the just embarking in search of love. She senses that she has reached the shore beyond the Rubicon. For the first time she doesn't feel like an outsider. She finally feels appreciated for who she is. She is the "apple of a man's eye." She desires the courage to go on.

It Took A Village

As you know, we humans bonded with significant others way back when we hunted and gathered in bands of buddies. I thank my charming wife and life companion, Jeannette, for her constant support of me and careful editing of this tale. She has been my courage.

We have walked on with family and friends clapping softly. My three sons, her four daughters, our brothers and sisters, our extended families, our friends and neighbors have been our village. Companions from former and present villages, like Gerry Feeney, Paul Friedman, Mary Lou Carlson, and the many unnamed have helped push this stone up the hill of its coming.

My thanks to Steve Simon, the Chicago/California, painter/poet, who also experienced the Red Rocks Fever. Like Carl and Sedona Schnebly, he left his home environment, came to the call. He now walks our trails, and eyes the hues in the mountain spaces. His cover painting of Kachina Woman resonates with my attempt to paint in words the encounter of female and male energy that happens in Red Rocks Country. His book *The Spirit of Sedona* rests on our living room coffee table. Anyone who opens it sees the energy of the land. Steve's cover reminds me what the tribe of **the fever** knows: we live in an ancient, still signaling place. Steve's art gives us a taste of the red rocks signals.

Those who visit can also share the blessing. We who live here walk the Blessing Way. I am grateful for the many smiles along the trails. It's our neighbors who make the red rocks country a true Blue Zone. Or maybe we need a book about the Crimson Zone.

I tip my cap of gratitude to my parents and the Mystery they believed in. They heard the Great Spirit Who still speaks in the wind and wilderness. Oh, for the courage to listen and see – with clear, kind eyes and silent, respecting ears. Come share the energy of the red rocks. It will turn your toes up!